S0-ACR-152

the AMAZING SPIDER-MAN Renew Your Vows

Are You Okay, Annie?

writer: JODY HOUSER

artist: SCOTT KOBLISH

color artist: RUTH REDMOND

letterer: VC's JOE CARAMAGNA

cover art: SCOTT KOBLISH & BRIAN REBER (#19), RYAN STEGMAN & BRIAN REBER (#20) and EDUARD PETROVICH (#21-23)

editors: HEATHER ANTOS & KATHLEEN WISNESKI

supervising editor: NICK LOWE

Spider-Man created by STAN LEE & STEVE DITKO

collection editor: MARK D. BEAZLEY
assistant editor: CAITLIN O'CONNELL
associate managing editor: KATERI WOODY
senior editor, special projects: JENNIFER GRÜNWALD
vp production & special projects: JEFF YOUNGQUIST
svp print, sales & marketing: DAVID GABRIEL
book designer: ADAM DEL RE

editor in chief: C.B. CEBULSKI
chief creative officer: JOE QUESADA
president: DAN BUCKLEY
executive producer: ALAN FINE

AMAZING SPIDER-MAN: RENEW YOUR VOWS VOL. 4 — ARE YOU OK, ANNIE? Contains material originally published in magazine form as AMAZING SPIDER-MAN: RENEW YOUR VOWS #19-23. First printing 2018. ISBN 978-1-302-91061-7. Published by MARVEL WORLDWIDE, INC., a subsidiary of MARVEL ENTERTAINMENT, LLC. OFFICE OF PUBLICATION: 135 West 50th Street, New York, NY 10020. **Printed in Canada.** DAN BUCKLEY, President, Marvel Entertainment; JOHN NEE, Publisher; JOE QUESADA, Chief Creative Officer; TOM BREVOORT, SVP of Publishing; DAVID BOGART, SVP of Business Affairs & Operations, Publishing & Partnership; DAVID GABRIEL, SVP of Sales & Marketing, Publishing; JEFF YOUNGQUIST, VP of Production & Special Projects; DAN CARR, Executive Director of Publishing Technology; ALEX MORALES, Director of Publishing Operations; DAN EDINGTON, Managing Editor; SUSAN CRESPI, Production Manager; STAN LEE, Chairman Emeritus. For information regarding advertising in Marvel Comics or on Marvel.com, please contact Vit DeBellis, Custom Solutions & Integrated Advertising Manager, at vdebellis@marvel.com. For Marvel subscription inquiries, please call 888-511-5480. **Manufactured between 9/28/2018 and 10/30/2018 by SOLISCO PRINTERS, SCOTT, QC, CANADA.**

10 9 8 7 6 5 4 3 2 1

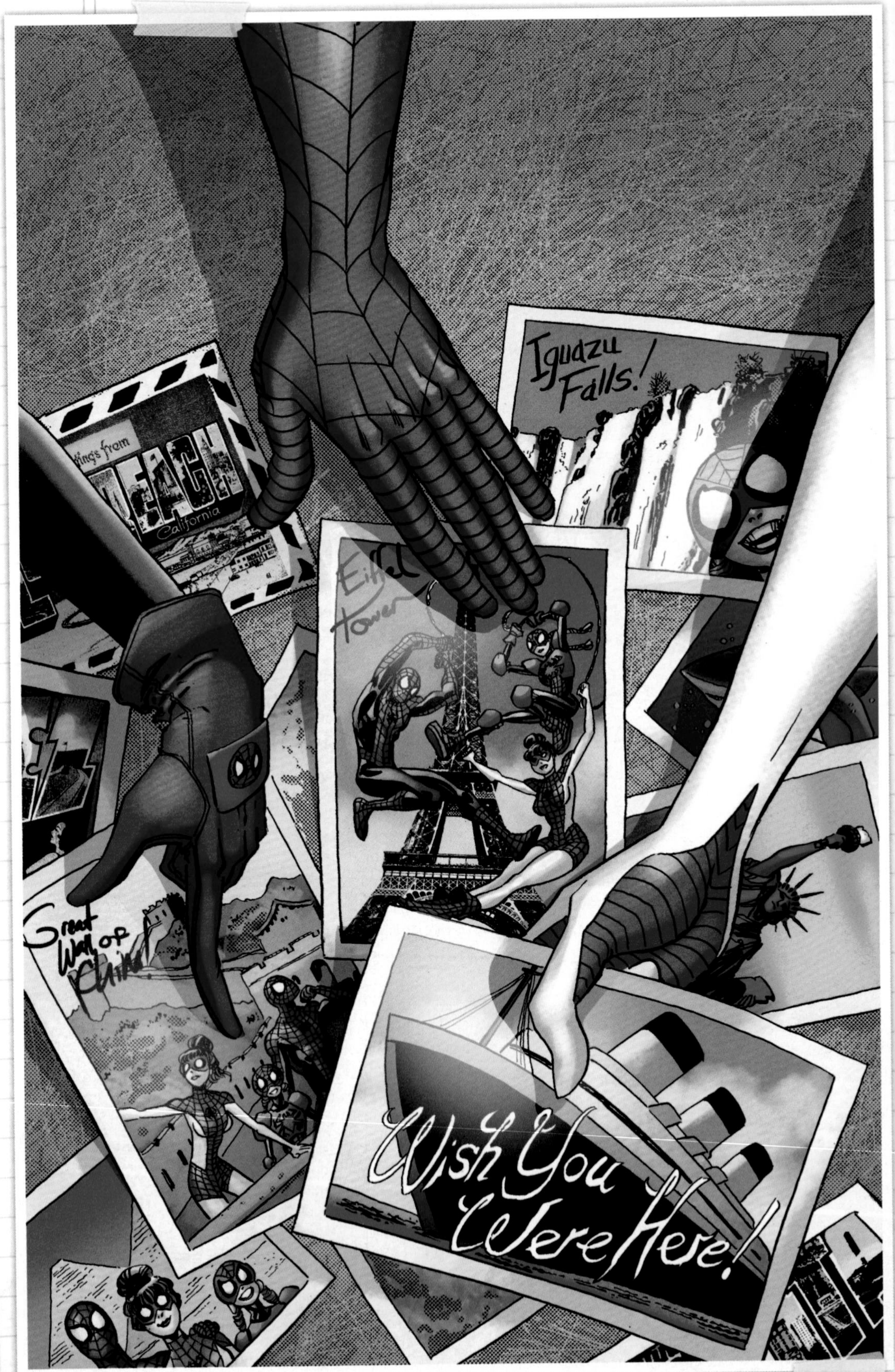
Iguazu Falls!
California
Eiffel Tower
Great Wall of China!
Wish You Were Here!

19: PARKER SUMMER VACATION

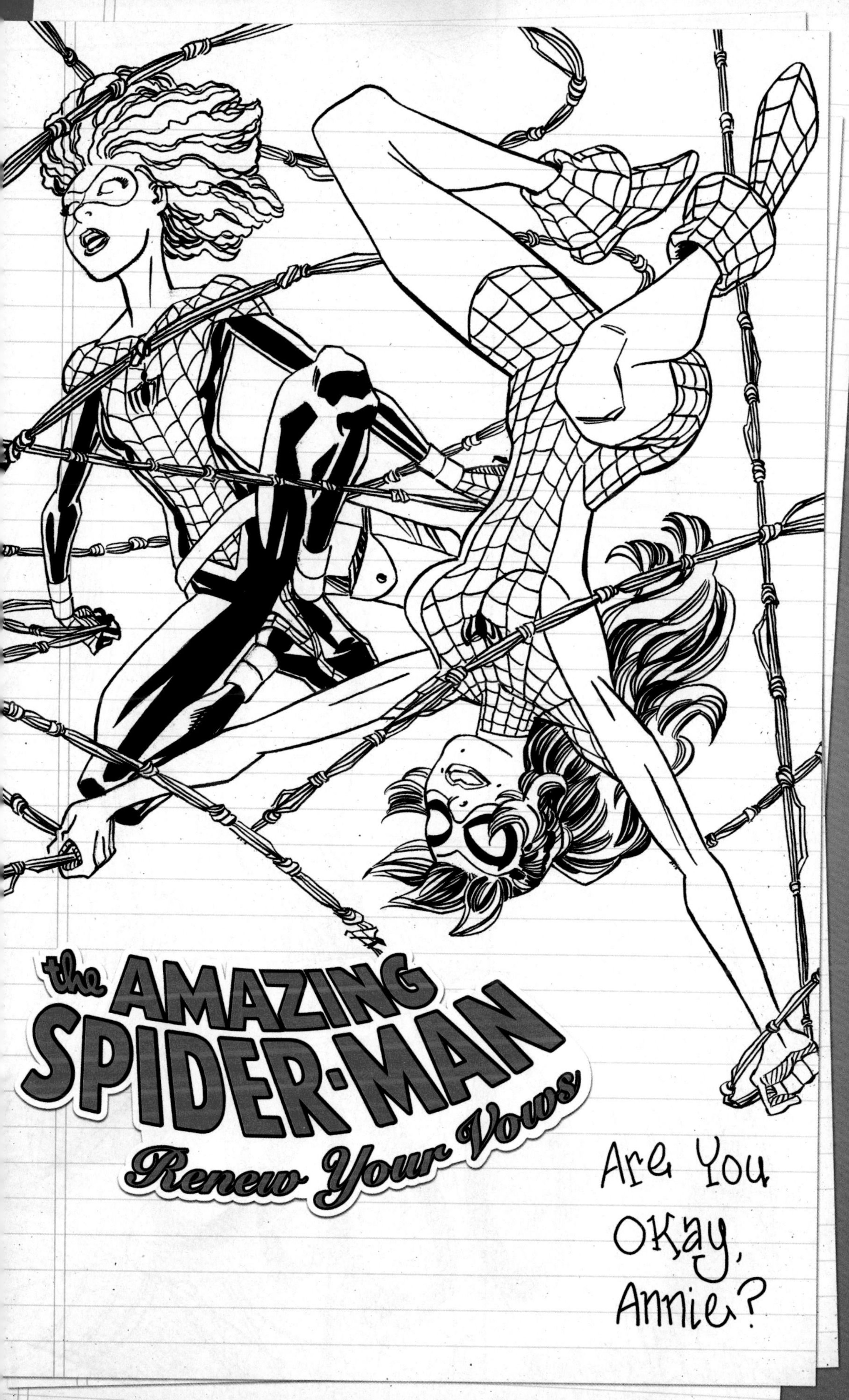
the AMAZING
SPIDER-MAN
Renew Your Vows
Are You
Okay,
Annie?

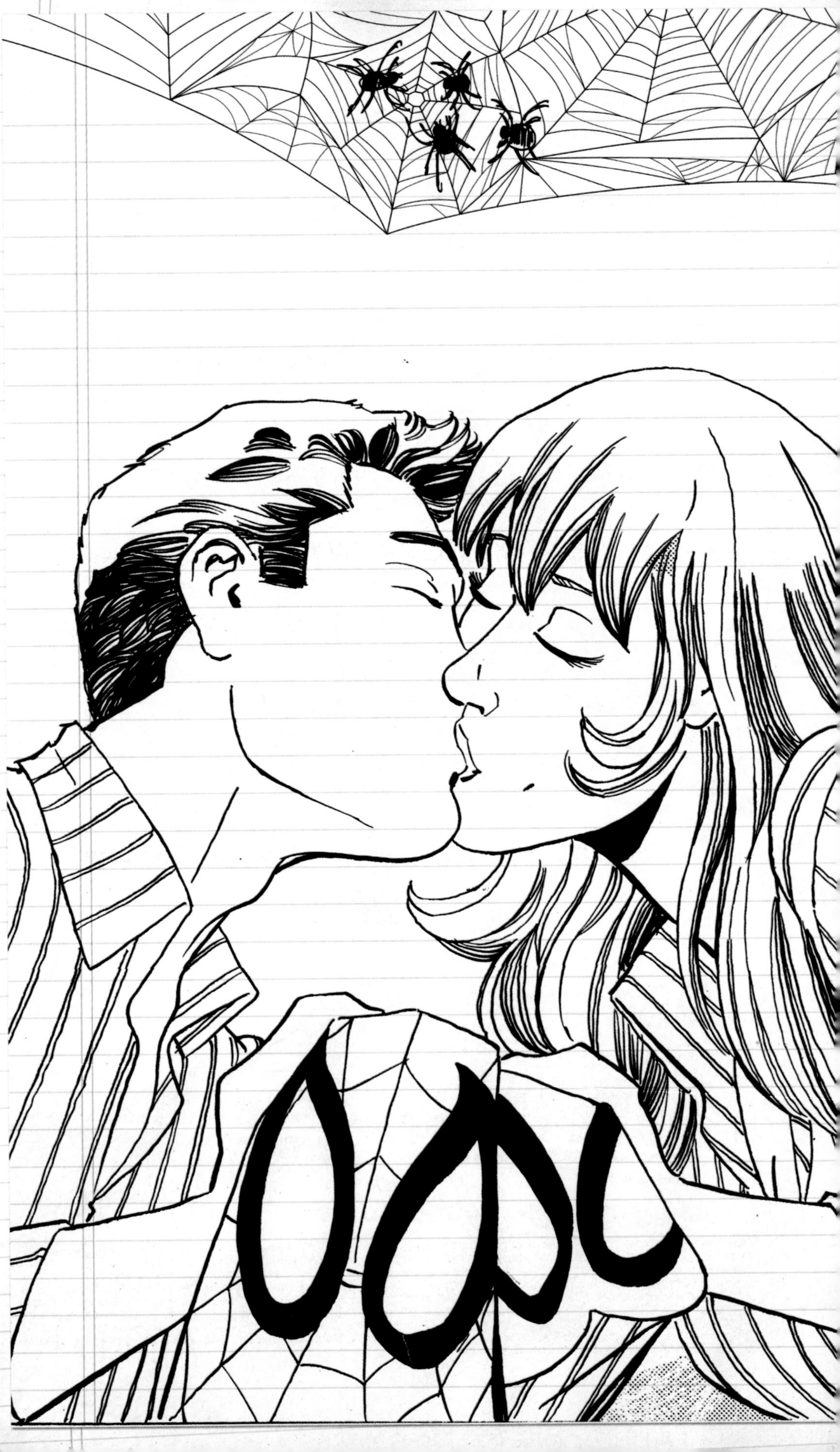

When **PETER PARKER** was bitten by a radioactive spider, he gained the proportional speed, strength and agility of a spider. Learning that with great power there must also come great responsibility, he became the crimefighting super hero **SPIDER-MAN**! With his wife, **MARY JANE**, and their teenage daughter, **ANNIE MAY**, the Parker family has become a force to be reckoned with!

Between photography gigs, substitute teaching, running a boutique, raising a teenage super-daughter and occasionally saving the world, Peter and MJ never seem to take a break. But once, eight years ago, the Spider-couple left Annie with a sitter and took the romantic trip of a lifetime!

- BACK 2 SCHOOL SHOPPING
- CONVINCE PARENTS 2 CHANGE CURFEW
- GET CLASS SCHEDULE
- PICK UP iBOOKS

= BEEP-BOOP
BEE-BOOP =

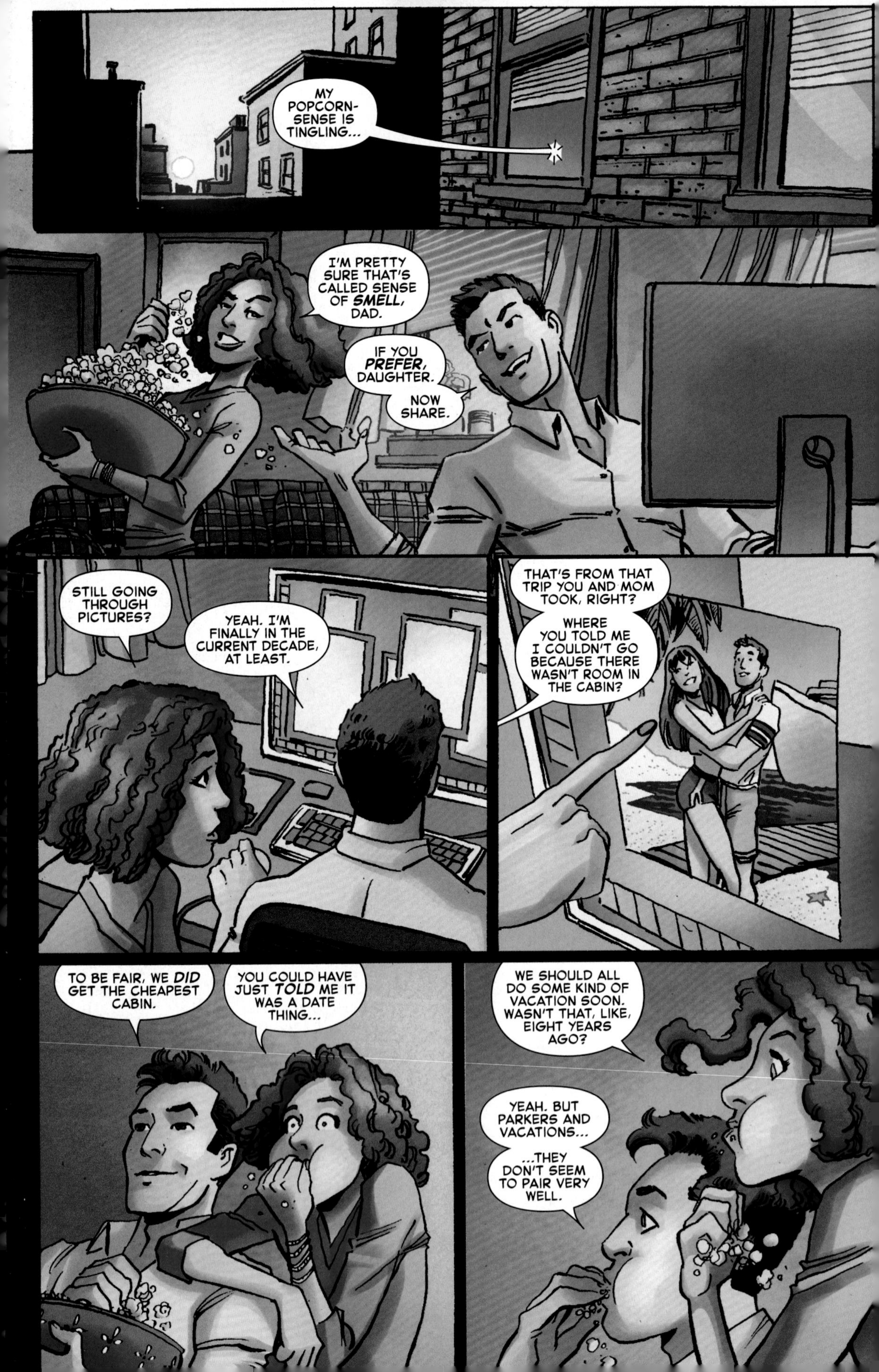
MY POPCORN-SENSE IS TINGLING...
I'M PRETTY SURE THAT'S CALLED SENSE OF *SMELL*, DAD.
IF YOU *PREFER*, DAUGHTER.
NOW SHARE.
STILL GOING THROUGH PICTURES?
YEAH. I'M FINALLY IN THE CURRENT DECADE, AT LEAST.
THAT'S FROM THAT TRIP YOU AND MOM TOOK, RIGHT?
WHERE YOU TOLD ME I COULDN'T GO BECAUSE THERE WASN'T ROOM IN THE CABIN?
TO BE FAIR, WE *DID* GET THE CHEAPEST CABIN.
YOU COULD HAVE JUST *TOLD* ME IT WAS A DATE THING...
WE SHOULD ALL DO SOME KIND OF VACATION SOON. WASN'T THAT, LIKE, EIGHT YEARS AGO?
YEAH. BUT PARKERS AND VACATIONS...
...THEY DON'T SEEM TO PAIR VERY WELL.

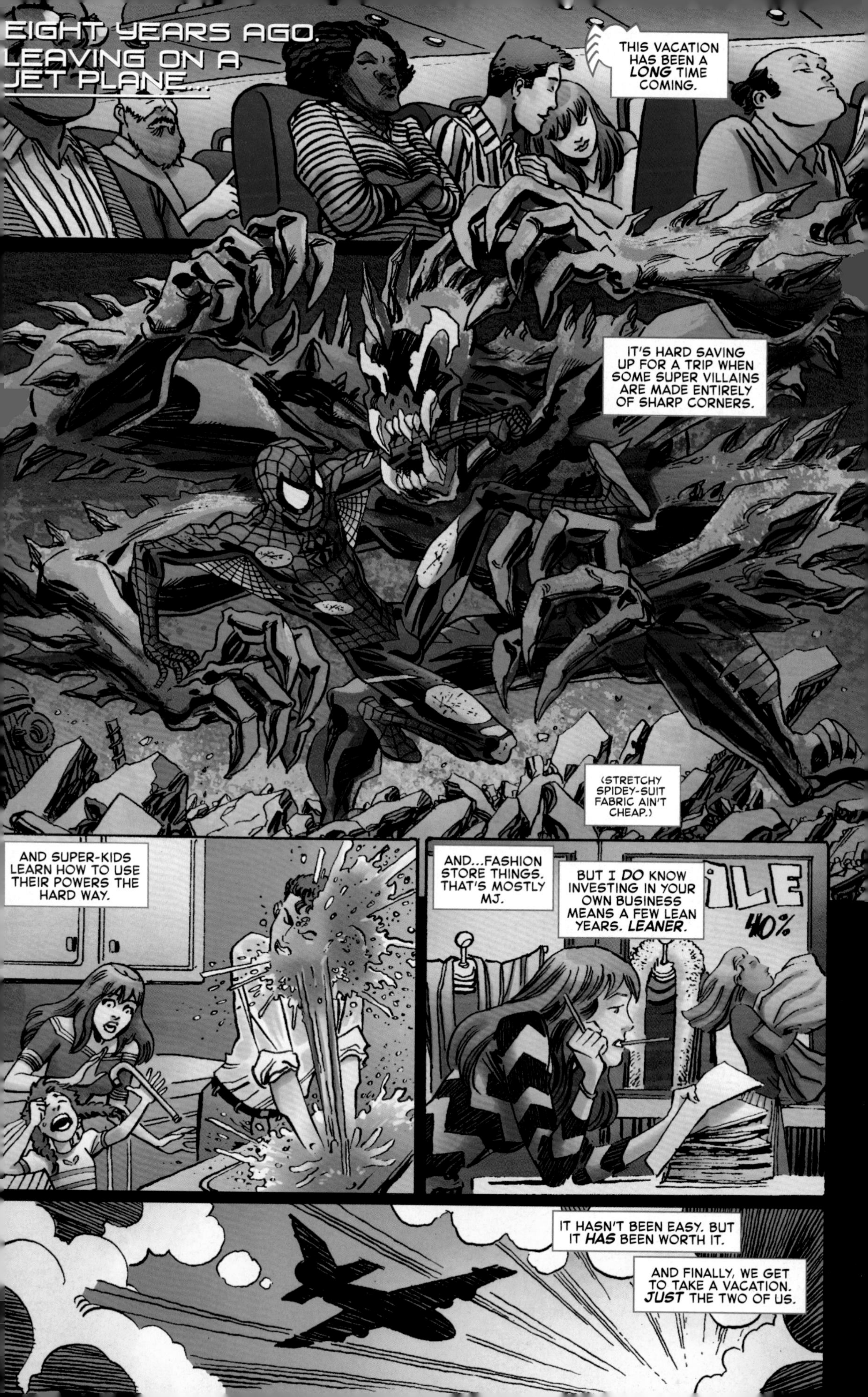
EIGHT YEARS AGO. LEAVING ON A JET PLANE...
THIS VACATION HAS BEEN A LONG TIME COMING.
IT'S HARD SAVING UP FOR A TRIP WHEN SOME SUPER VILLAINS ARE MADE ENTIRELY OF SHARP CORNERS.
(STRETCHY SPIDEY-SUIT FABRIC AIN'T CHEAP.)
AND SUPER-KIDS LEARN HOW TO USE THEIR POWERS THE HARD WAY.
AND...FASHION STORE THINGS. THAT'S MOSTLY MJ.
BUT I DO KNOW INVESTING IN YOUR OWN BUSINESS MEANS A FEW LEAN YEARS. LEANER.
ILE
40%
IT HASN'T BEEN EASY. BUT IT HAS BEEN WORTH IT.
AND FINALLY, WE GET TO TAKE A VACATION. JUST THE TWO OF US.

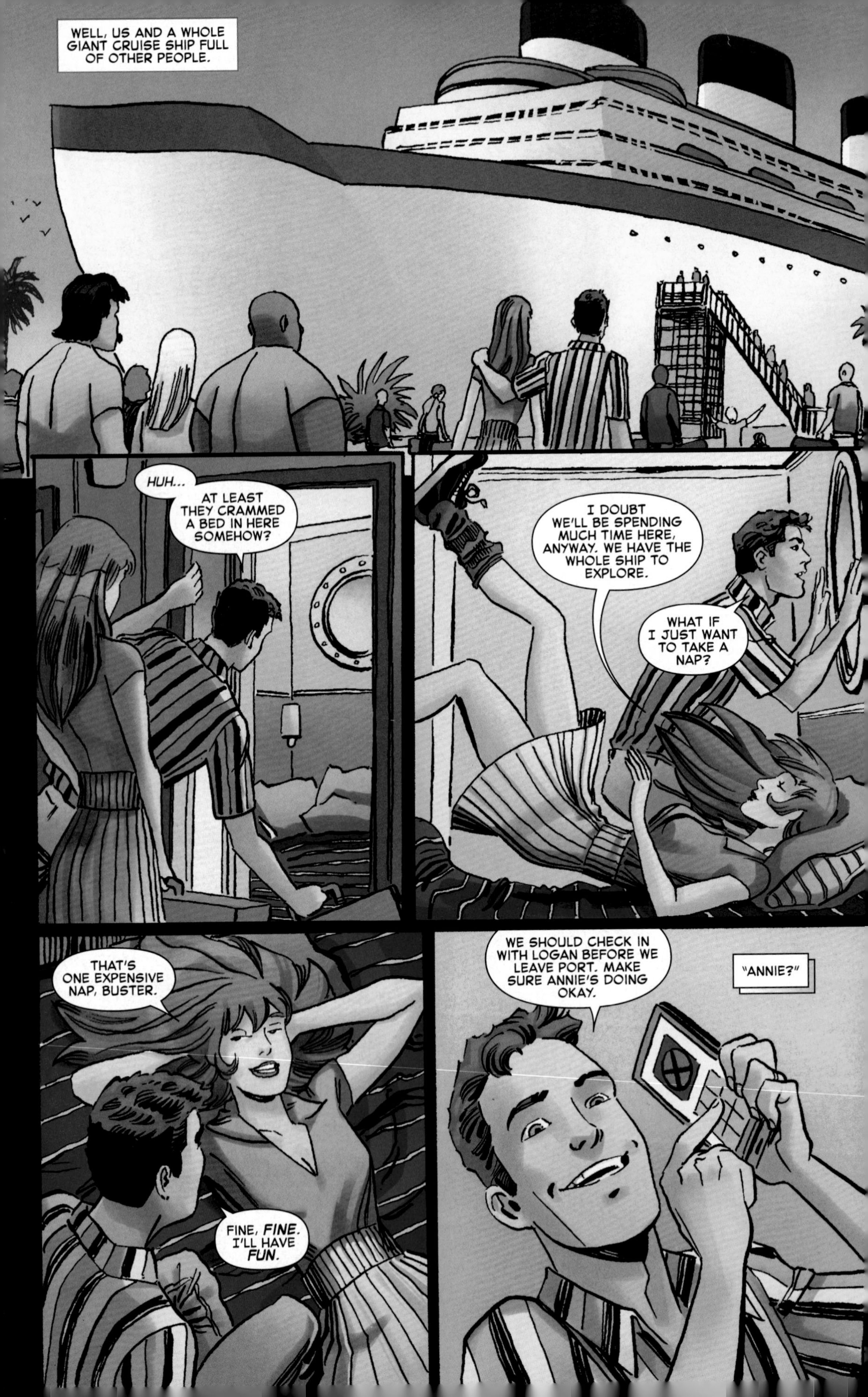
WELL, US AND A WHOLE GIANT CRUISE SHIP FULL OF OTHER PEOPLE.
HUH...
AT LEAST THEY CRAMMED A BED IN HERE SOMEHOW?
I DOUBT WE'LL BE SPENDING MUCH TIME HERE, ANYWAY. WE HAVE THE WHOLE SHIP TO EXPLORE.
WHAT IF I JUST WANT TO TAKE A NAP?
THAT'S ONE EXPENSIVE NAP, BUSTER.
FINE, FINE. I'LL HAVE FUN.
WE SHOULD CHECK IN WITH LOGAN BEFORE WE LEAVE PORT. MAKE SURE ANNIE'S DOING OKAY.
"ANNIE?"

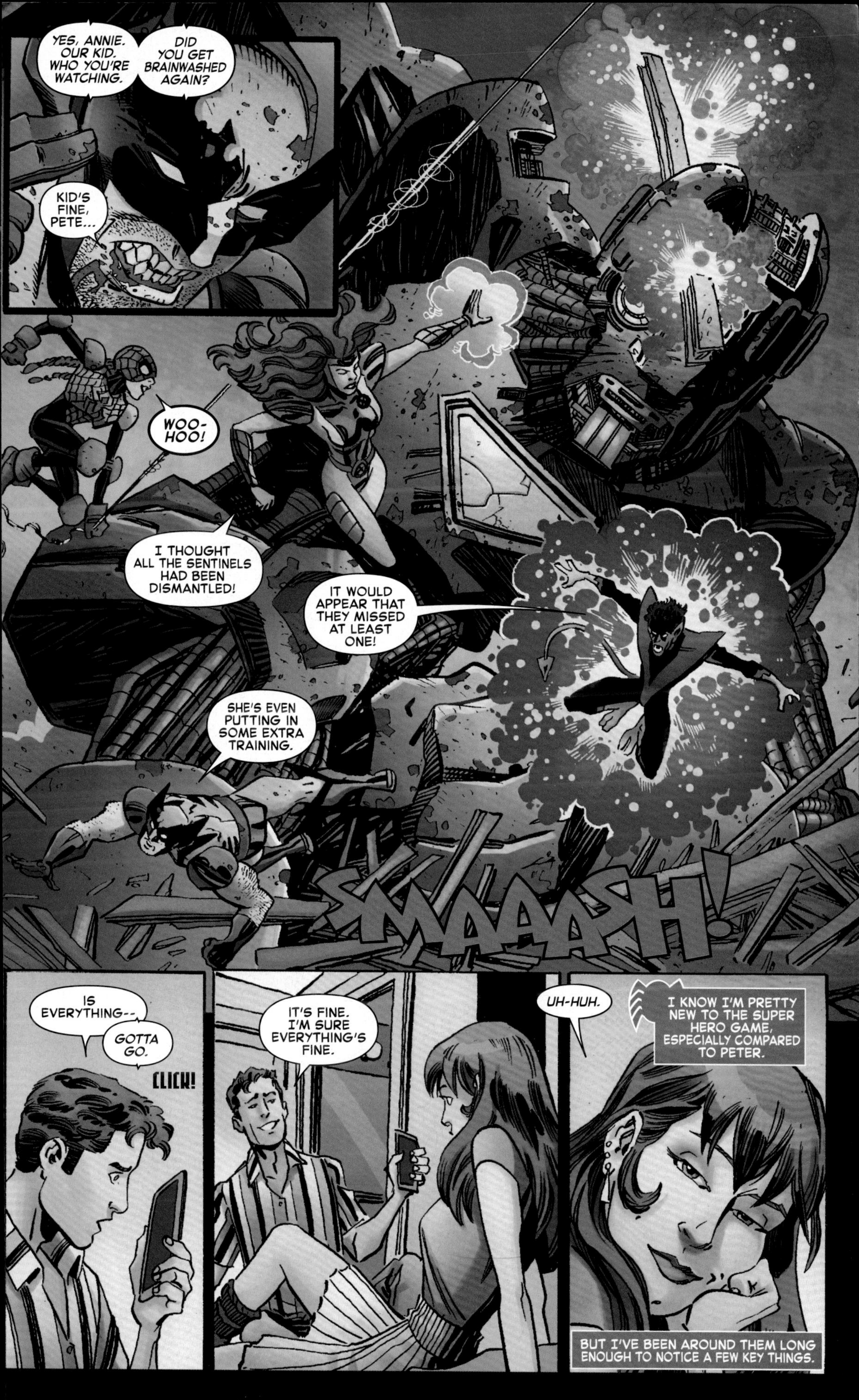

YES, ANNIE. OUR KID. WHO YOU'RE WATCHING.
DID YOU GET BRAINWASHED AGAIN?
KID'S FINE, PETE...
WOO-HOO!
I THOUGHT ALL THE SENTINELS HAD BEEN DISMANTLED!
IT WOULD APPEAR THAT THEY MISSED AT LEAST ONE!
SHE'S EVEN PUTTING IN SOME EXTRA TRAINING.
SMAAASH!
IS EVERYTHING--
GOTTA GO.
CLICK!
IT'S FINE. I'M SURE EVERYTHING'S FINE.
UH-HUH.
I KNOW I'M PRETTY NEW TO THE SUPER HERO GAME, ESPECIALLY COMPARED TO PETER.
BUT I'VE BEEN AROUND THEM LONG ENOUGH TO NOTICE A FEW KEY THINGS.

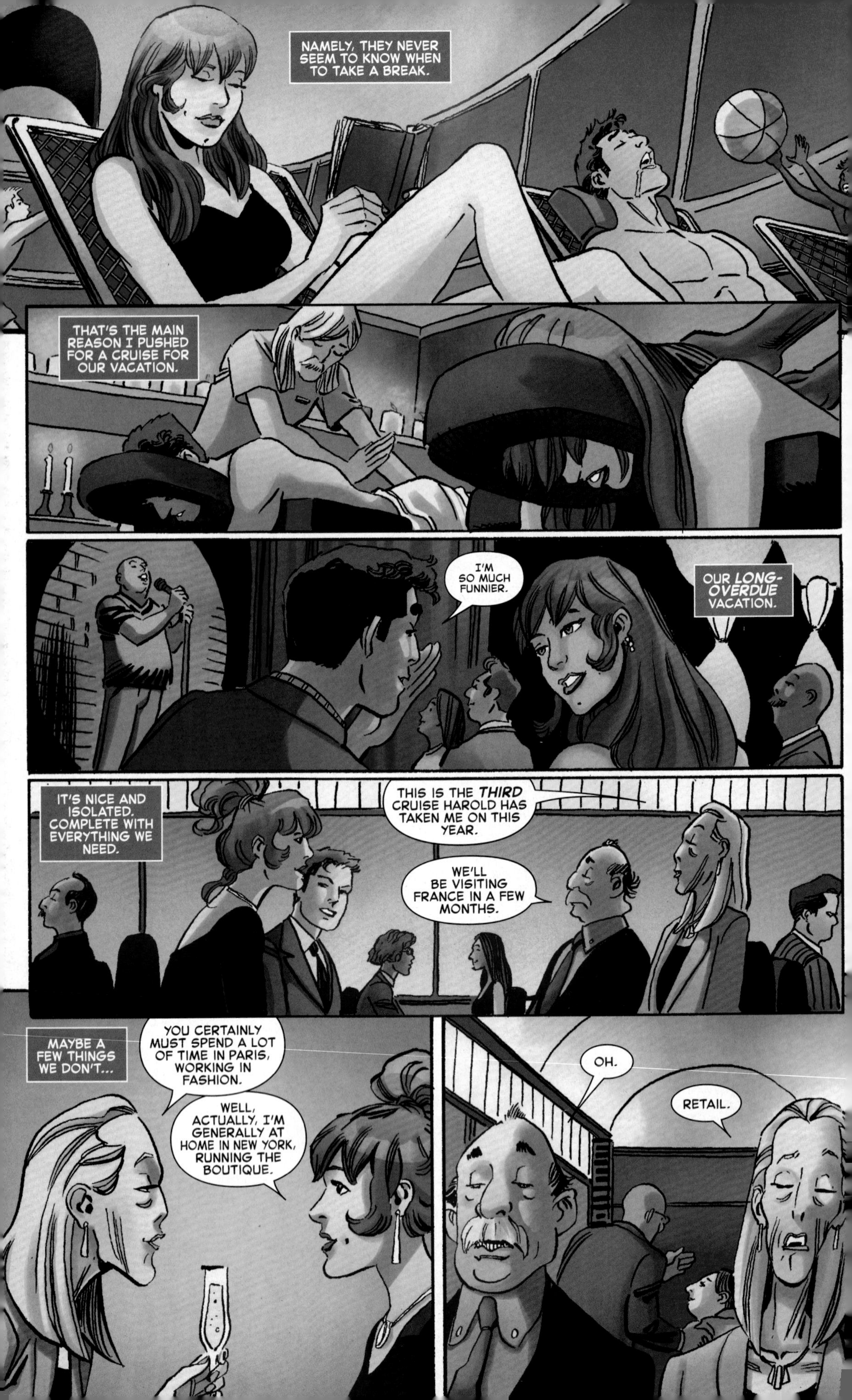
NAMELY, THEY NEVER SEEM TO KNOW WHEN TO TAKE A BREAK.
THAT'S THE MAIN REASON I PUSHED FOR A CRUISE FOR OUR VACATION.
I'M SO MUCH FUNNIER.
OUR LONG-OVERDUE VACATION.
IT'S NICE AND ISOLATED. COMPLETE WITH EVERYTHING WE NEED.
THIS IS THE THIRD CRUISE HAROLD HAS TAKEN ME ON THIS YEAR.
WE'LL BE VISITING FRANCE IN A FEW MONTHS.
MAYBE A FEW THINGS WE DON'T...
YOU CERTAINLY MUST SPEND A LOT OF TIME IN PARIS, WORKING IN FASHION.
WELL, ACTUALLY, I'M GENERALLY AT HOME IN NEW YORK, RUNNING THE BOUTIQUE.
OH.
RETAIL.

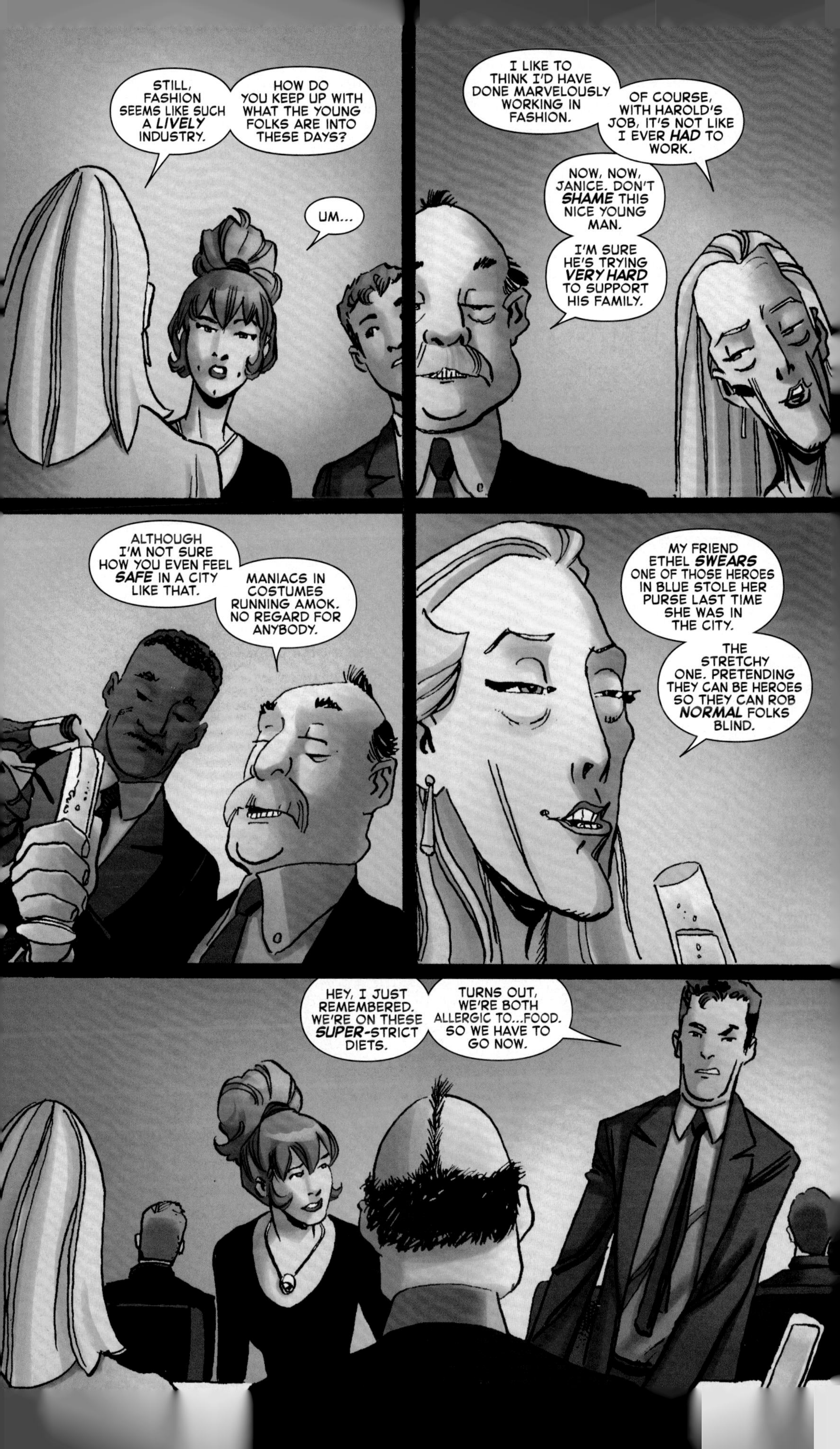
STILL, FASHION SEEMS LIKE SUCH A *LIVELY* INDUSTRY.
HOW DO YOU KEEP UP WITH WHAT THE YOUNG FOLKS ARE INTO THESE DAYS?
UM...
I LIKE TO THINK I'D HAVE DONE MARVELOUSLY WORKING IN FASHION.
OF COURSE, WITH HAROLD'S JOB, IT'S NOT LIKE I EVER *HAD* TO WORK.
NOW, NOW, JANICE. DON'T *SHAME* THIS NICE YOUNG MAN.
I'M SURE HE'S TRYING *VERY HARD* TO SUPPORT HIS FAMILY.
ALTHOUGH I'M NOT SURE HOW YOU EVEN FEEL *SAFE* IN A CITY LIKE THAT.
MANIACS IN COSTUMES RUNNING AMOK. NO REGARD FOR ANYBODY.
MY FRIEND ETHEL *SWEARS* ONE OF THOSE HEROES IN BLUE STOLE HER PURSE LAST TIME SHE WAS IN THE CITY.
THE STRETCHY ONE. PRETENDING THEY CAN BE HEROES SO THEY CAN ROB *NORMAL* FOLKS BLIND.
HEY, I JUST REMEMBERED. WE'RE ON THESE *SUPER*-STRICT DIETS.
TURNS OUT, WE'RE BOTH ALLERGIC TO...FOOD. SO WE HAVE TO GO NOW.

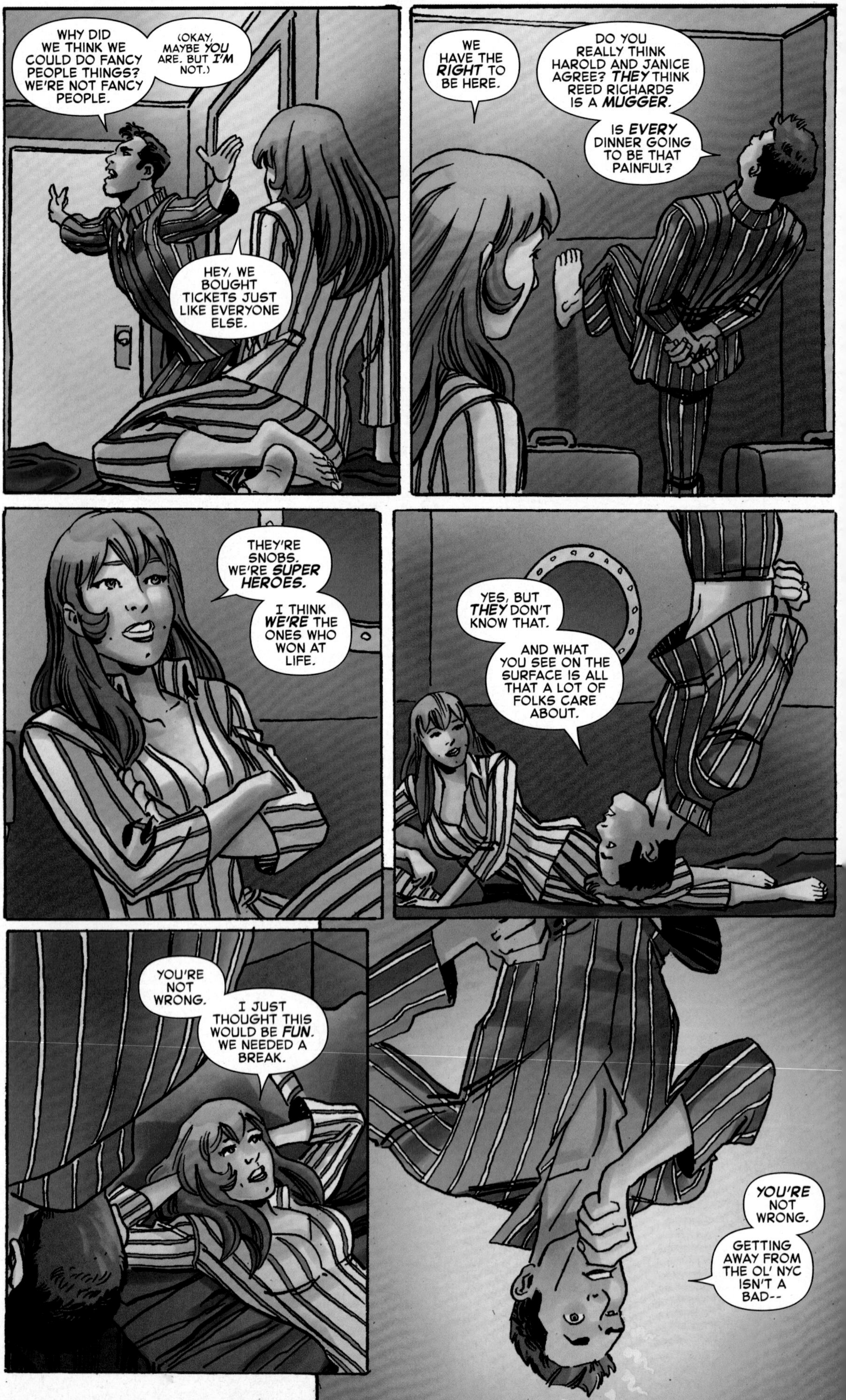
WHY DID WE THINK WE COULD DO FANCY PEOPLE THINGS? WE'RE NOT FANCY PEOPLE.
(OKAY, MAYBE YOU ARE. BUT I'M NOT.)
HEY, WE BOUGHT TICKETS JUST LIKE EVERYONE ELSE.
WE HAVE THE RIGHT TO BE HERE.
DO YOU REALLY THINK HAROLD AND JANICE AGREE? THEY THINK REED RICHARDS IS A MUGGER.
IS EVERY DINNER GOING TO BE THAT PAINFUL?
THEY'RE SNOBS. WE'RE SUPER HEROES.
I THINK WE'RE THE ONES WHO WON AT LIFE.
YES, BUT THEY DON'T KNOW THAT.
AND WHAT YOU SEE ON THE SURFACE IS ALL THAT A LOT OF FOLKS CARE ABOUT.
YOU'RE NOT WRONG.
I JUST THOUGHT THIS WOULD BE FUN. WE NEEDED A BREAK.
YOU'RE NOT WRONG.
GETTING AWAY FROM THE OL' NYC ISN'T A BAD--

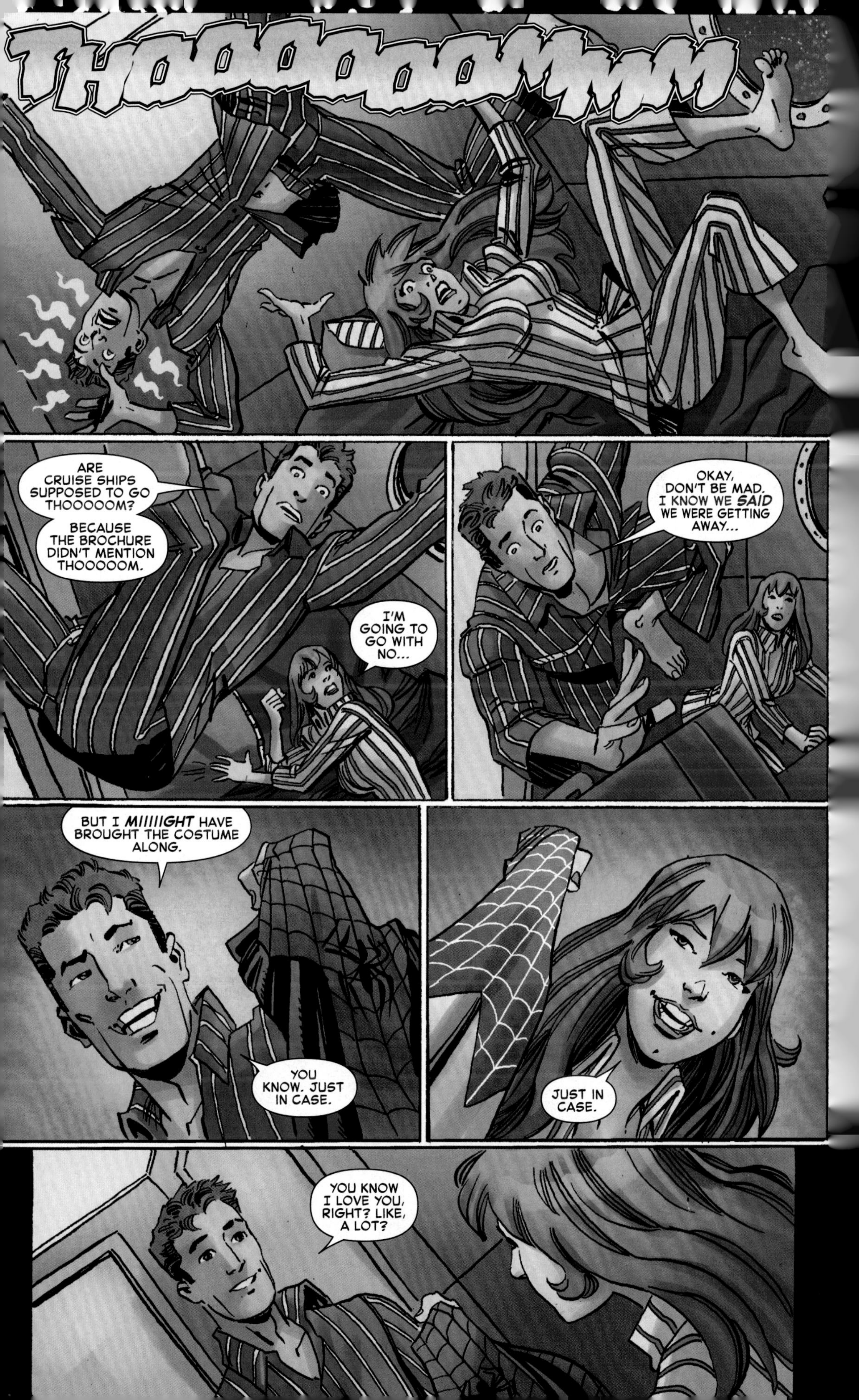
THOOOOOOMMM
ARE CRUISE SHIPS SUPPOSED TO GO THOOOOOM?
BECAUSE THE BROCHURE DIDN'T MENTION THOOOOOM.
I'M GOING TO GO WITH NO...
OKAY, DON'T BE MAD. I KNOW WE SAID WE WERE GETTING AWAY...
BUT I MIIIIIGHT HAVE BROUGHT THE COSTUME ALONG.
YOU KNOW. JUST IN CASE.
JUST IN CASE.
YOU KNOW I LOVE YOU, RIGHT? LIKE, A LOT?

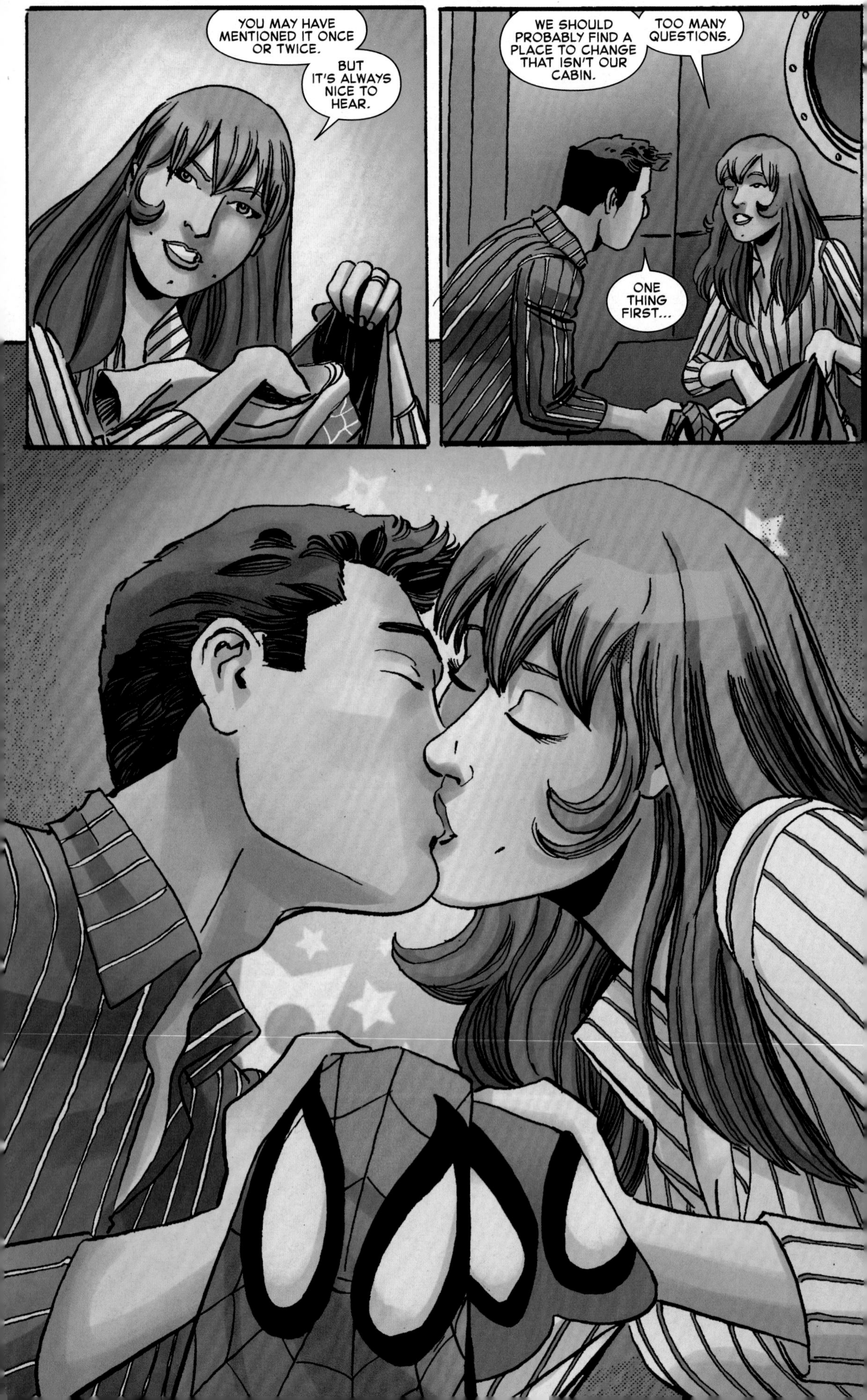
YOU MAY HAVE MENTIONED IT ONCE OR TWICE.
BUT IT'S ALWAYS NICE TO HEAR.
WE SHOULD PROBABLY FIND A PLACE TO CHANGE THAT ISN'T OUR CABIN.
TOO MANY QUESTIONS.
ONE THING FIRST...

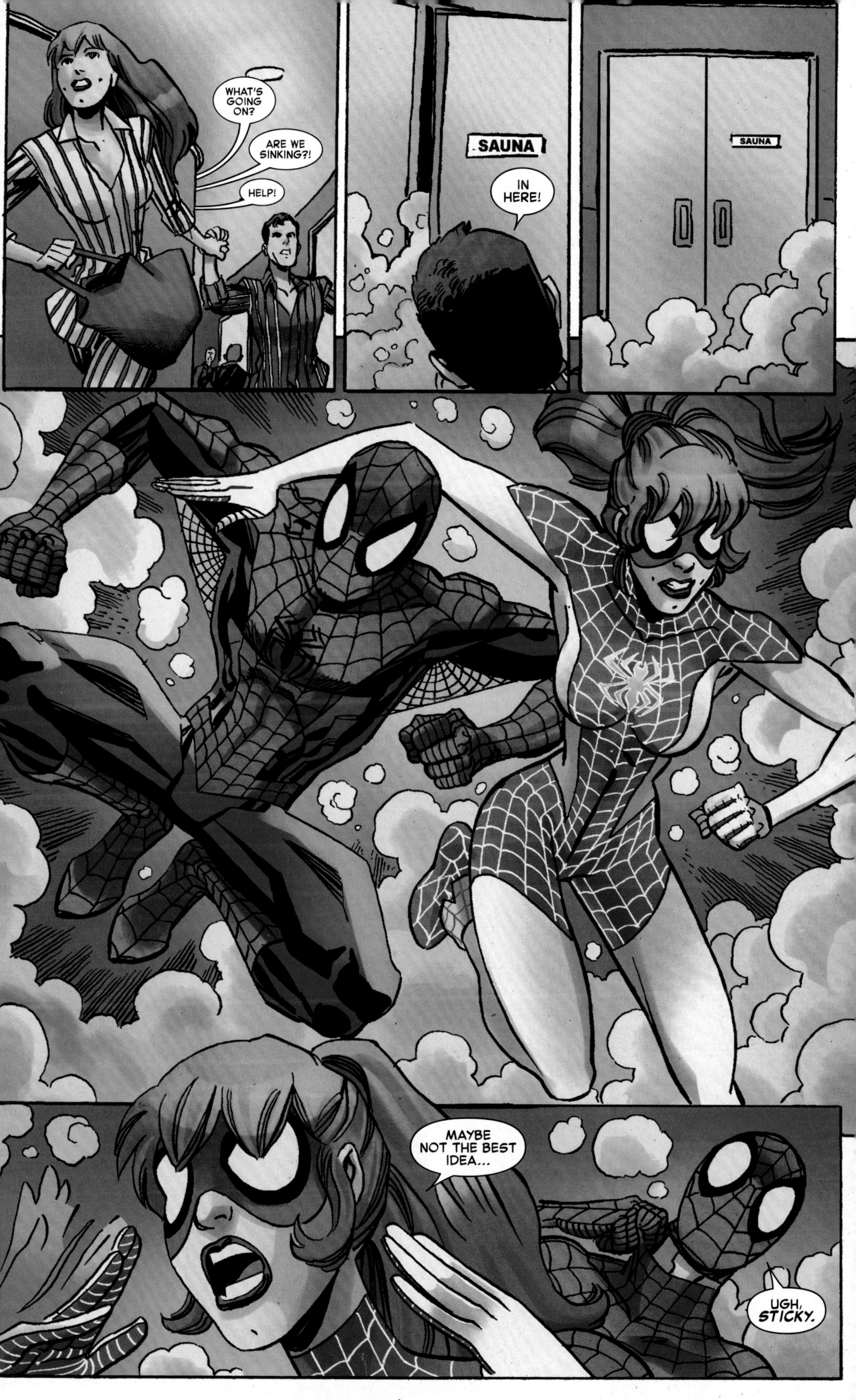
WHAT'S GOING ON?
ARE WE SINKING?!
HELP!
SAUNA
IN HERE!
SAUNA
MAYBE NOT THE BEST IDEA...
UGH, STICKY.

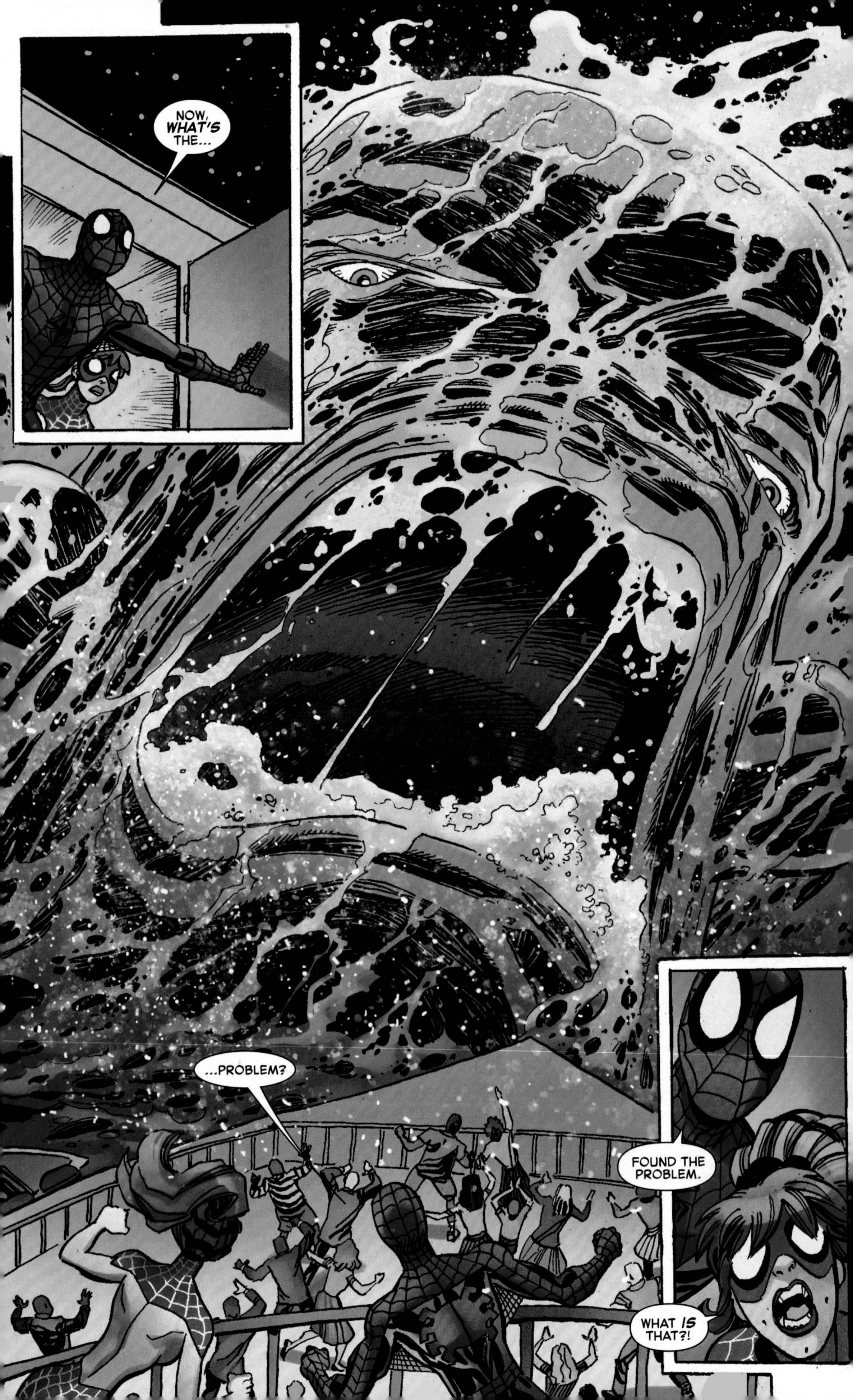
NOW, WHAT'S THE...
...PROBLEM?
FOUND THE PROBLEM.
WHAT IS THAT?!

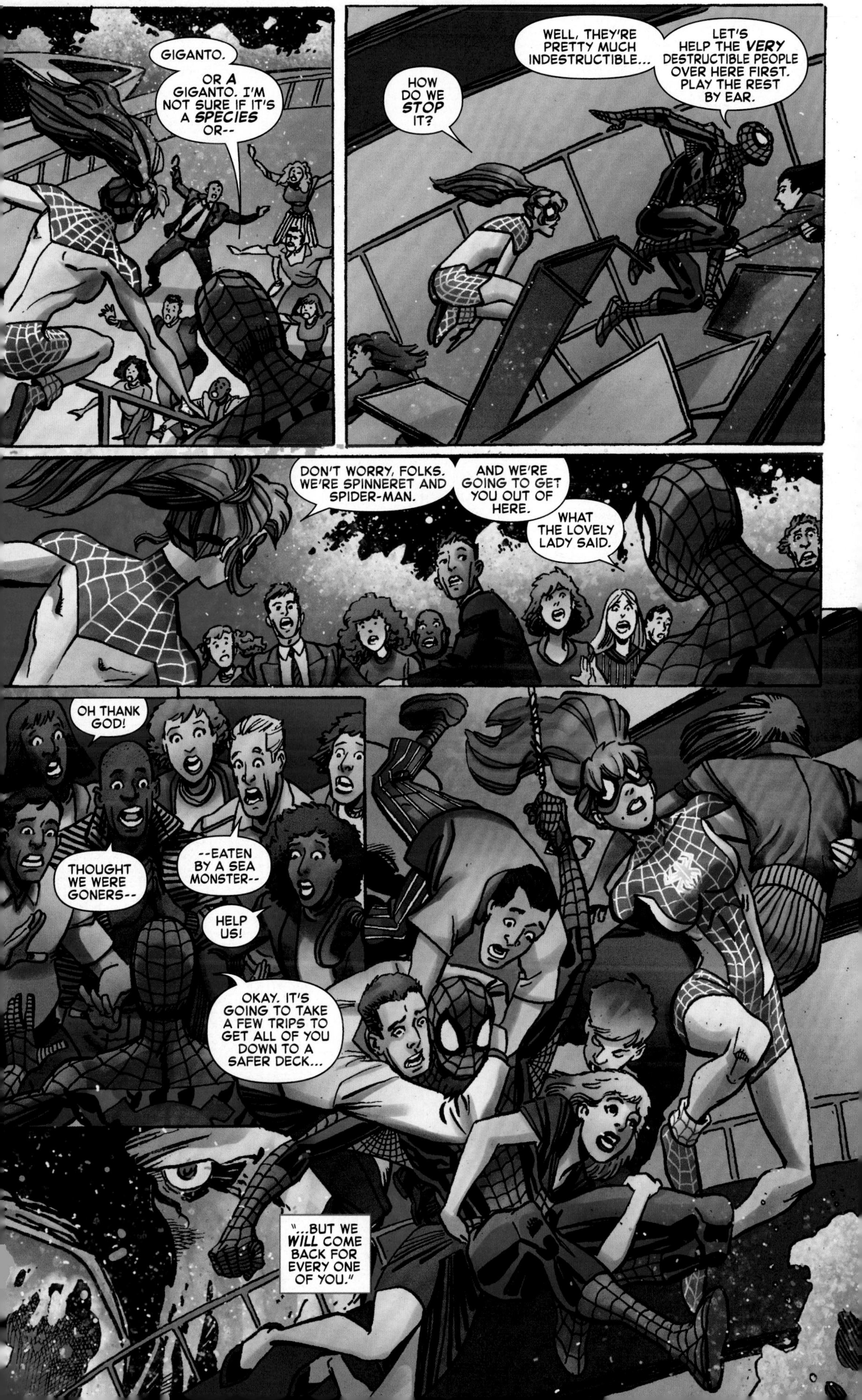
GIGANTO.
OR A GIGANTO. I'M NOT SURE IF IT'S A SPECIES OR--
HOW DO WE STOP IT?
WELL, THEY'RE PRETTY MUCH INDESTRUCTIBLE...
LET'S HELP THE VERY DESTRUCTIBLE PEOPLE OVER HERE FIRST. PLAY THE REST BY EAR.
DON'T WORRY, FOLKS. WE'RE SPINNERET AND SPIDER-MAN.
AND WE'RE GOING TO GET YOU OUT OF HERE.
WHAT THE LOVELY LADY SAID.
OH THANK GOD!
THOUGHT WE WERE GONERS--
--EATEN BY A SEA MONSTER--
HELP US!
OKAY. IT'S GOING TO TAKE A FEW TRIPS TO GET ALL OF YOU DOWN TO A SAFER DECK...
"...BUT WE WILL COME BACK FOR EVERY ONE OF YOU."

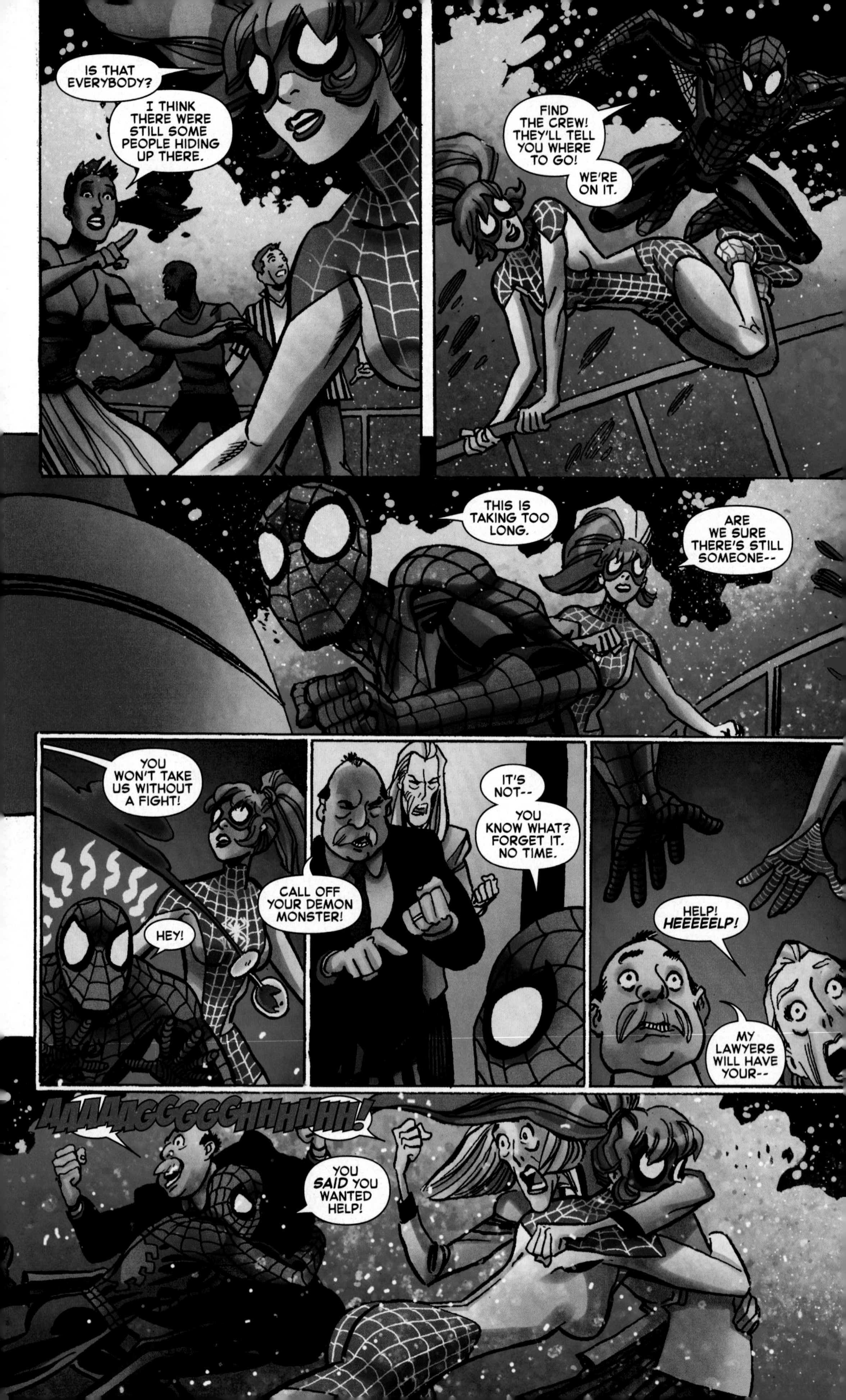
IS THAT EVERYBODY?
I THINK THERE WERE STILL SOME PEOPLE HIDING UP THERE.
FIND THE CREW! THEY'LL TELL YOU WHERE TO GO!
WE'RE ON IT.
THIS IS TAKING TOO LONG.
ARE WE SURE THERE'S STILL SOMEONE--
YOU WON'T TAKE US WITHOUT A FIGHT!
HEY!
CALL OFF YOUR DEMON MONSTER!
IT'S NOT--
YOU KNOW WHAT? FORGET IT. NO TIME.
HELP! HEEEEELP!
MY LAWYERS WILL HAVE YOUR--
AAAAAGGGGGGHHHHHH!
YOU SAID YOU WANTED HELP!

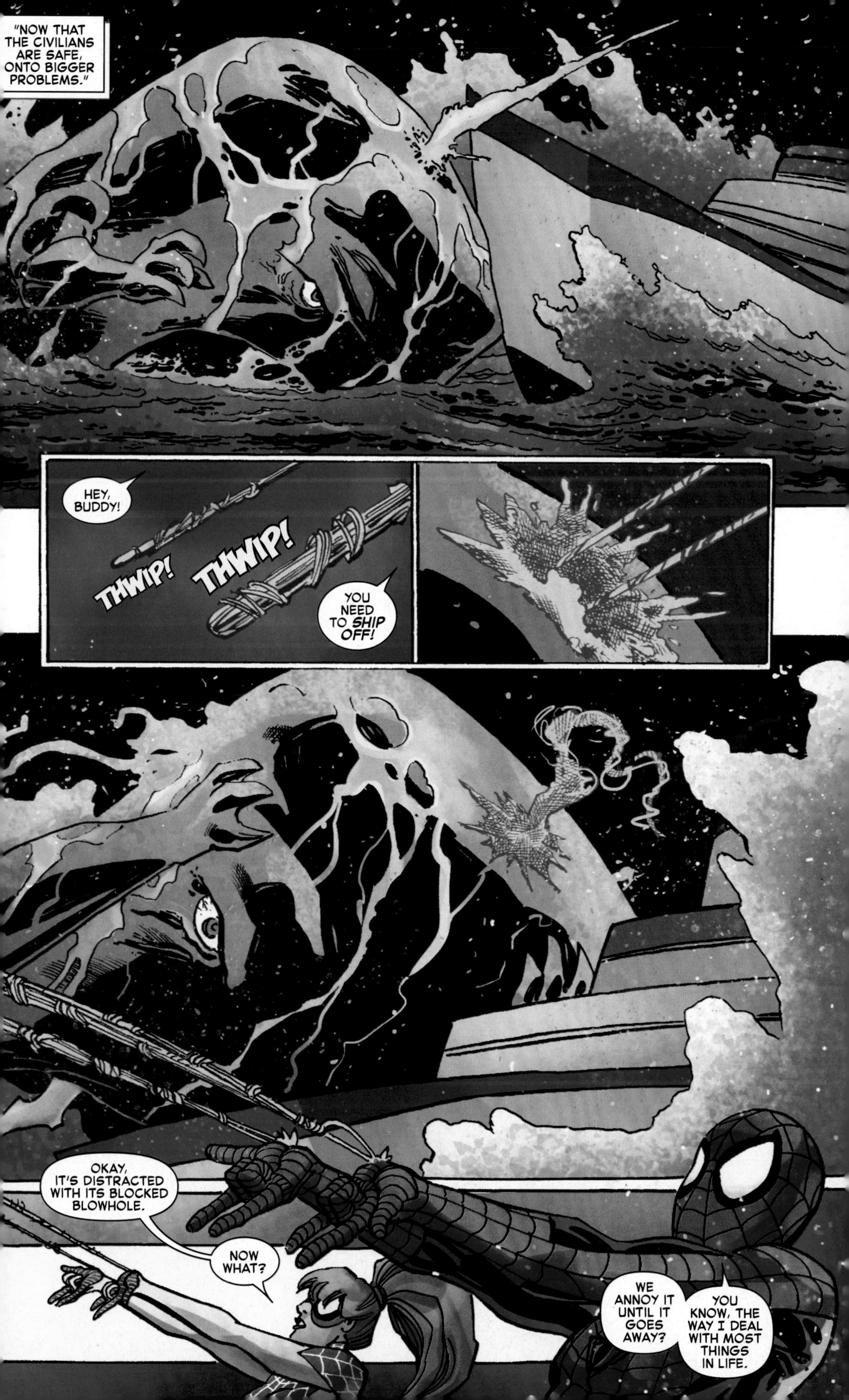
"NOW THAT THE CIVILIANS ARE SAFE, ONTO BIGGER PROBLEMS."
HEY, BUDDY!
THWIP!
THWIP!
YOU NEED TO SHIP OFF!
OKAY, IT'S DISTRACTED WITH ITS BLOCKED BLOWHOLE.
NOW WHAT?
WE ANNOY IT UNTIL IT GOES AWAY?
YOU KNOW, THE WAY I DEAL WITH MOST THINGS IN LIFE.

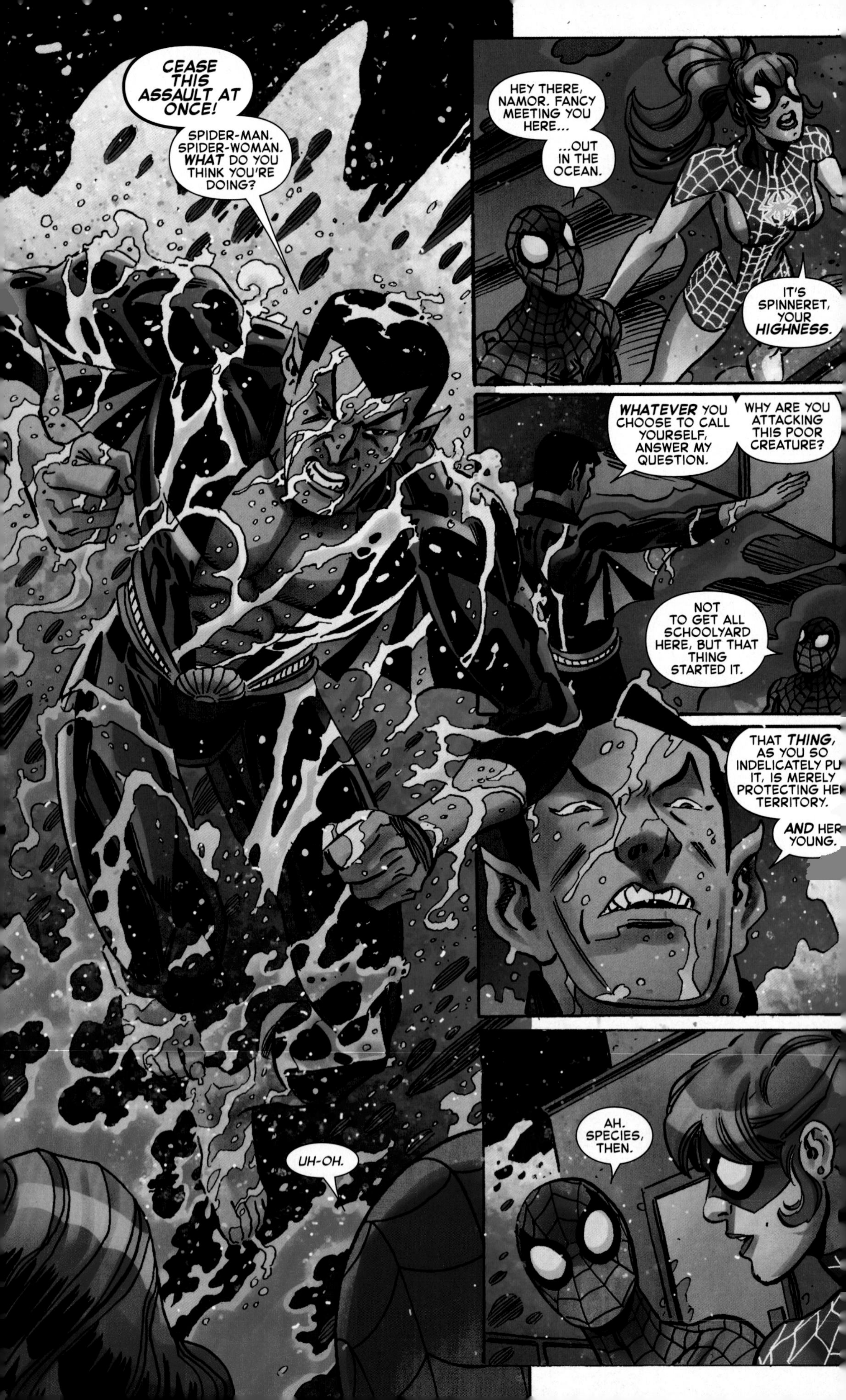
CEASE THIS ASSAULT AT ONCE!
SPIDER-MAN. SPIDER-WOMAN. WHAT DO YOU THINK YOU'RE DOING?
HEY THERE, NAMOR. FANCY MEETING YOU HERE...
...OUT IN THE OCEAN.
IT'S SPINNERET, YOUR HIGHNESS.
WHATEVER YOU CHOOSE TO CALL YOURSELF, ANSWER MY QUESTION.
WHY ARE YOU ATTACKING THIS POOR CREATURE?
NOT TO GET ALL SCHOOLYARD HERE, BUT THAT THING STARTED IT.
THAT THING, AS YOU SO INDELICATELY PU IT, IS MERELY PROTECTING HE TERRITORY.
AND HER YOUNG.
UH-OH.
AH. SPECIES, THEN.

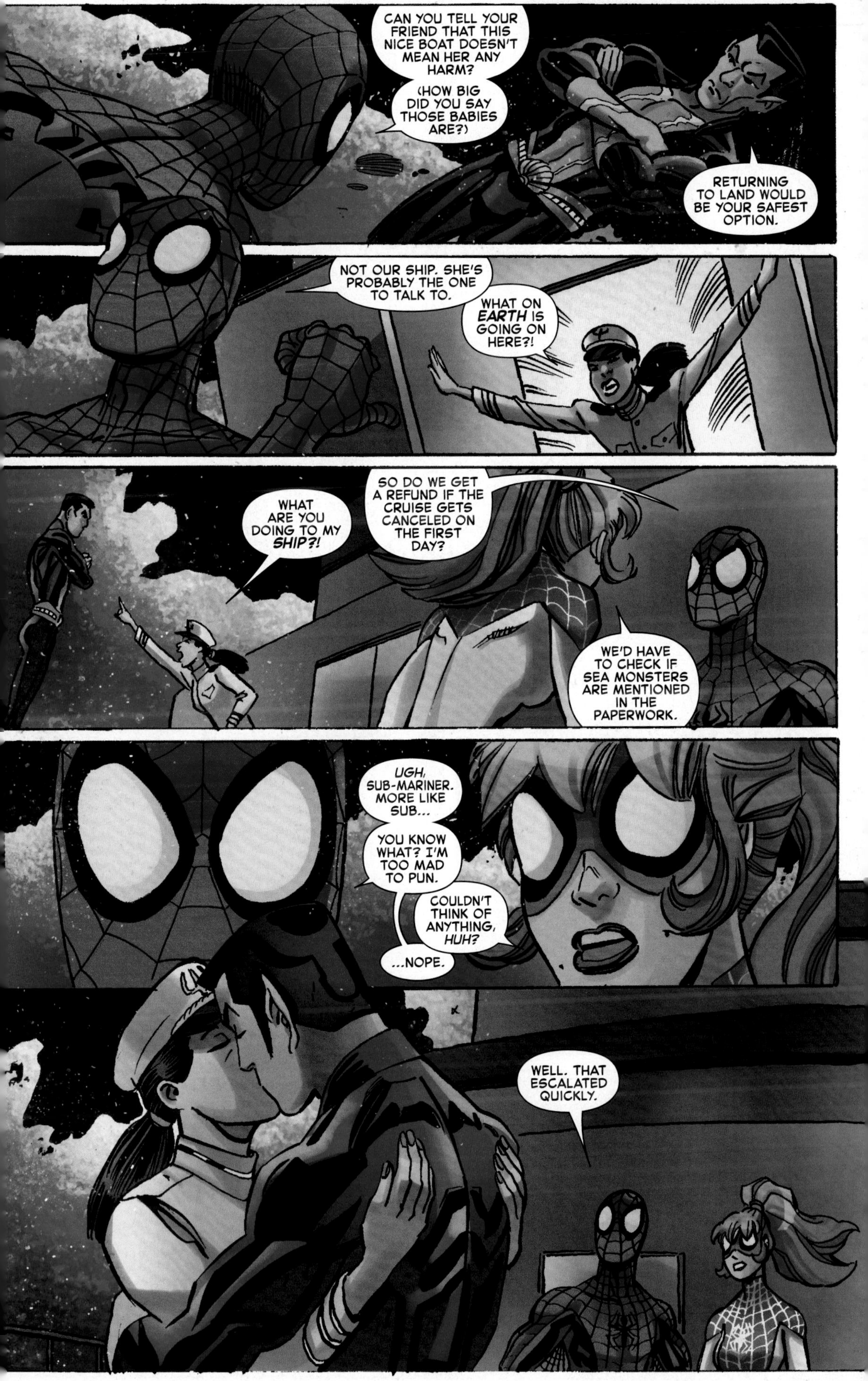
CAN YOU TELL YOUR FRIEND THAT THIS NICE BOAT DOESN'T MEAN HER ANY HARM?
(HOW BIG DID YOU SAY THOSE BABIES ARE?)
RETURNING TO LAND WOULD BE YOUR SAFEST OPTION.
NOT OUR SHIP. SHE'S PROBABLY THE ONE TO TALK TO.
WHAT ON *EARTH* IS GOING ON HERE?!
WHAT ARE YOU DOING TO MY *SHIP?!*
SO DO WE GET A REFUND IF THE CRUISE GETS CANCELED ON THE FIRST DAY?
WE'D HAVE TO CHECK IF SEA MONSTERS ARE MENTIONED IN THE PAPERWORK.
UGH, SUB-MARINER. MORE LIKE SUB...
YOU KNOW WHAT? I'M TOO MAD TO PUN.
COULDN'T THINK OF ANYTHING, *HUH?*
...NOPE.
WELL. THAT ESCALATED QUICKLY.

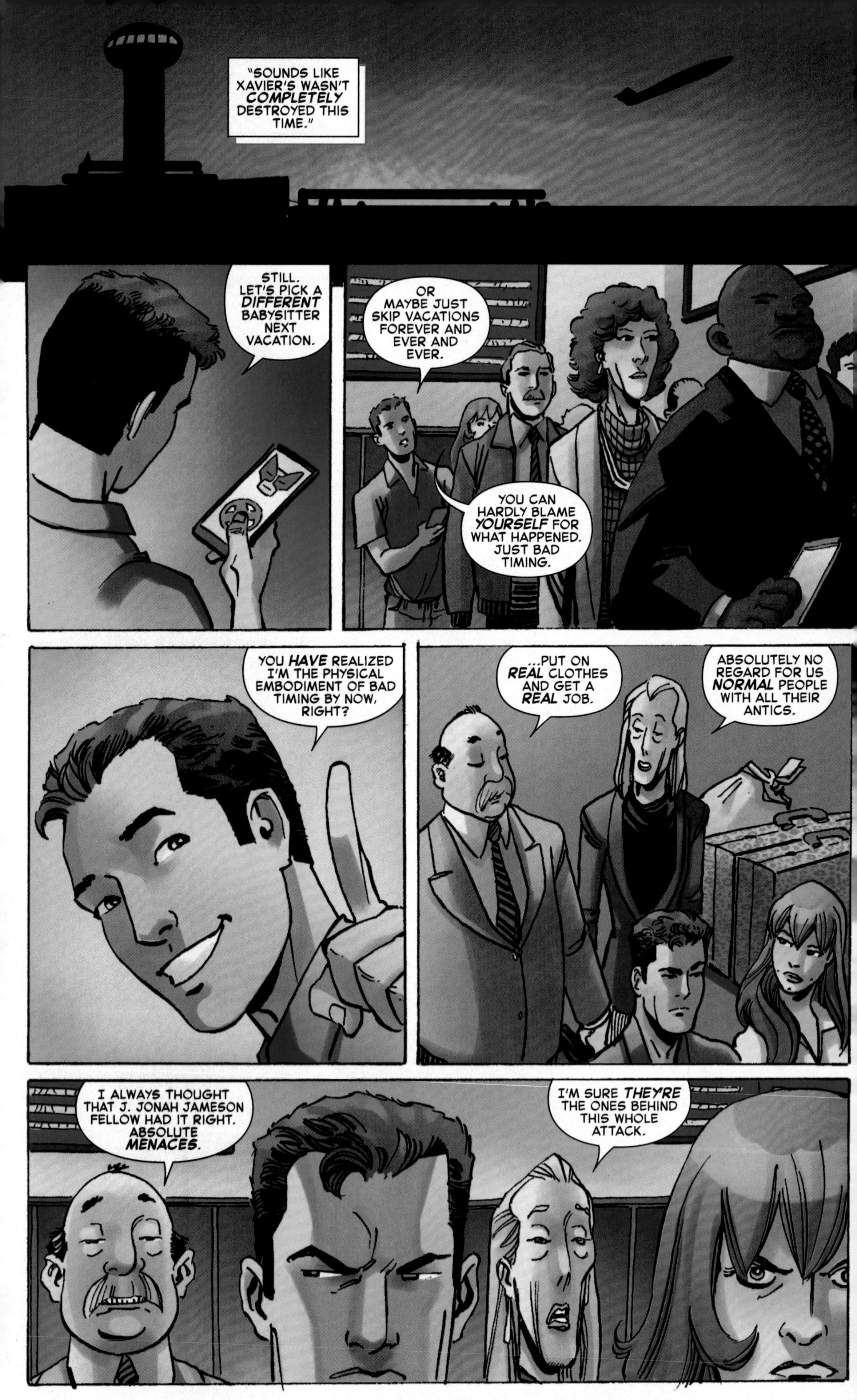
"SOUNDS LIKE XAVIER'S WASN'T COMPLETELY DESTROYED THIS TIME."
STILL. LET'S PICK A DIFFERENT BABYSITTER NEXT VACATION.
OR MAYBE JUST SKIP VACATIONS FOREVER AND EVER AND EVER.
YOU CAN HARDLY BLAME YOURSELF FOR WHAT HAPPENED. JUST BAD TIMING.
YOU HAVE REALIZED I'M THE PHYSICAL EMBODIMENT OF BAD TIMING BY NOW, RIGHT?
ABSOLUTELY NO REGARD FOR US NORMAL PEOPLE WITH ALL THEIR ANTICS.
...PUT ON REAL CLOTHES AND GET A REAL JOB.
I ALWAYS THOUGHT THAT J. JONAH JAMESON FELLOW HAD IT RIGHT. ABSOLUTE MENACES.
I'M SURE THEY'RE THE ONES BEHIND THIS WHOLE ATTACK.

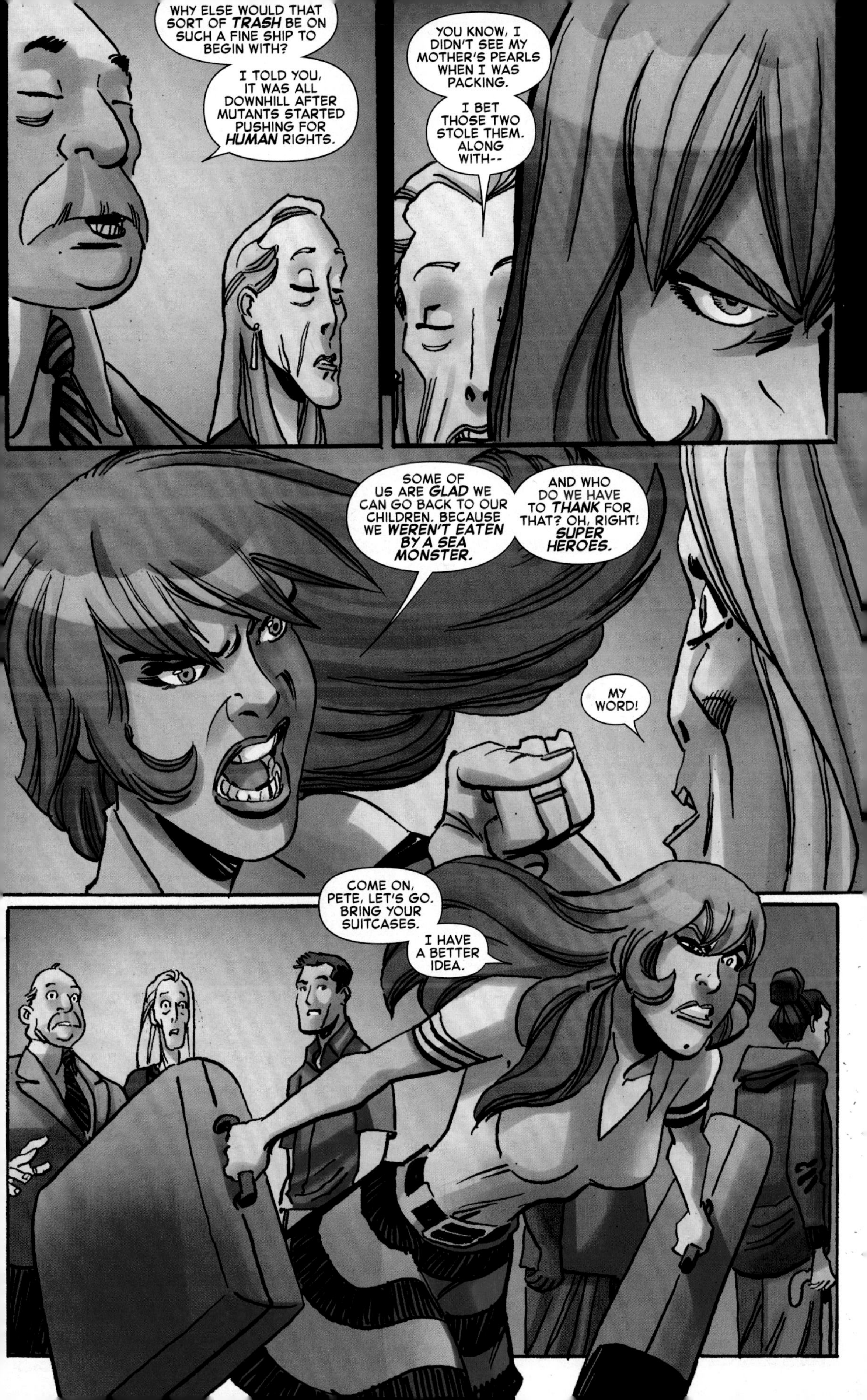
WHY ELSE WOULD THAT SORT OF TRASH BE ON SUCH A FINE SHIP TO BEGIN WITH?
I TOLD YOU, IT WAS ALL DOWNHILL AFTER MUTANTS STARTED PUSHING FOR HUMAN RIGHTS.
YOU KNOW, I DIDN'T SEE MY MOTHER'S PEARLS WHEN I WAS PACKING.
I BET THOSE TWO STOLE THEM. ALONG WITH--
SOME OF US ARE GLAD WE CAN GO BACK TO OUR CHILDREN. BECAUSE WE WEREN'T EATEN BY A SEA MONSTER.
AND WHO DO WE HAVE TO THANK FOR THAT? OH, RIGHT! SUPER HEROES.
MY WORD!
COME ON, PETE, LET'S GO. BRING YOUR SUITCASES.
I HAVE A BETTER IDEA.

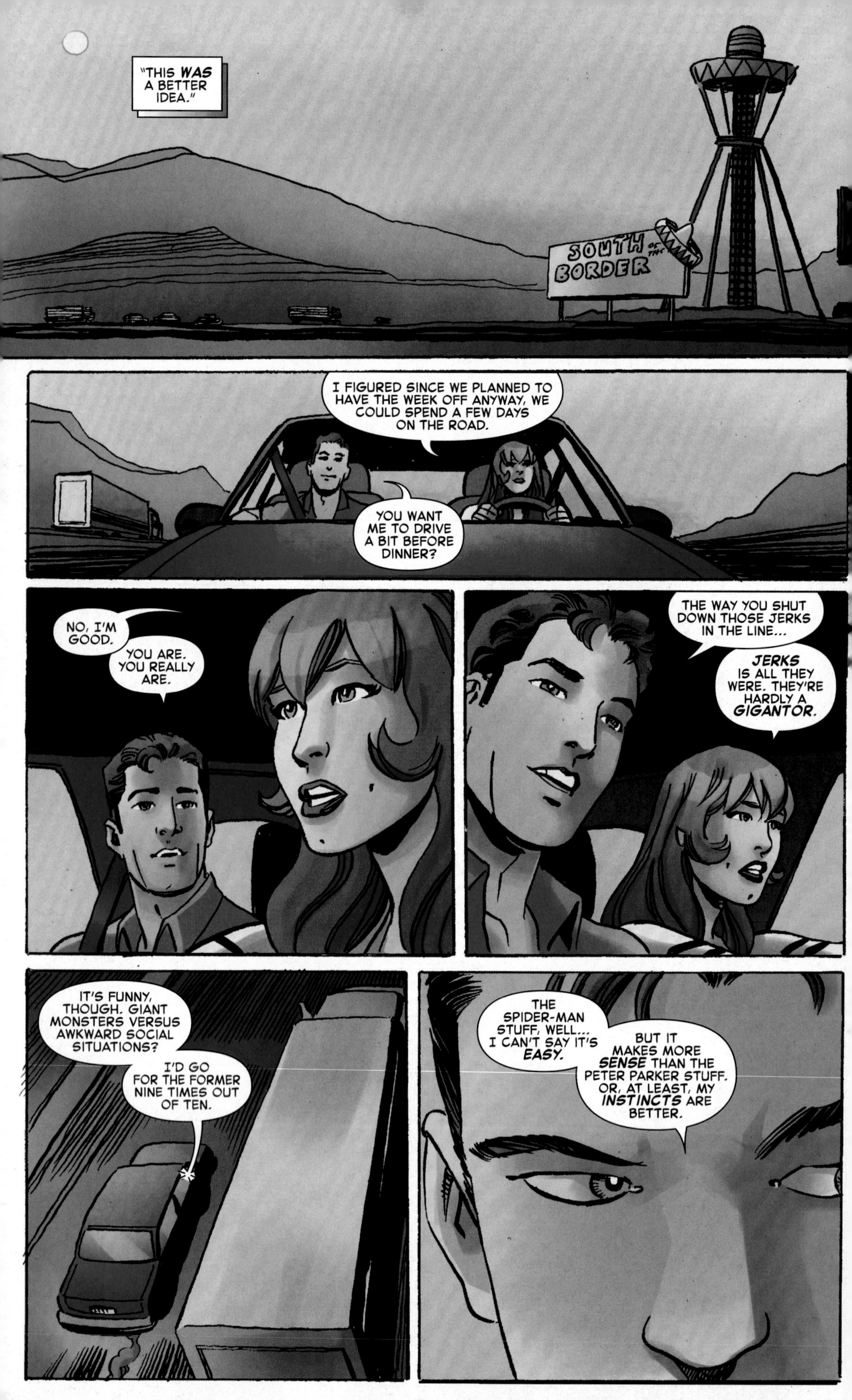
"THIS WAS A BETTER IDEA."
SOUTH OF THE BORDER
I FIGURED SINCE WE PLANNED TO HAVE THE WEEK OFF ANYWAY, WE COULD SPEND A FEW DAYS ON THE ROAD.
YOU WANT ME TO DRIVE A BIT BEFORE DINNER?
NO, I'M GOOD.
YOU ARE. YOU REALLY ARE.
THE WAY YOU SHUT DOWN THOSE JERKS IN THE LINE...
JERKS IS ALL THEY WERE. THEY'RE HARDLY A GIGANTOR.
IT'S FUNNY, THOUGH. GIANT MONSTERS VERSUS AWKWARD SOCIAL SITUATIONS?
I'D GO FOR THE FORMER NINE TIMES OUT OF TEN.
THE SPIDER-MAN STUFF, WELL... I CAN'T SAY IT'S EASY.
BUT IT MAKES MORE SENSE THAN THE PETER PARKER STUFF. OR, AT LEAST, MY INSTINCTS ARE BETTER.

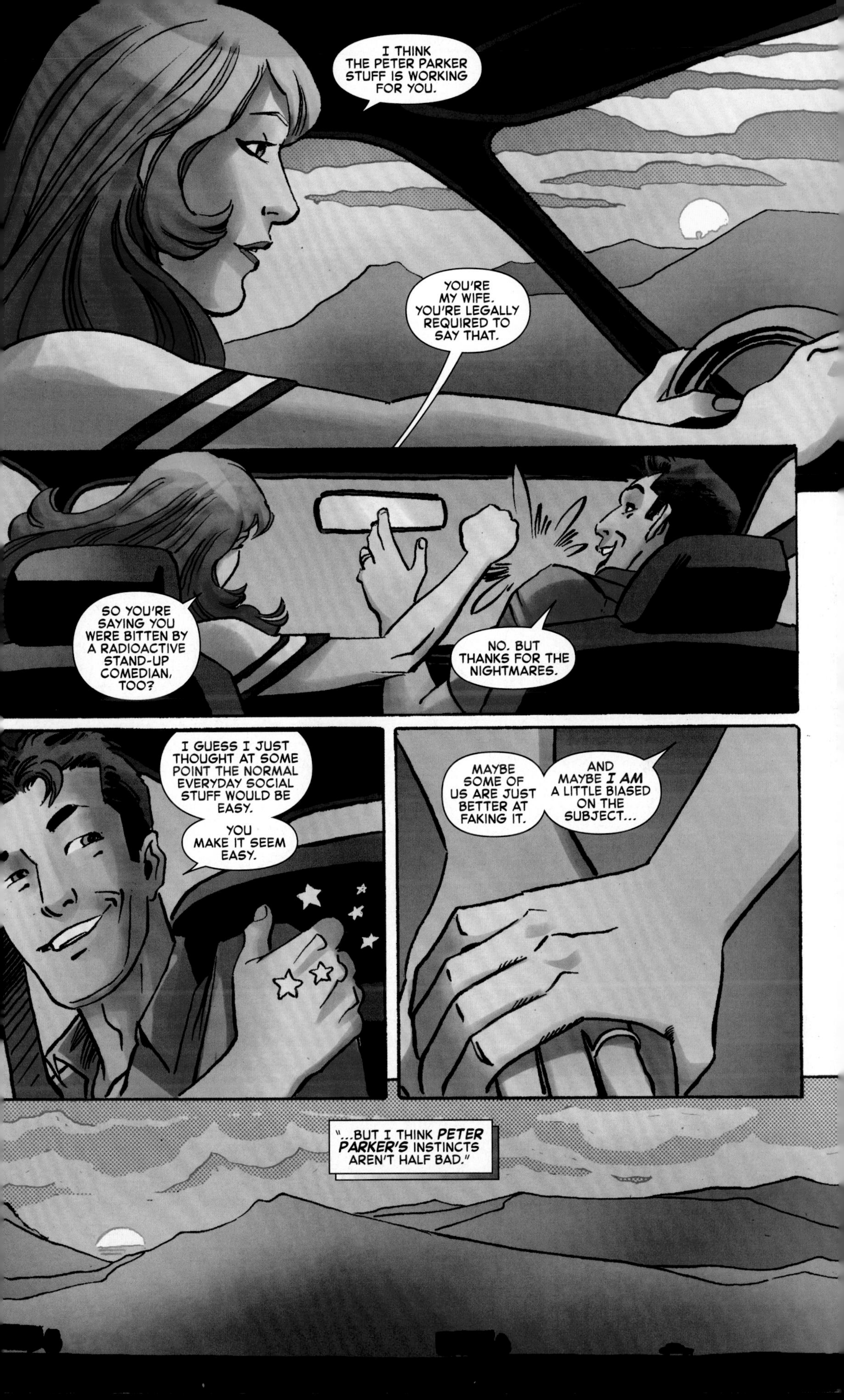

I THINK THE PETER PARKER STUFF IS WORKING FOR YOU.
YOU'RE MY WIFE. YOU'RE LEGALLY REQUIRED TO SAY THAT.
SO YOU'RE SAYING YOU WERE BITTEN BY A RADIOACTIVE STAND-UP COMEDIAN, TOO?
NO. BUT THANKS FOR THE NIGHTMARES.
I GUESS I JUST THOUGHT AT SOME POINT THE NORMAL EVERYDAY SOCIAL STUFF WOULD BE EASY.
YOU MAKE IT SEEM EASY.
MAYBE SOME OF US ARE JUST BETTER AT FAKING IT.
AND MAYBE *I AM* A LITTLE BIASED ON THE SUBJECT...
"...BUT I THINK *PETER PARKER'S* INSTINCTS AREN'T HALF BAD."

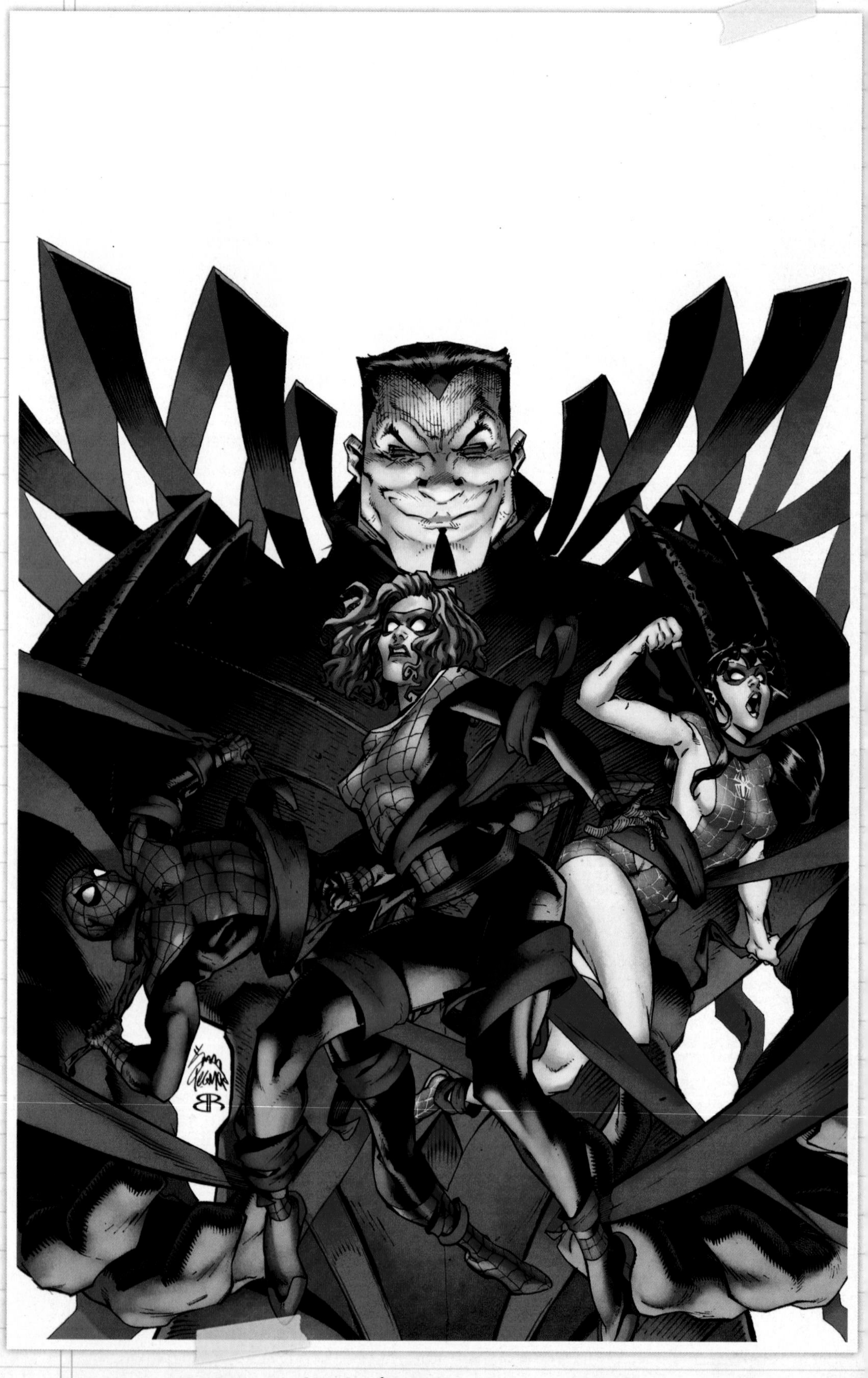

20: WEIRD SCIENCE — PART 1

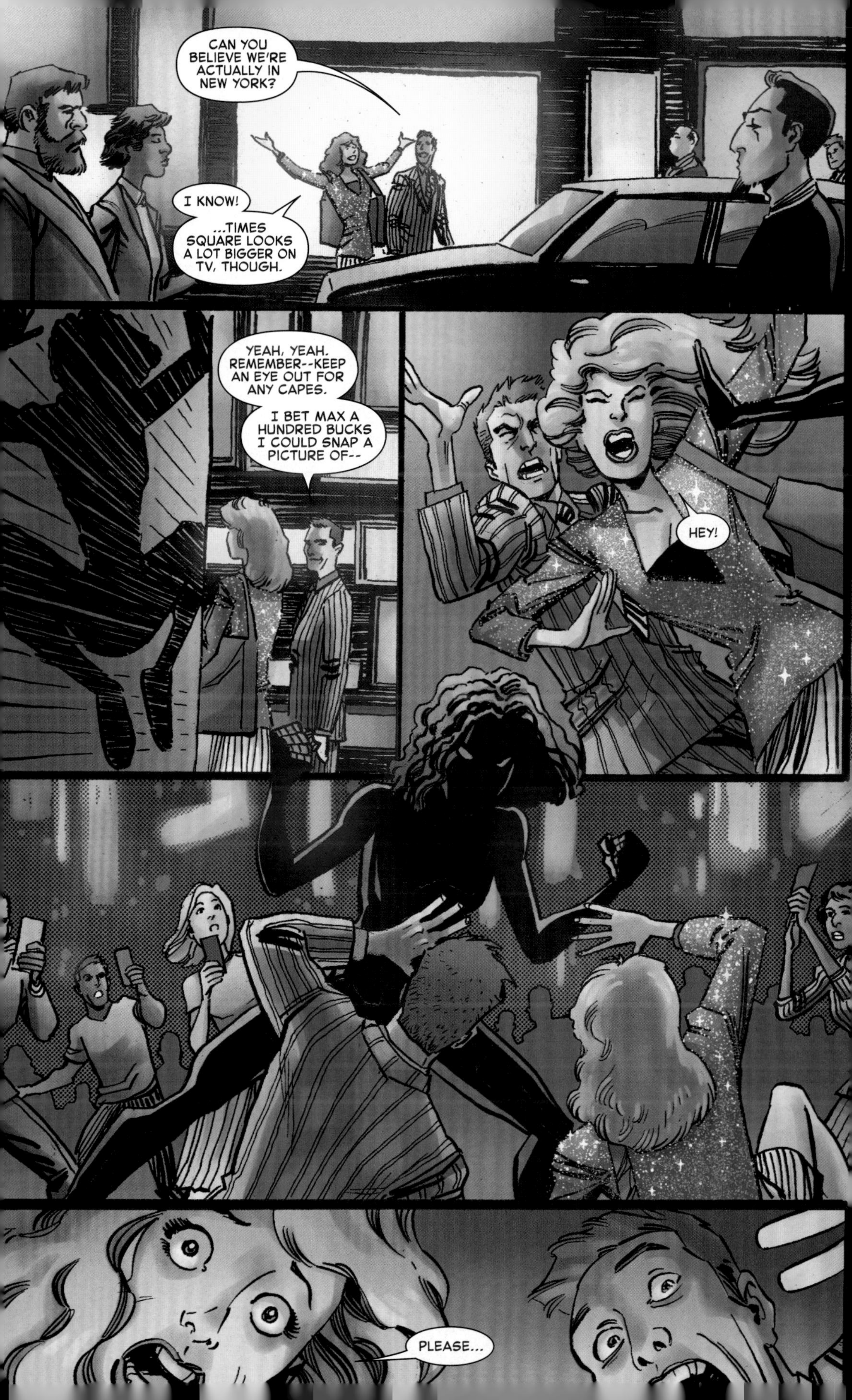
CAN YOU BELIEVE WE'RE ACTUALLY IN NEW YORK?
I KNOW!
...TIMES SQUARE LOOKS A LOT BIGGER ON TV, THOUGH.
YEAH, YEAH. REMEMBER--KEEP AN EYE OUT FOR ANY CAPES.
I BET MAX A HUNDRED BUCKS I COULD SNAP A PICTURE OF--
HEY!
PLEASE...

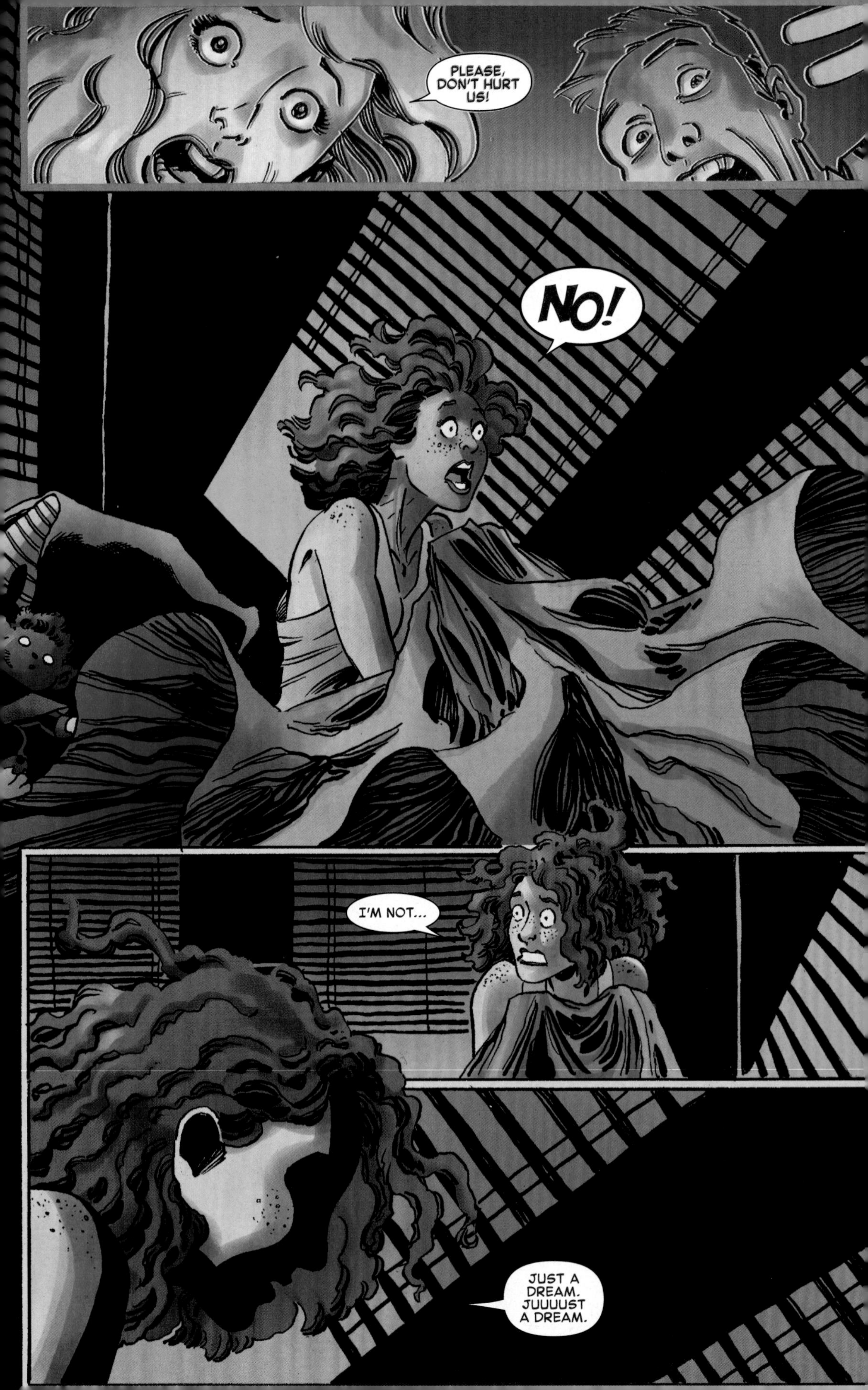
PLEASE, DON'T HURT US!
NO!
I'M NOT...
JUST A DREAM. JUUUUST A DREAM.

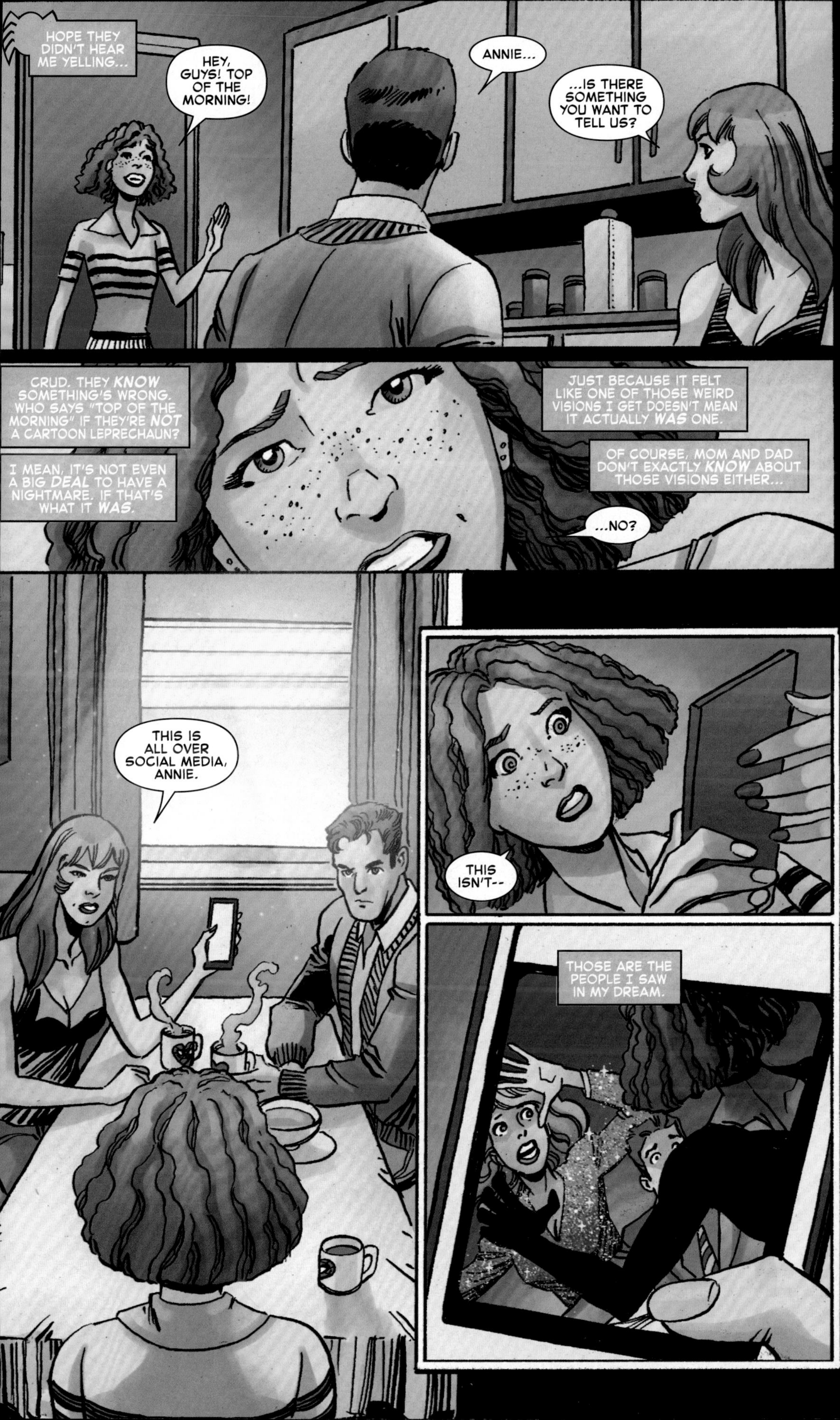
HOPE THEY DIDN'T HEAR ME YELLING...
HEY, GUYS! TOP OF THE MORNING!
ANNIE...
...IS THERE SOMETHING YOU WANT TO TELL US?
CRUD. THEY KNOW SOMETHING'S WRONG. WHO SAYS "TOP OF THE MORNING" IF THEY'RE NOT A CARTOON LEPRECHAUN?
I MEAN, IT'S NOT EVEN A BIG DEAL TO HAVE A NIGHTMARE. IF THAT'S WHAT IT WAS.
JUST BECAUSE IT FELT LIKE ONE OF THOSE WEIRD VISIONS I GET DOESN'T MEAN IT ACTUALLY WAS ONE.
OF COURSE, MOM AND DAD DON'T EXACTLY KNOW ABOUT THOSE VISIONS EITHER...
...NO?
THIS IS ALL OVER SOCIAL MEDIA, ANNIE.
THIS ISN'T--
THOSE ARE THE PEOPLE I SAW IN MY DREAM.

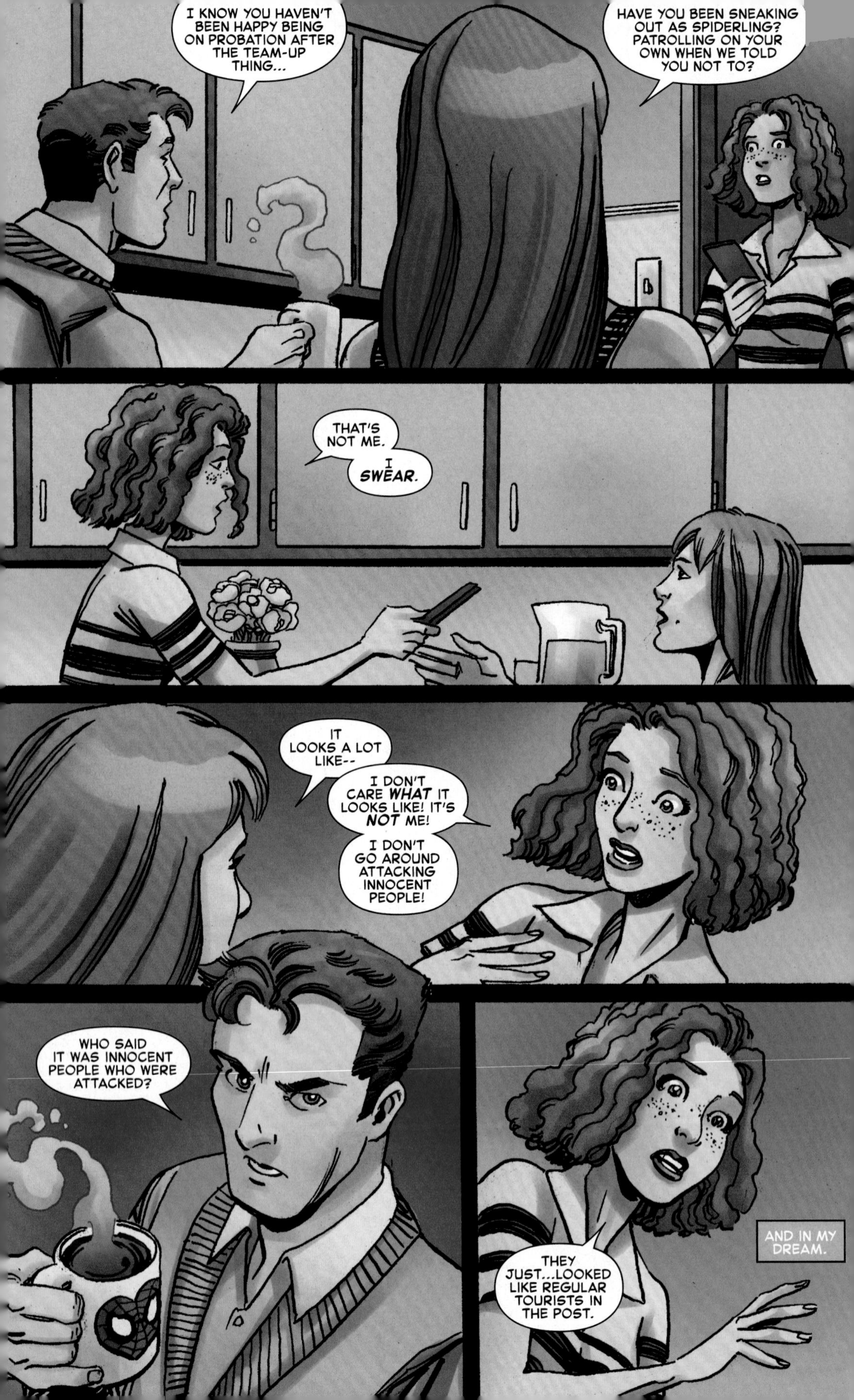

I KNOW YOU HAVEN'T BEEN HAPPY BEING ON PROBATION AFTER THE TEAM-UP THING...
HAVE YOU BEEN SNEAKING OUT AS SPIDERLING? PATROLLING ON YOUR OWN WHEN WE TOLD YOU NOT TO?
THAT'S NOT ME.
I SWEAR.
IT LOOKS A LOT LIKE--
I DON'T CARE WHAT IT LOOKS LIKE! IT'S NOT ME!
I DON'T GO AROUND ATTACKING INNOCENT PEOPLE!
WHO SAID IT WAS INNOCENT PEOPLE WHO WERE ATTACKED?
THEY JUST...LOOKED LIKE REGULAR TOURISTS IN THE POST.
AND IN MY DREAM.

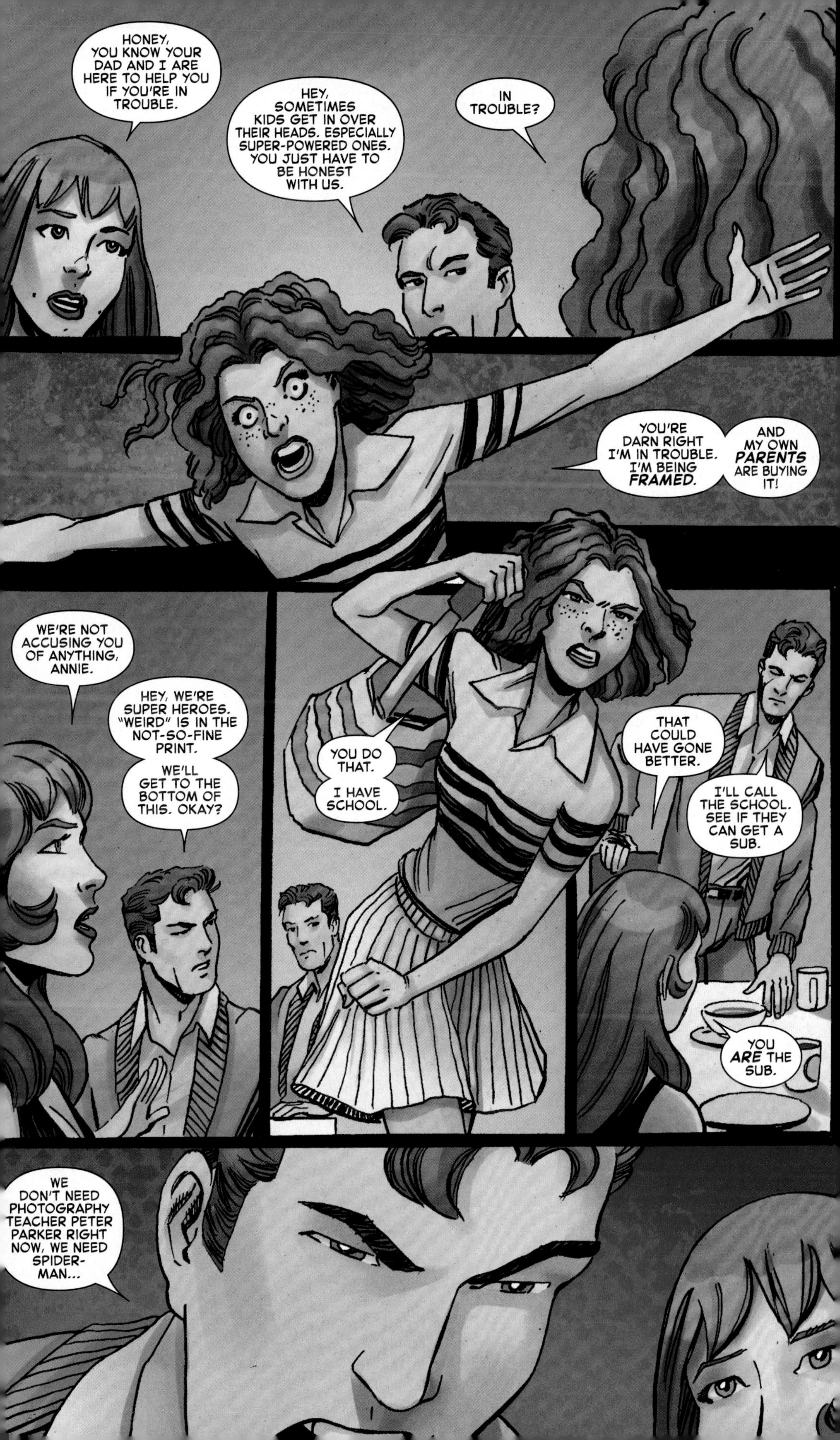
HONEY, YOU KNOW YOUR DAD AND I ARE HERE TO HELP YOU IF YOU'RE IN TROUBLE.
HEY, SOMETIMES KIDS GET IN OVER THEIR HEADS. ESPECIALLY SUPER-POWERED ONES. YOU JUST HAVE TO BE HONEST WITH US.
IN TROUBLE?
YOU'RE DARN RIGHT I'M IN TROUBLE. I'M BEING FRAMED.
AND MY OWN PARENTS ARE BUYING IT!
WE'RE NOT ACCUSING YOU OF ANYTHING, ANNIE.
HEY, WE'RE SUPER HEROES. "WEIRD" IS IN THE NOT-SO-FINE PRINT.
WE'LL GET TO THE BOTTOM OF THIS. OKAY?
YOU DO THAT.
I HAVE SCHOOL.
THAT COULD HAVE GONE BETTER.
I'LL CALL THE SCHOOL. SEE IF THEY CAN GET A SUB.
YOU ARE THE SUB.
WE DON'T NEED PHOTOGRAPHY TEACHER PETER PARKER RIGHT NOW, WE NEED SPIDER-MAN...

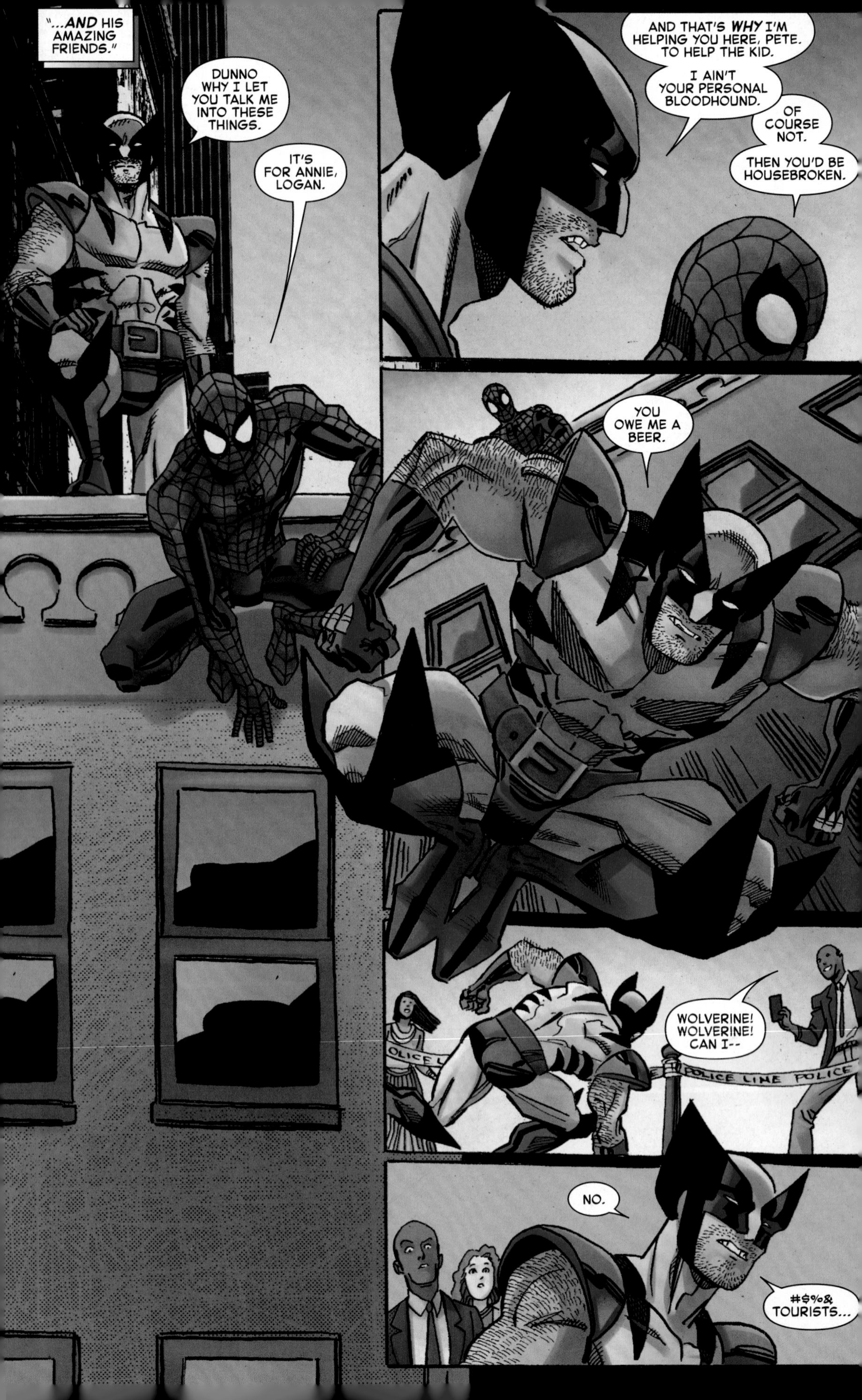
"...AND HIS AMAZING FRIENDS."
DUNNO WHY I LET YOU TALK ME INTO THESE THINGS.
IT'S FOR ANNIE, LOGAN.
AND THAT'S WHY I'M HELPING YOU HERE, PETE. TO HELP THE KID.
I AIN'T YOUR PERSONAL BLOODHOUND.
OF COURSE NOT.
THEN YOU'D BE HOUSEBROKEN.
YOU OWE ME A BEER.
WOLVERINE! WOLVERINE! CAN I--
POLICE LINE POLICE
NO.
#$%& TOURISTS...

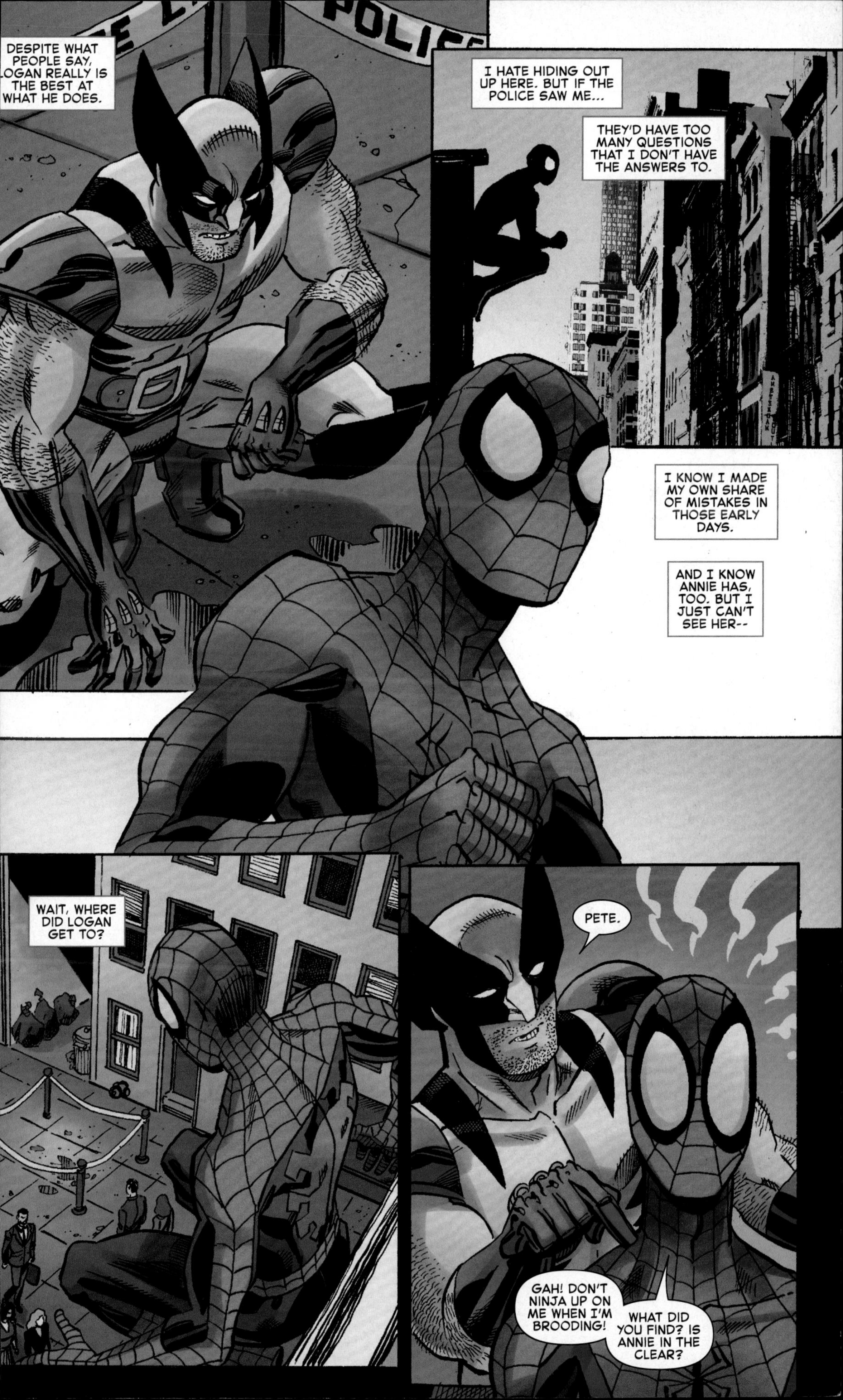

POLICE
DESPITE WHAT PEOPLE SAY, LOGAN REALLY IS THE BEST AT WHAT HE DOES.
I HATE HIDING OUT UP HERE. BUT IF THE POLICE SAW ME...
THEY'D HAVE TOO MANY QUESTIONS THAT I DON'T HAVE THE ANSWERS TO.
I KNOW I MADE MY OWN SHARE OF MISTAKES IN THOSE EARLY DAYS.
AND I KNOW ANNIE HAS, TOO. BUT I JUST CAN'T SEE HER--
WAIT, WHERE DID LOGAN GET TO?
PETE.
GAH! DON'T NINJA UP ON ME WHEN I'M BROODING!
WHAT DID YOU FIND? IS ANNIE IN THE CLEAR?

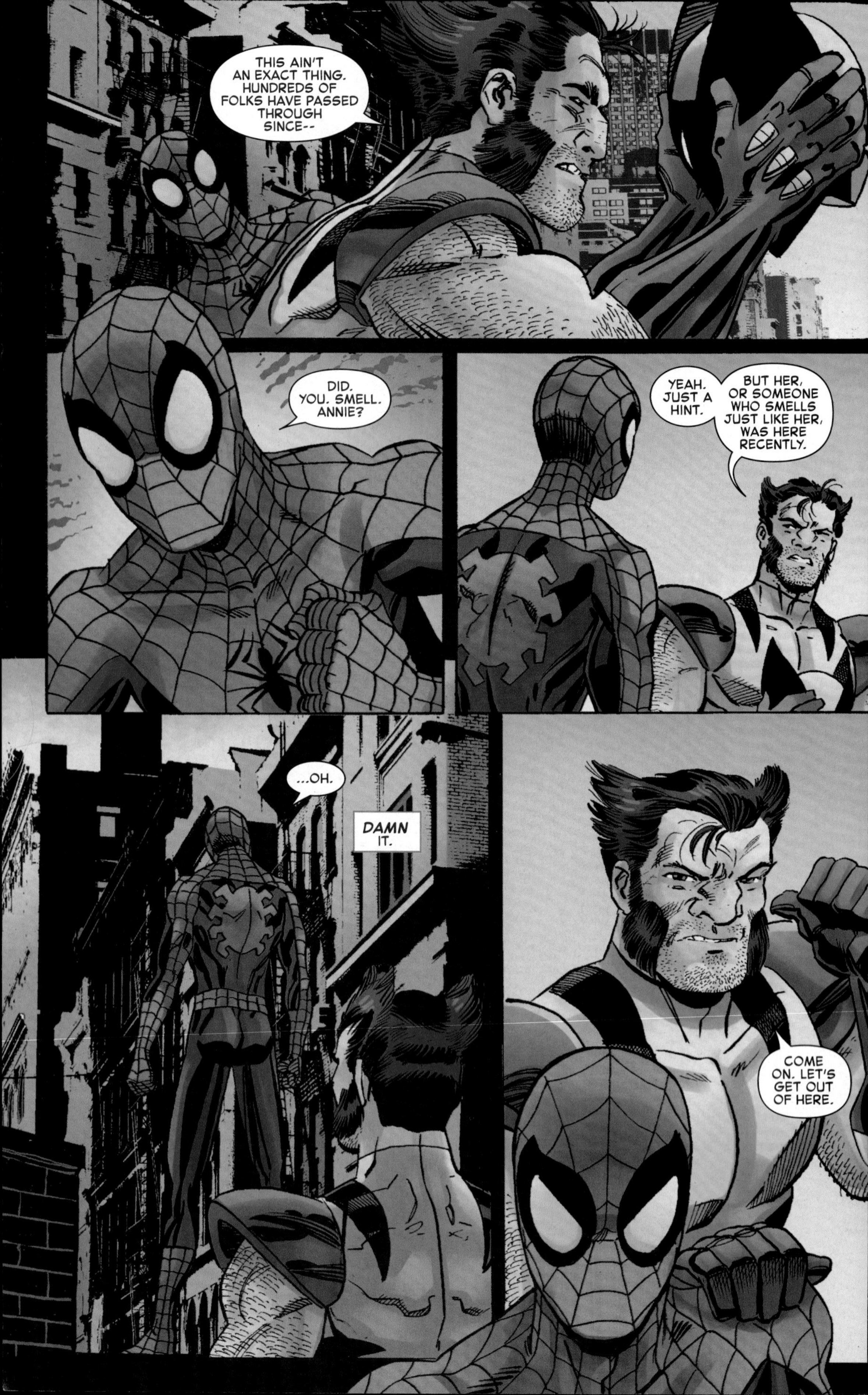
THIS AIN'T AN EXACT THING. HUNDREDS OF FOLKS HAVE PASSED THROUGH SINCE--
DID. YOU. SMELL. ANNIE?
YEAH. JUST A HINT.
BUT HER, OR SOMEONE WHO SMELLS JUST LIKE HER, WAS HERE RECENTLY.
...OH.
DAMN IT.
COME ON. LET'S GET OUT OF HERE.

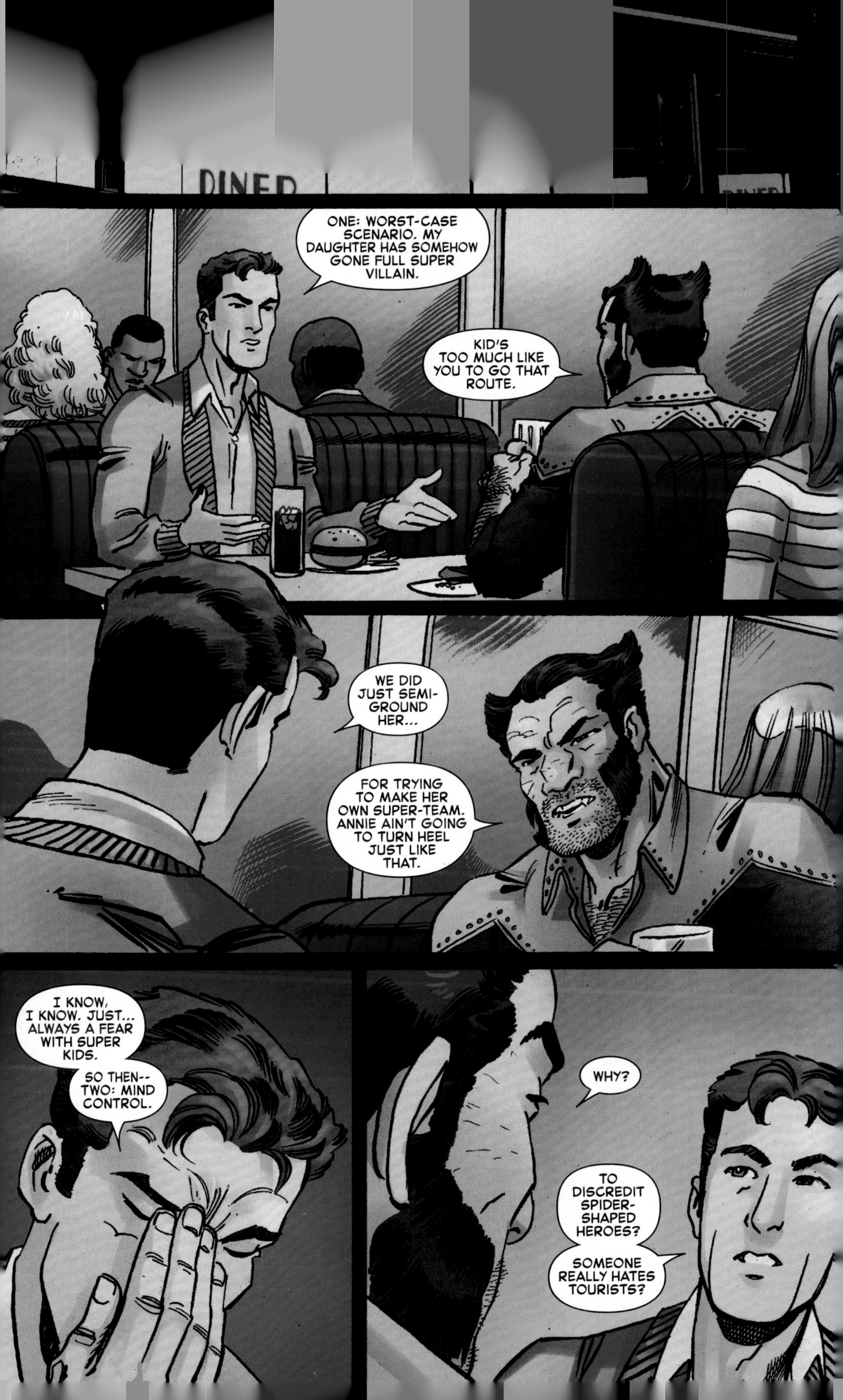
DINER
ONE: WORST-CASE SCENARIO. MY DAUGHTER HAS SOMEHOW GONE FULL SUPER VILLAIN.
KID'S TOO MUCH LIKE YOU TO GO THAT ROUTE.
WE DID JUST SEMI-GROUND HER...
FOR TRYING TO MAKE HER OWN SUPER-TEAM. ANNIE AIN'T GOING TO TURN HEEL JUST LIKE THAT.
I KNOW, I KNOW. JUST... ALWAYS A FEAR WITH SUPER KIDS.
SO THEN-- TWO: MIND CONTROL.
WHY?
TO DISCREDIT SPIDER-SHAPED HEROES?
SOMEONE REALLY HATES TOURISTS?

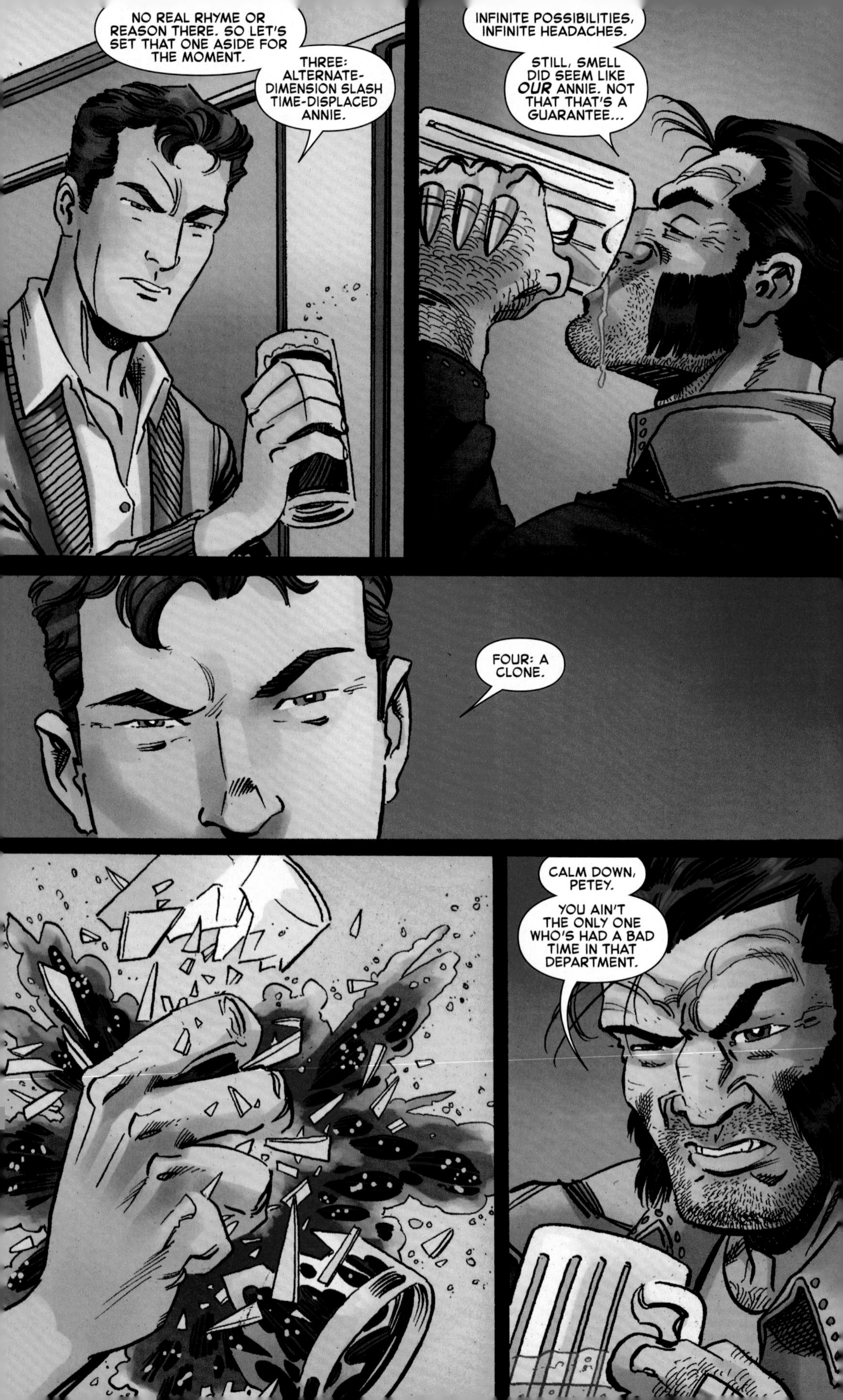
NO REAL RHYME OR REASON THERE. SO LET'S SET THAT ONE ASIDE FOR THE MOMENT.
THREE: ALTERNATE-DIMENSION SLASH TIME-DISPLACED ANNIE.
INFINITE POSSIBILITIES, INFINITE HEADACHES.
STILL, SMELL DID SEEM LIKE OUR ANNIE. NOT THAT THAT'S A GUARANTEE...
FOUR: A CLONE.
CALM DOWN, PETEY.
YOU AIN'T THE ONLY ONE WHO'S HAD A BAD TIME IN THAT DEPARTMENT.

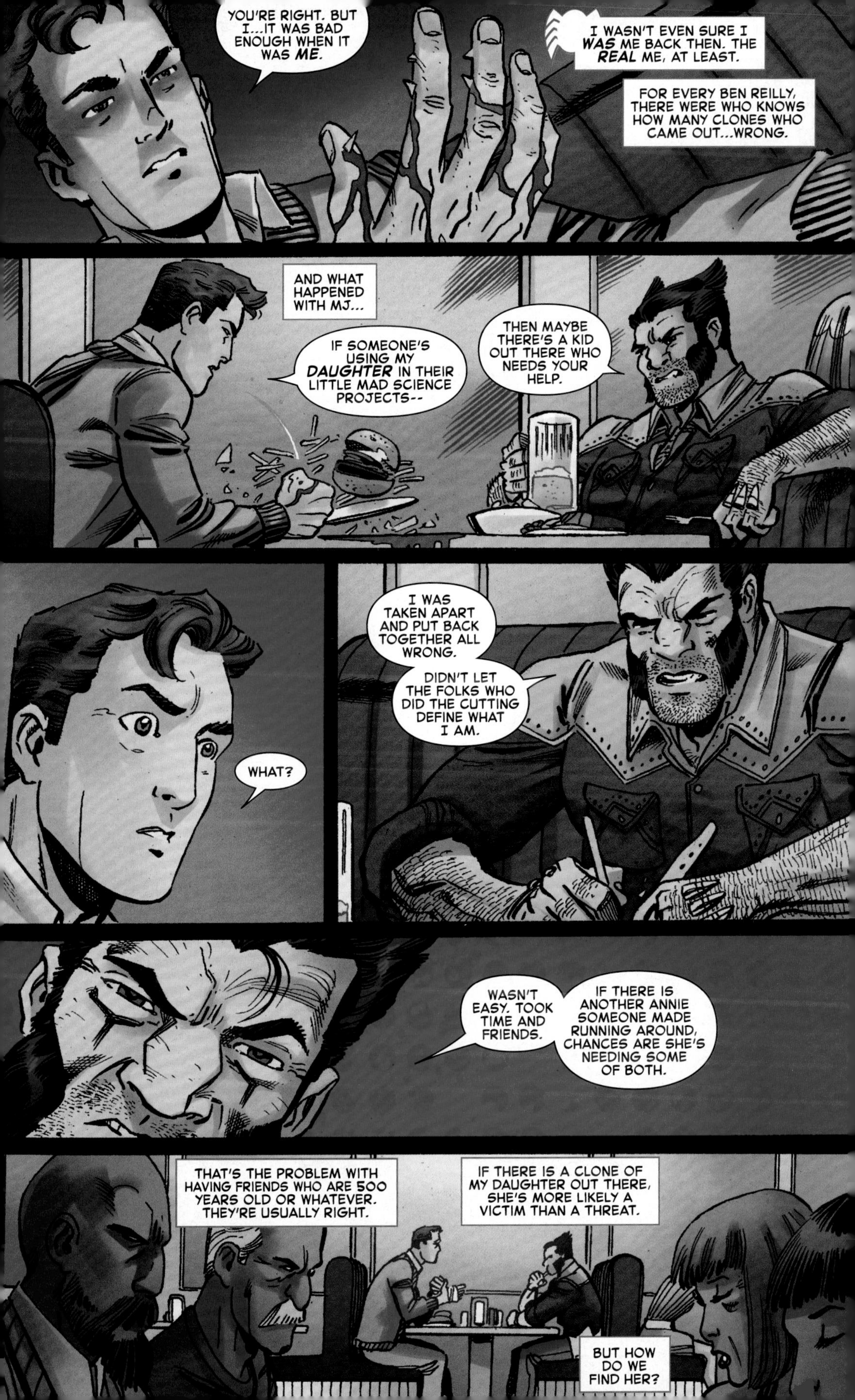

YOU'RE RIGHT. BUT I...IT WAS BAD ENOUGH WHEN IT WAS ME.
I WASN'T EVEN SURE I WAS ME BACK THEN. THE REAL ME, AT LEAST.
FOR EVERY BEN REILLY, THERE WERE WHO KNOWS HOW MANY CLONES WHO CAME OUT...WRONG.
AND WHAT HAPPENED WITH MJ...
IF SOMEONE'S USING MY DAUGHTER IN THEIR LITTLE MAD SCIENCE PROJECTS--
THEN MAYBE THERE'S A KID OUT THERE WHO NEEDS YOUR HELP.
WHAT?
I WAS TAKEN APART AND PUT BACK TOGETHER ALL WRONG.
DIDN'T LET THE FOLKS WHO DID THE CUTTING DEFINE WHAT I AM.
WASN'T EASY. TOOK TIME AND FRIENDS.
IF THERE IS ANOTHER ANNIE SOMEONE MADE RUNNING AROUND, CHANCES ARE SHE'S NEEDING SOME OF BOTH.
THAT'S THE PROBLEM WITH HAVING FRIENDS WHO ARE 500 YEARS OLD OR WHATEVER. THEY'RE USUALLY RIGHT.
IF THERE IS A CLONE OF MY DAUGHTER OUT THERE, SHE'S MORE LIKELY A VICTIM THAN A THREAT.
BUT HOW DO WE FIND HER?

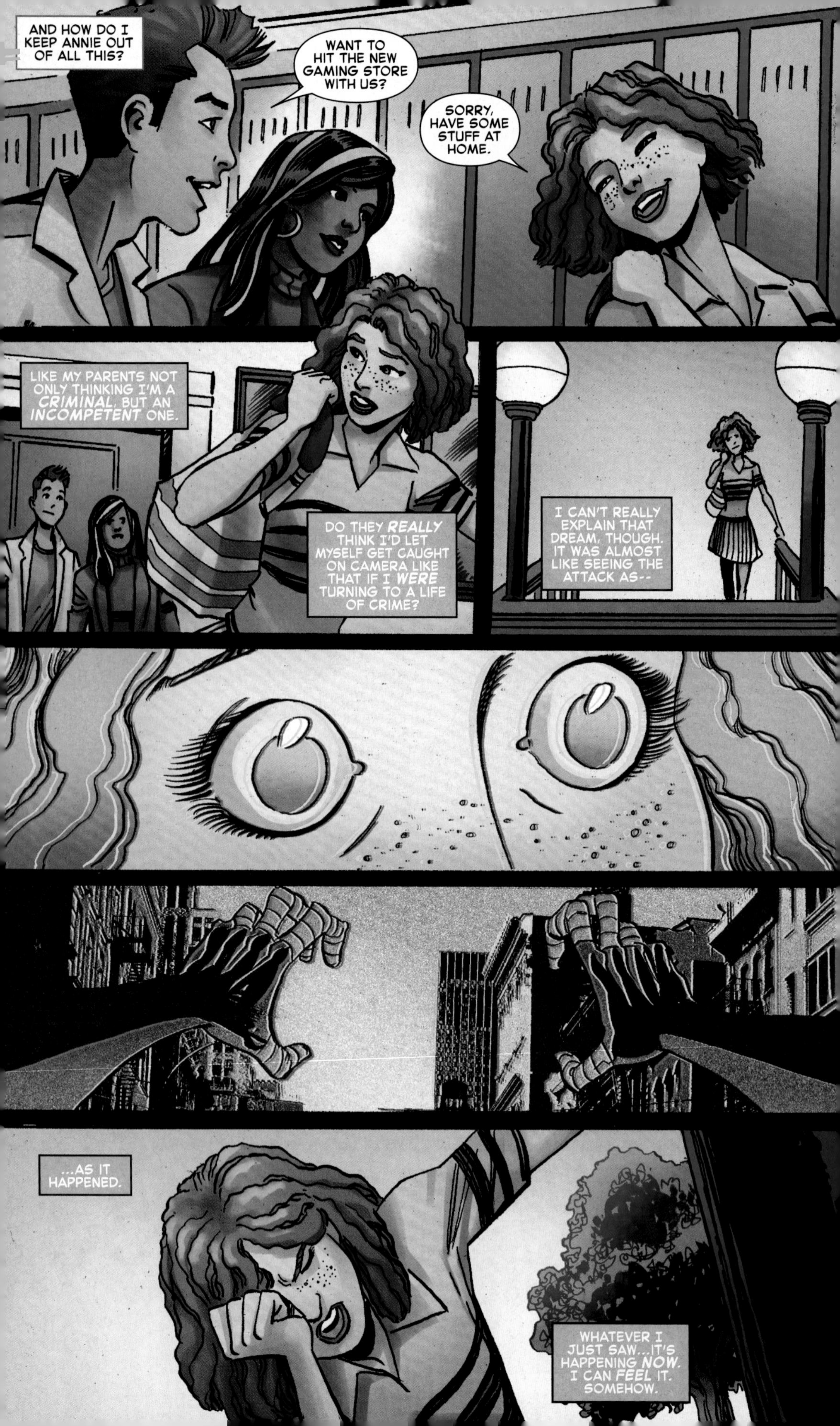
AND HOW DO I KEEP ANNIE OUT OF ALL THIS?
WANT TO HIT THE NEW GAMING STORE WITH US?
SORRY, HAVE SOME STUFF AT HOME.
LIKE MY PARENTS NOT ONLY THINKING I'M A CRIMINAL, BUT AN INCOMPETENT ONE.
DO THEY REALLY THINK I'D LET MYSELF GET CAUGHT ON CAMERA LIKE THAT IF I WERE TURNING TO A LIFE OF CRIME?
I CAN'T REALLY EXPLAIN THAT DREAM, THOUGH. IT WAS ALMOST LIKE SEEING THE ATTACK AS--
...AS IT HAPPENED.
WHATEVER I JUST SAW...IT'S HAPPENING NOW. I CAN FEEL IT. SOMEHOW.

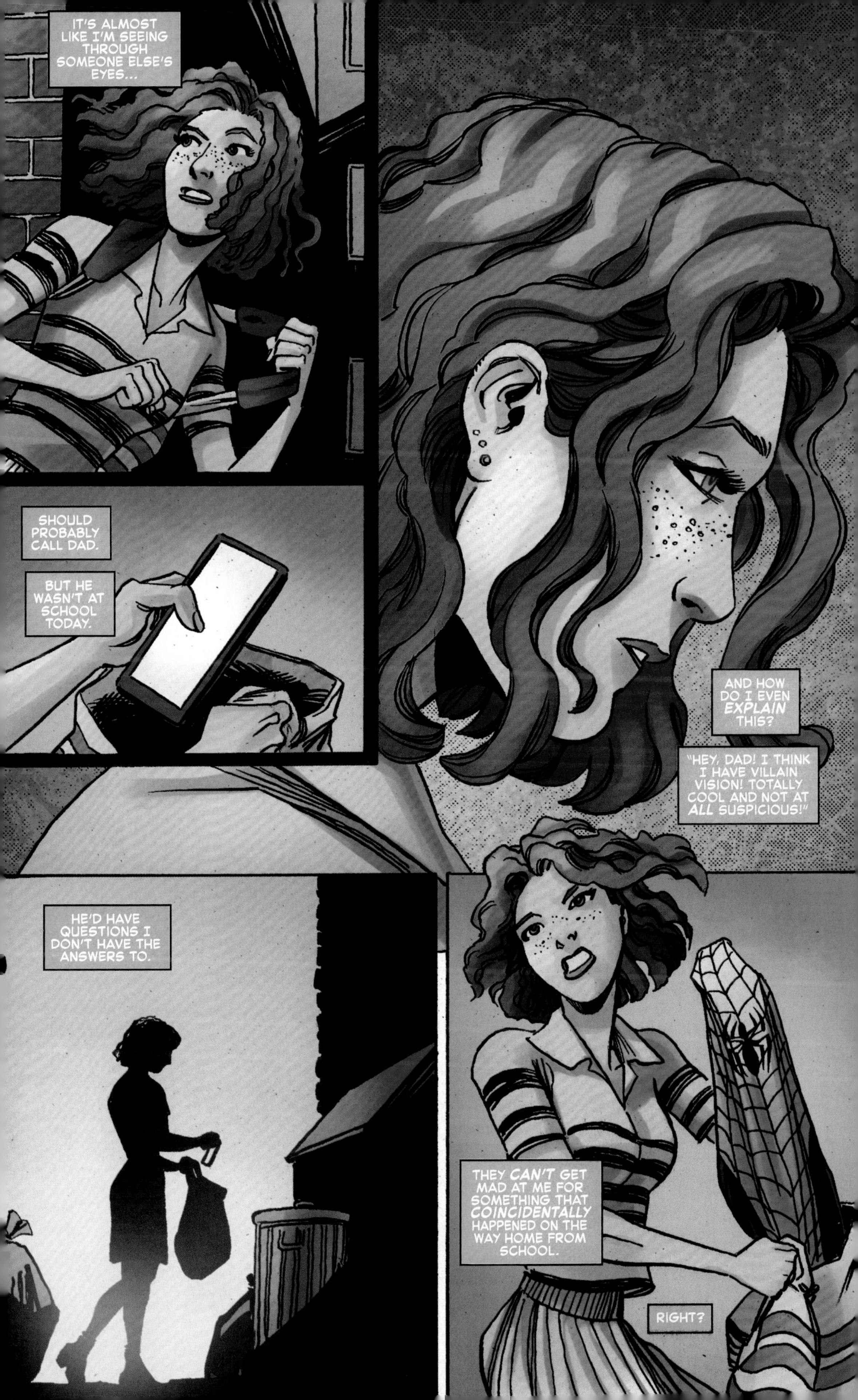
IT'S ALMOST LIKE I'M SEEING THROUGH SOMEONE ELSE'S EYES...
SHOULD PROBABLY CALL DAD.
BUT HE WASN'T AT SCHOOL TODAY.
AND HOW DO I EVEN *EXPLAIN* THIS?
"HEY, DAD! I THINK I HAVE VILLAIN VISION! TOTALLY COOL AND NOT AT *ALL* SUSPICIOUS!"
HE'D HAVE QUESTIONS I DON'T HAVE THE ANSWERS TO.
THEY *CAN'T* GET MAD AT ME FOR SOMETHING THAT *COINCIDENTALLY* HAPPENED ON THE WAY HOME FROM SCHOOL.
RIGHT?

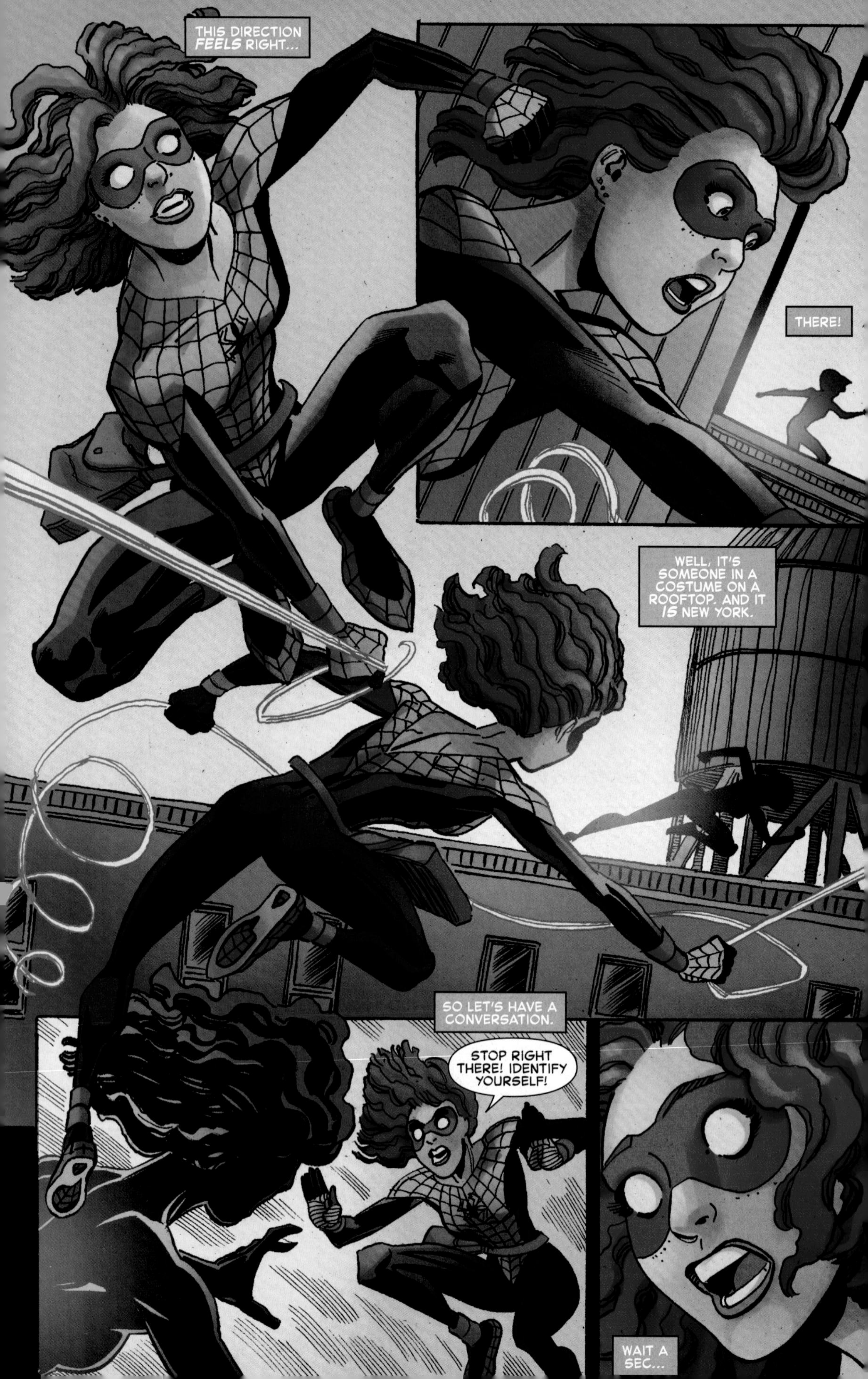
THIS DIRECTION *FEELS* RIGHT...
THERE!
WELL, IT'S SOMEONE IN A COSTUME ON A ROOFTOP. AND IT *IS* NEW YORK.
SO LET'S HAVE A CONVERSATION.
STOP RIGHT THERE! IDENTIFY YOURSELF!
WAIT A SEC...

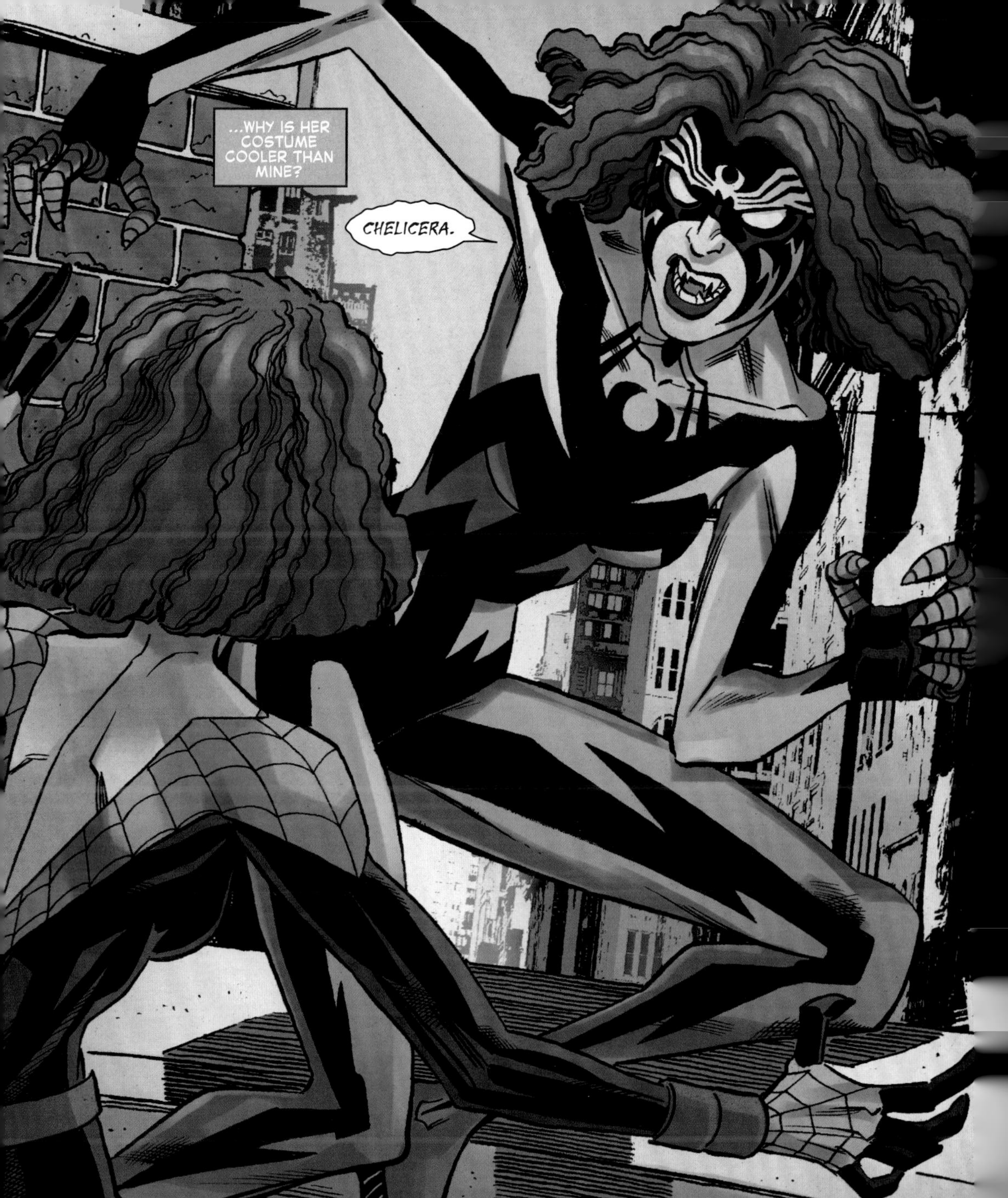
...WHY IS HER COSTUME COOLER THAN MINE?
CHELICERA.

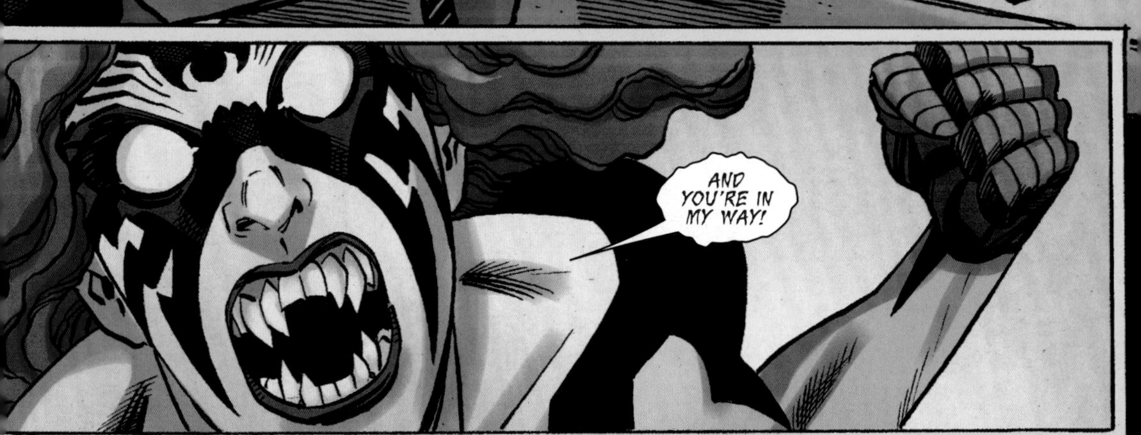
AND YOU'RE IN MY WAY!

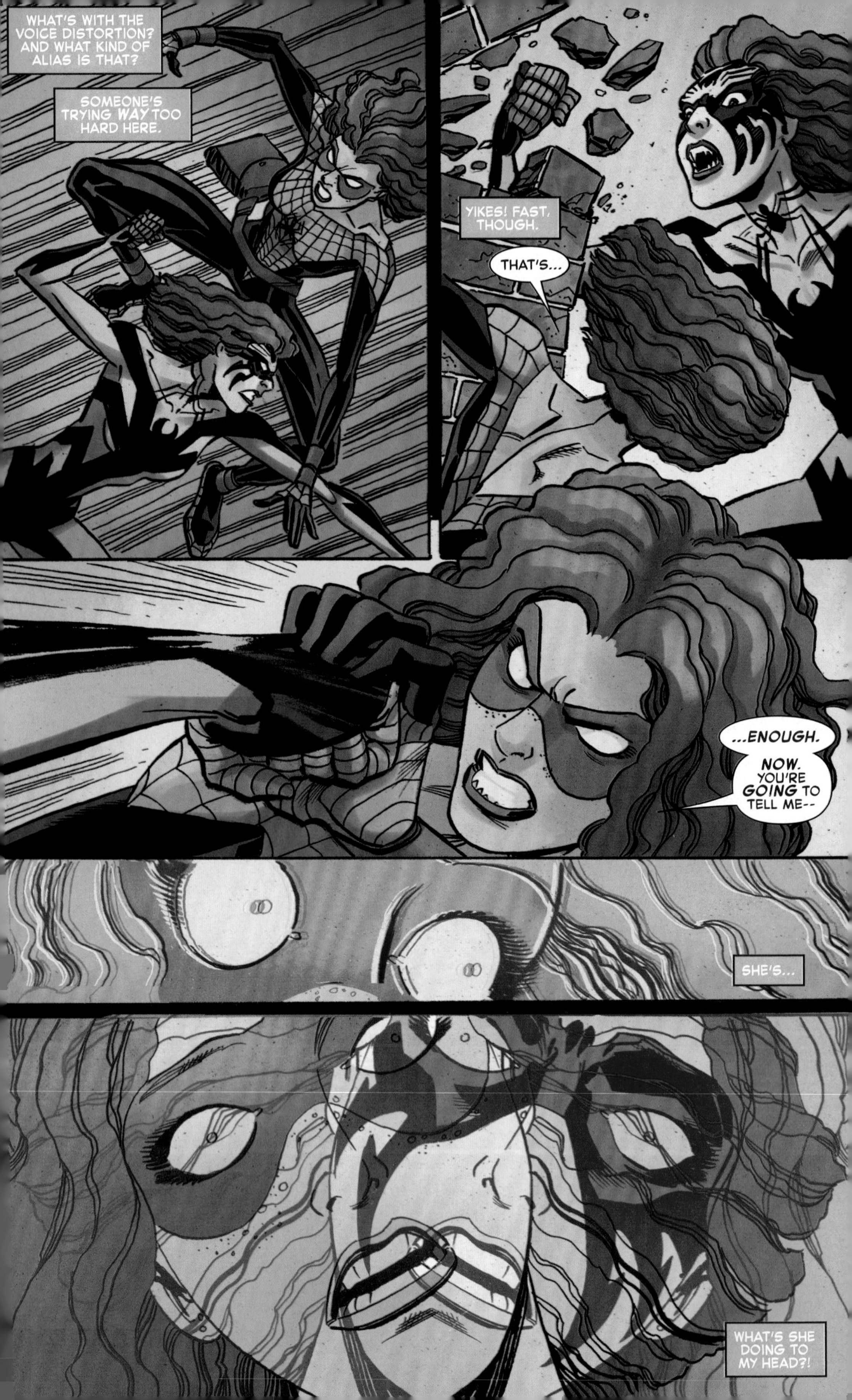
WHAT'S WITH THE VOICE DISTORTION? AND WHAT KIND OF ALIAS IS THAT?
SOMEONE'S TRYING WAY TOO HARD HERE.
YIKES! FAST, THOUGH.
THAT'S...
...ENOUGH.
NOW. YOU'RE GOING TO TELL ME--
SHE'S...
WHAT'S SHE DOING TO MY HEAD?!

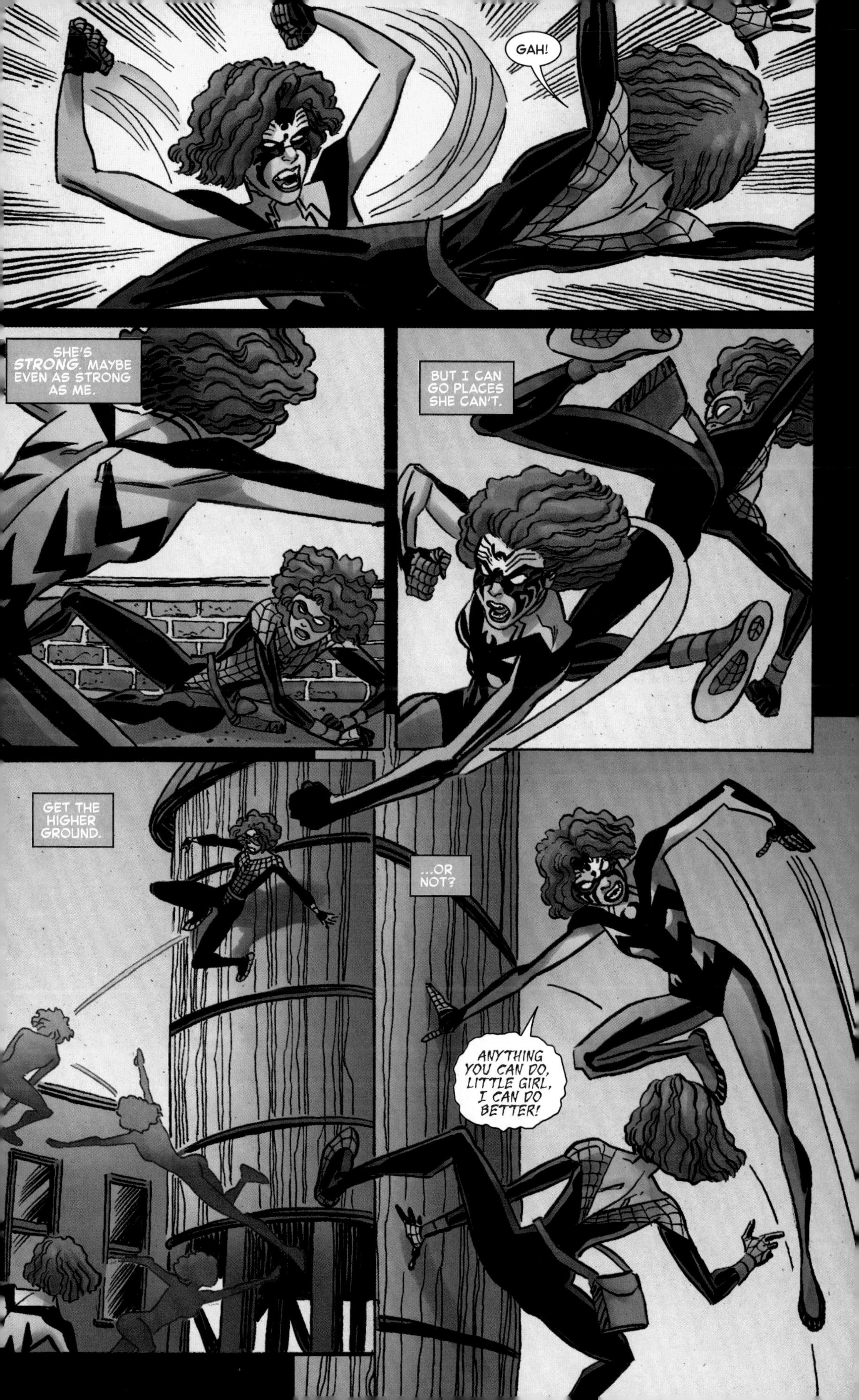
GAH!
SHE'S STRONG. MAYBE EVEN AS STRONG AS ME.
BUT I CAN GO PLACES SHE CAN'T.
GET THE HIGHER GROUND.
...OR NOT?
ANYTHING YOU CAN DO, LITTLE GIRL, I CAN DO BETTER!

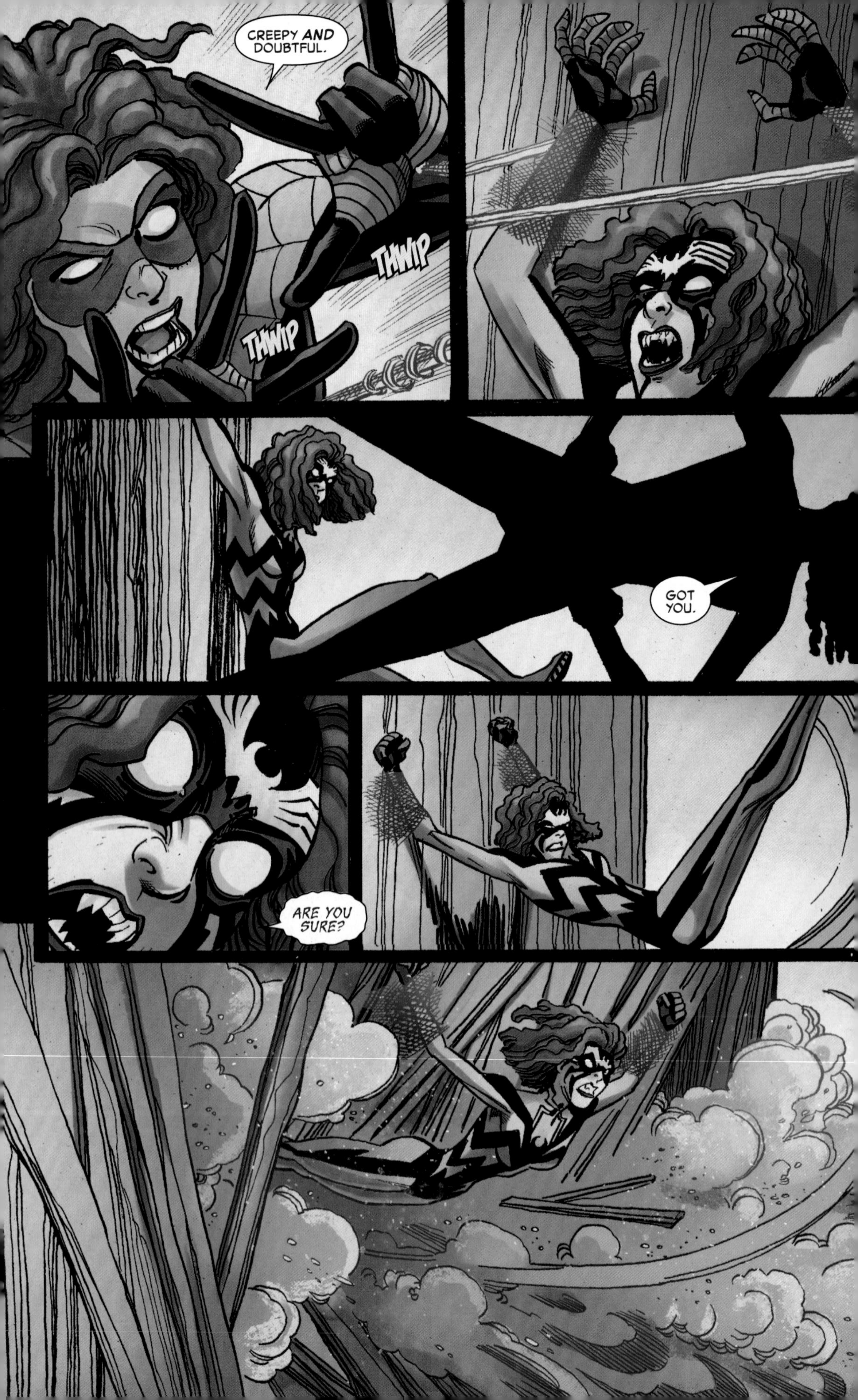
CREEPY AND DOUBTFUL.
THWIP
THWIP
GOT YOU.
ARE YOU SURE?

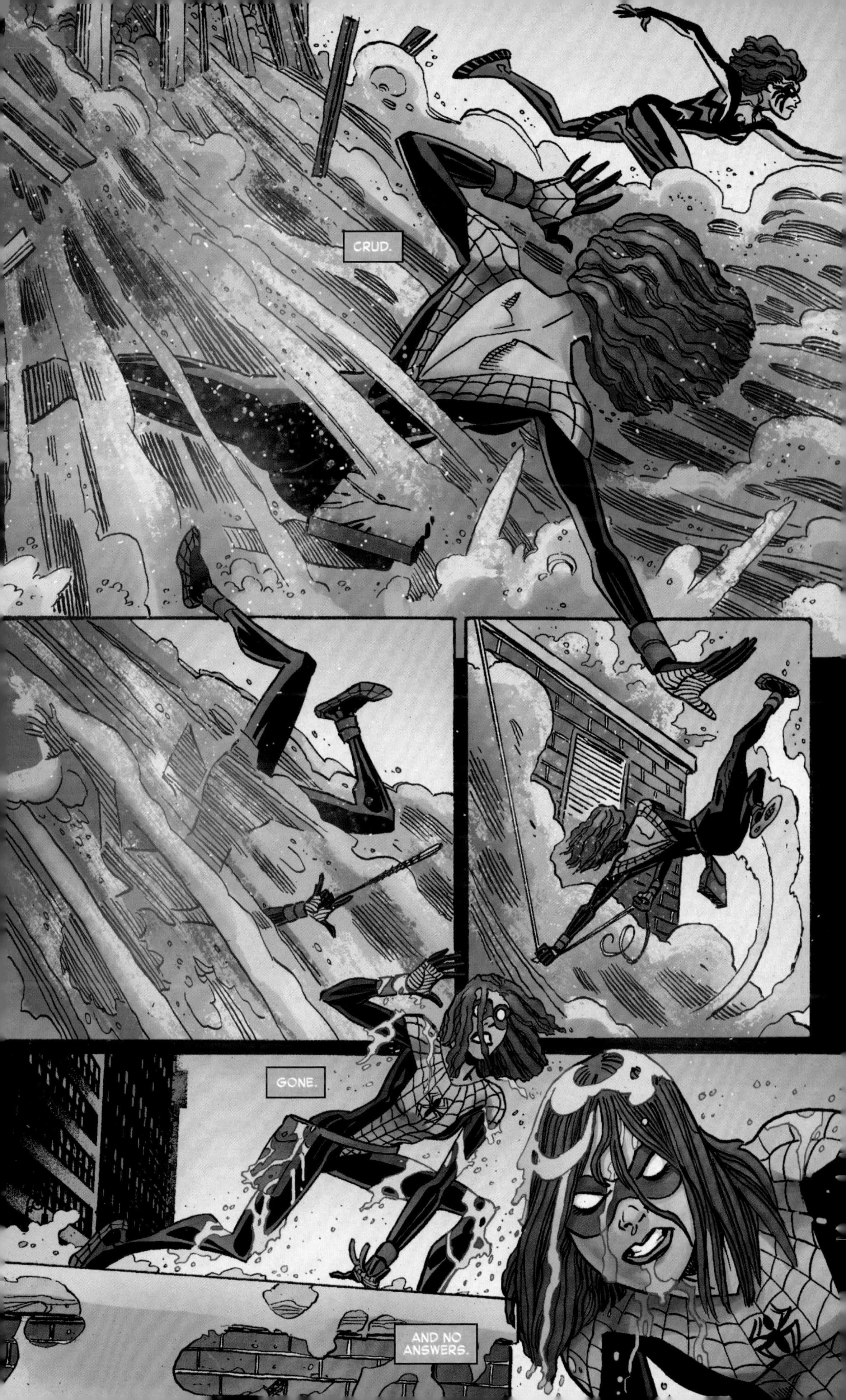
CRUD.
GONE.
AND NO ANSWERS.

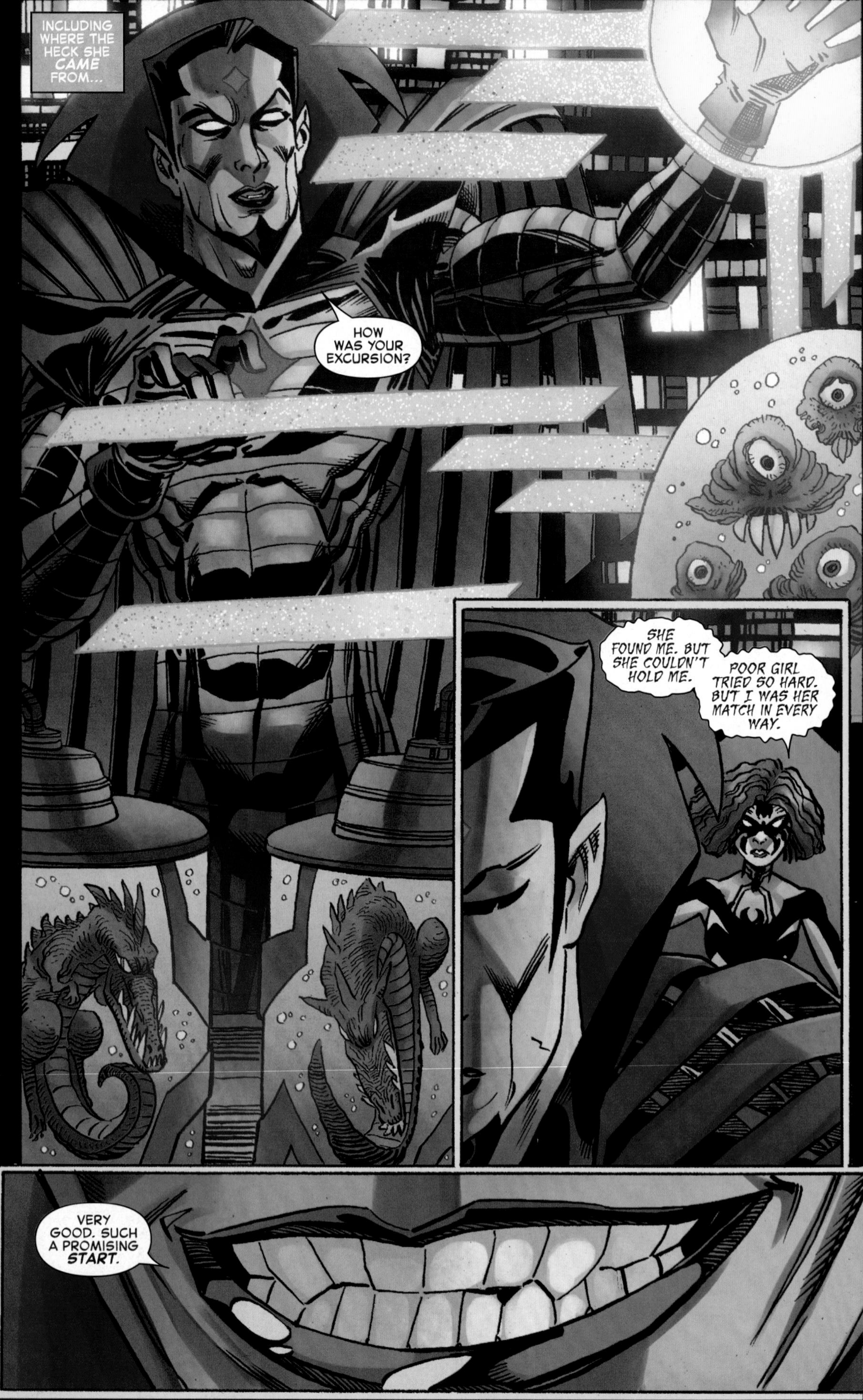

INCLUDING WHERE THE HECK SHE CAME FROM...
HOW WAS YOUR EXCURSION?
SHE FOUND ME. BUT SHE COULDN'T HOLD ME.
POOR GIRL TRIED SO HARD. BUT I WAS HER MATCH IN EVERY WAY.
VERY GOOD. SUCH A PROMISING START.

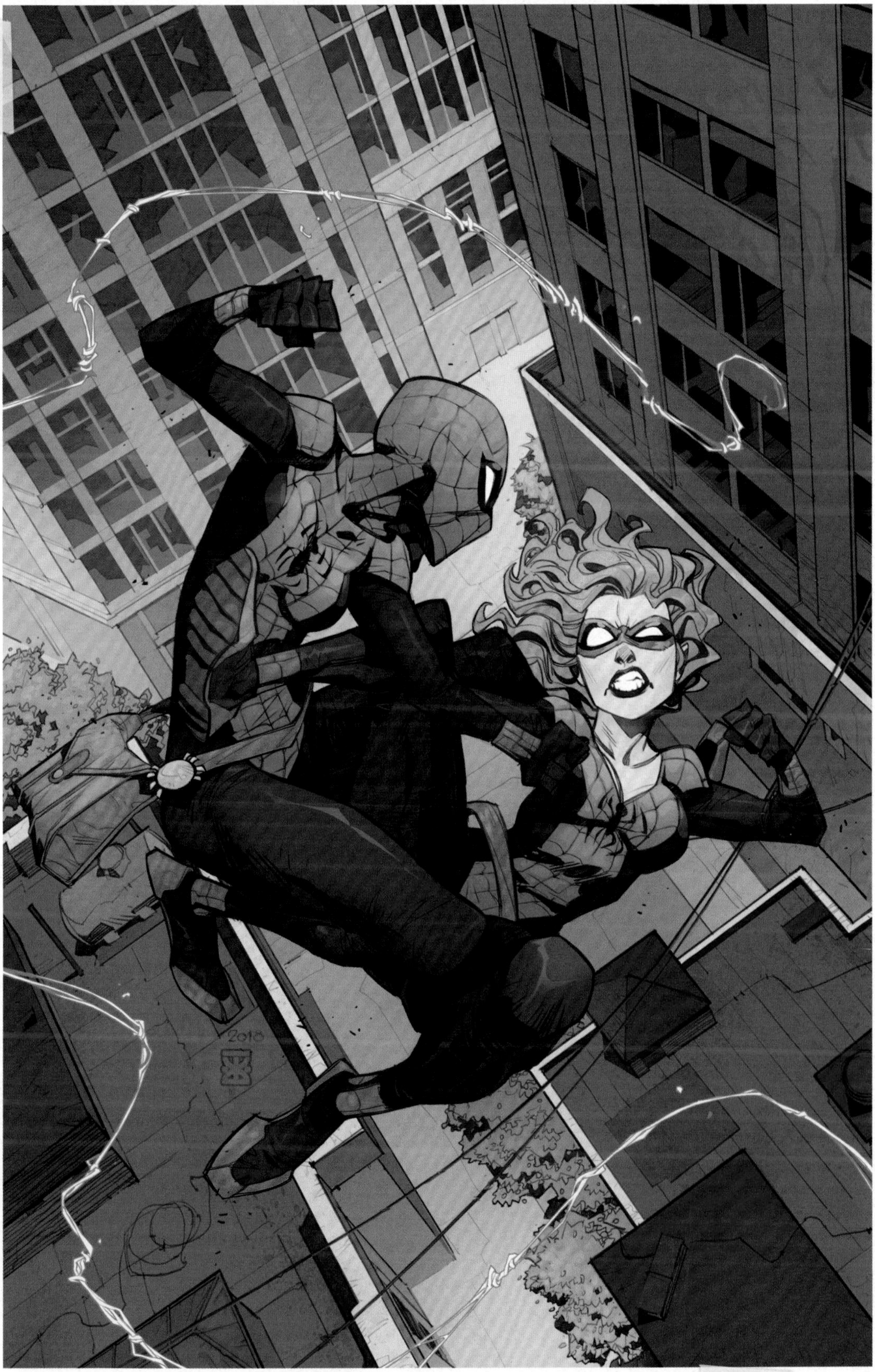

21: WEIRD SCIENCE — PART 2

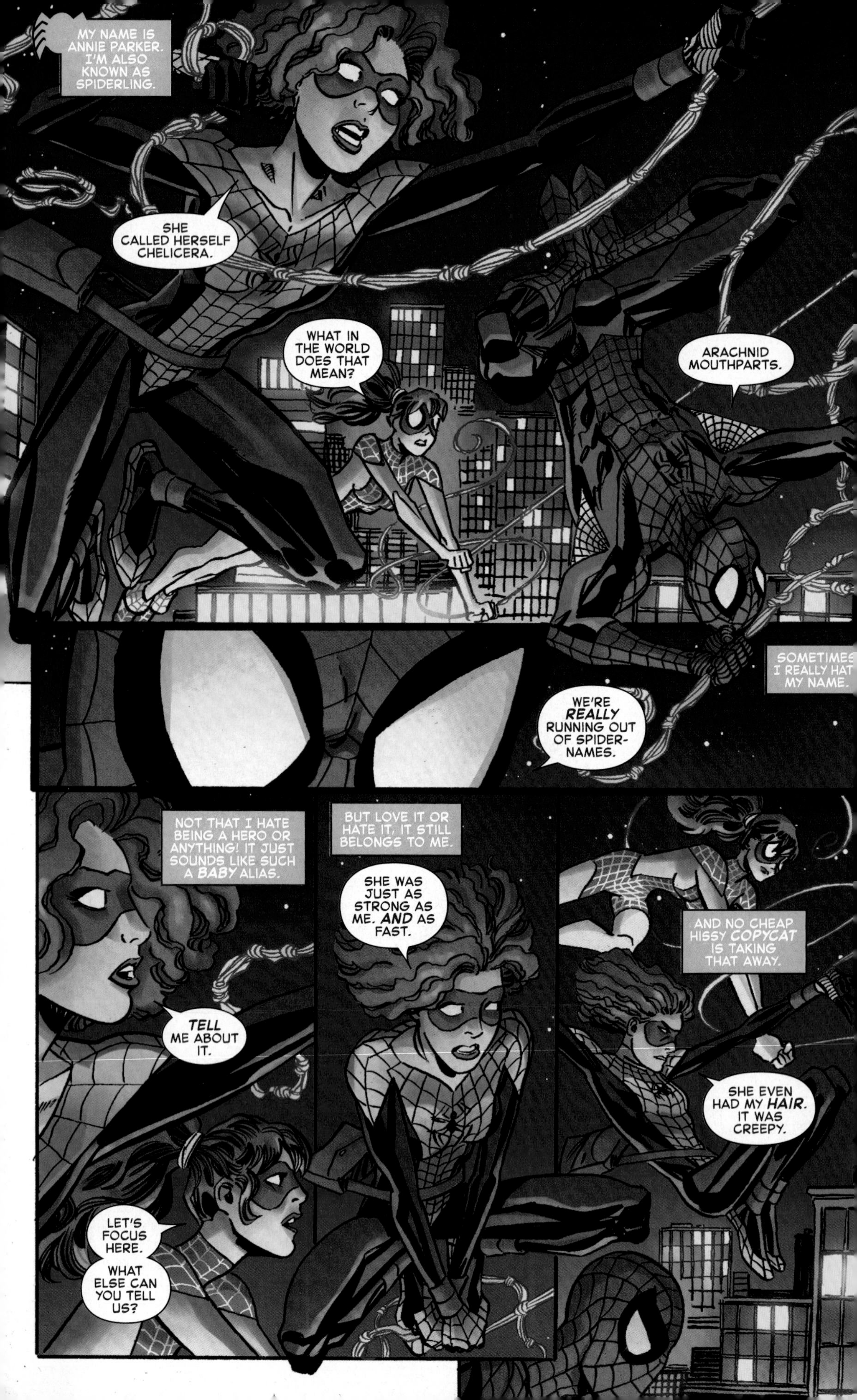

MY NAME IS ANNIE PARKER. I'M ALSO KNOWN AS SPIDERLING.
SHE CALLED HERSELF CHELICERA.
WHAT IN THE WORLD DOES THAT MEAN?
ARACHNID MOUTHPARTS.
SOMETIMES I REALLY HAT MY NAME.
WE'RE *REALLY* RUNNING OUT OF SPIDER-NAMES.
NOT THAT I HATE BEING A HERO OR ANYTHING! IT JUST SOUNDS LIKE SUCH A *BABY* ALIAS.
TELL ME ABOUT IT.
LET'S FOCUS HERE.
WHAT ELSE CAN YOU TELL US?
BUT LOVE IT OR HATE IT, IT STILL BELONGS TO ME.
SHE WAS JUST AS STRONG AS ME. *AND* AS FAST.
AND NO CHEAP HISSY *COPYCAT* IS TAKING THAT AWAY.
SHE EVEN HAD MY *HAIR*. IT WAS CREEPY.

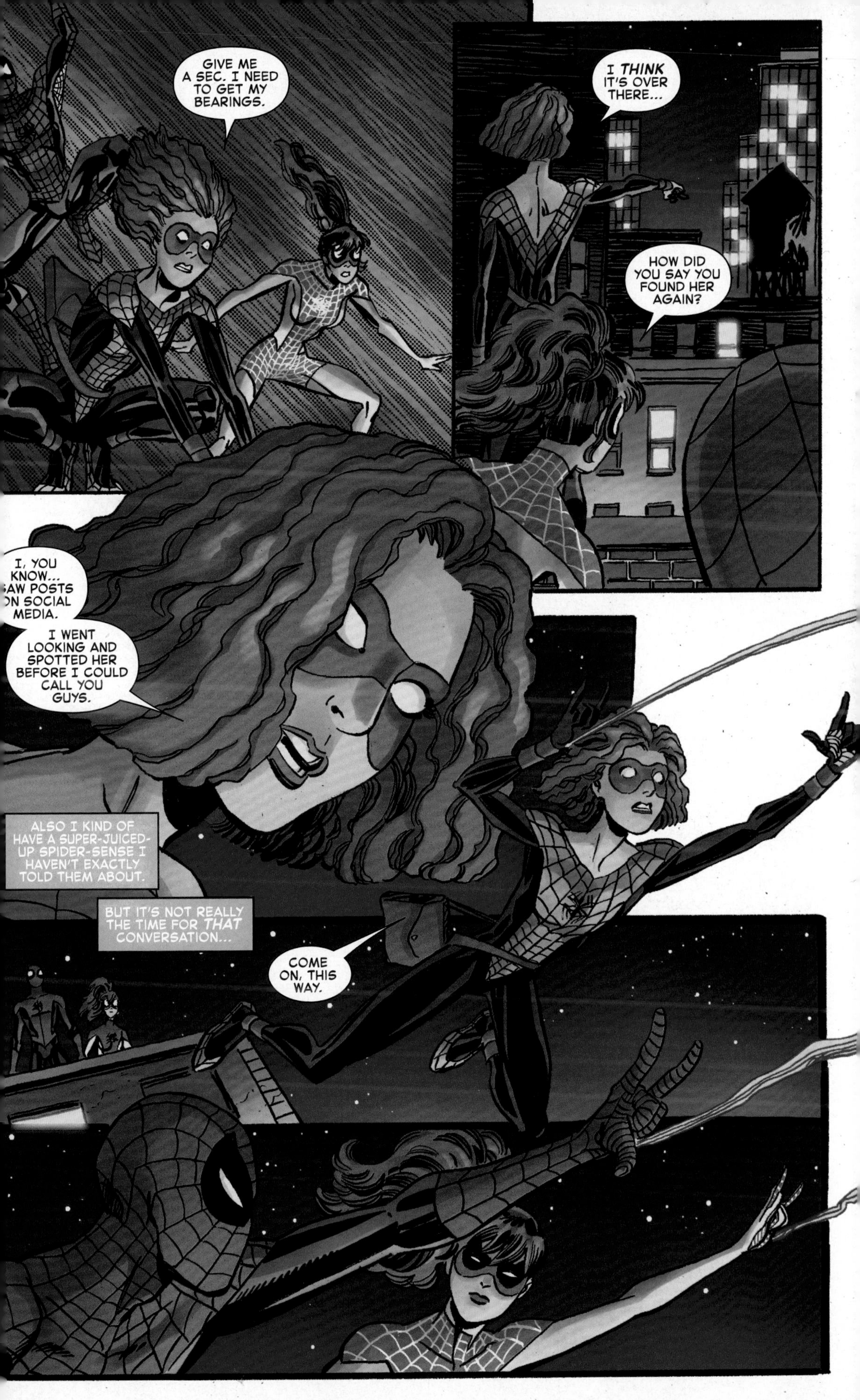
GIVE ME A SEC. I NEED TO GET MY BEARINGS.
I *THINK* IT'S OVER THERE...
HOW DID YOU SAY YOU FOUND HER AGAIN?
I, YOU KNOW... SAW POSTS ON SOCIAL MEDIA.
I WENT LOOKING AND SPOTTED HER BEFORE I COULD CALL YOU GUYS.
ALSO I KIND OF HAVE A SUPER-JUICED-UP SPIDER-SENSE I HAVEN'T EXACTLY TOLD THEM ABOUT.
BUT IT'S NOT REALLY THE TIME FOR *THAT* CONVERSATION...
COME ON, THIS WAY.

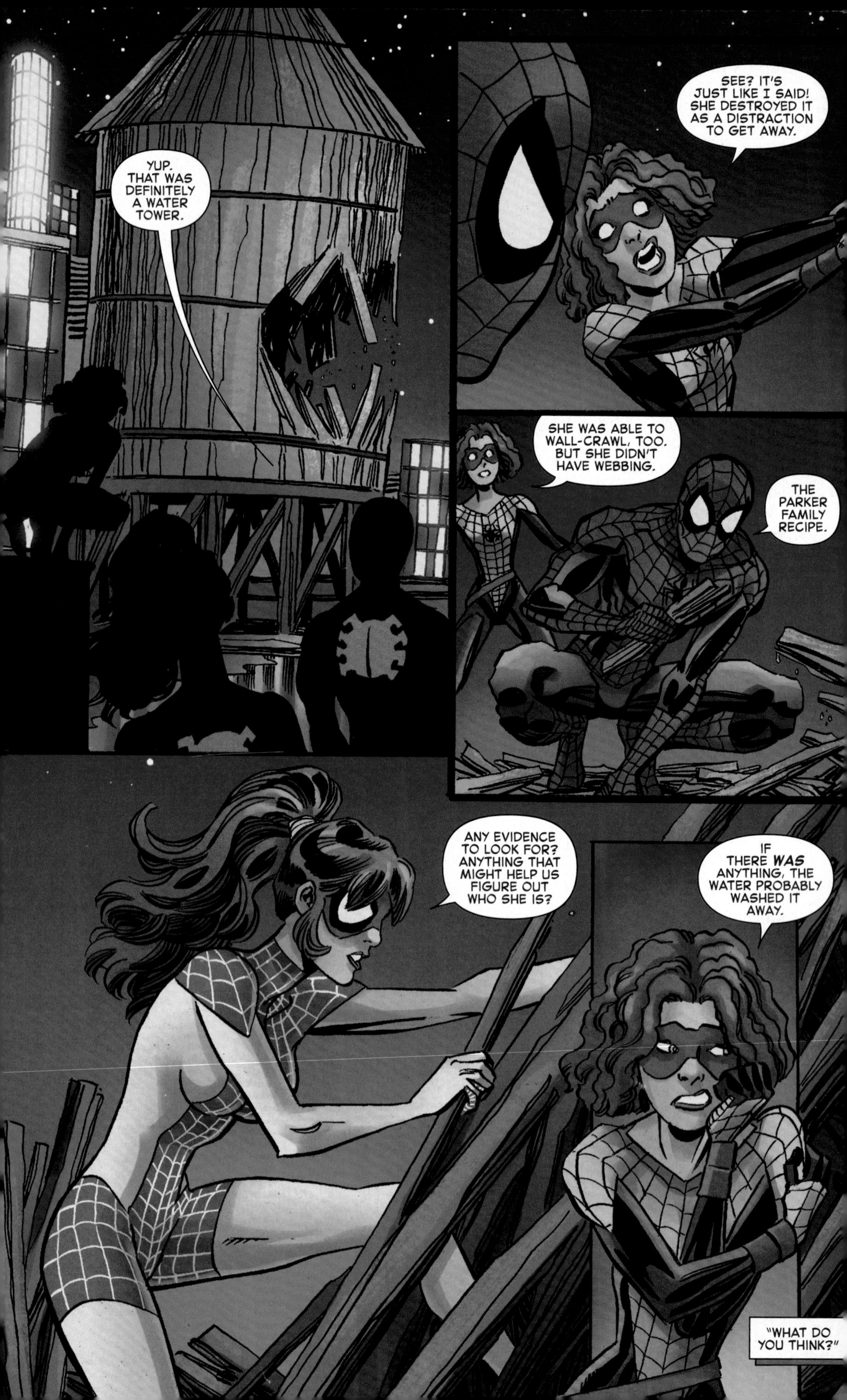
YUP. THAT WAS DEFINITELY A WATER TOWER.
SEE? IT'S JUST LIKE I SAID! SHE DESTROYED IT AS A DISTRACTION TO GET AWAY.
SHE WAS ABLE TO WALL-CRAWL, TOO. BUT SHE DIDN'T HAVE WEBBING.
THE PARKER FAMILY RECIPE.
ANY EVIDENCE TO LOOK FOR? ANYTHING THAT MIGHT HELP US FIGURE OUT WHO SHE IS?
IF THERE *WAS* ANYTHING, THE WATER PROBABLY WASHED IT AWAY.
"WHAT DO YOU THINK?"

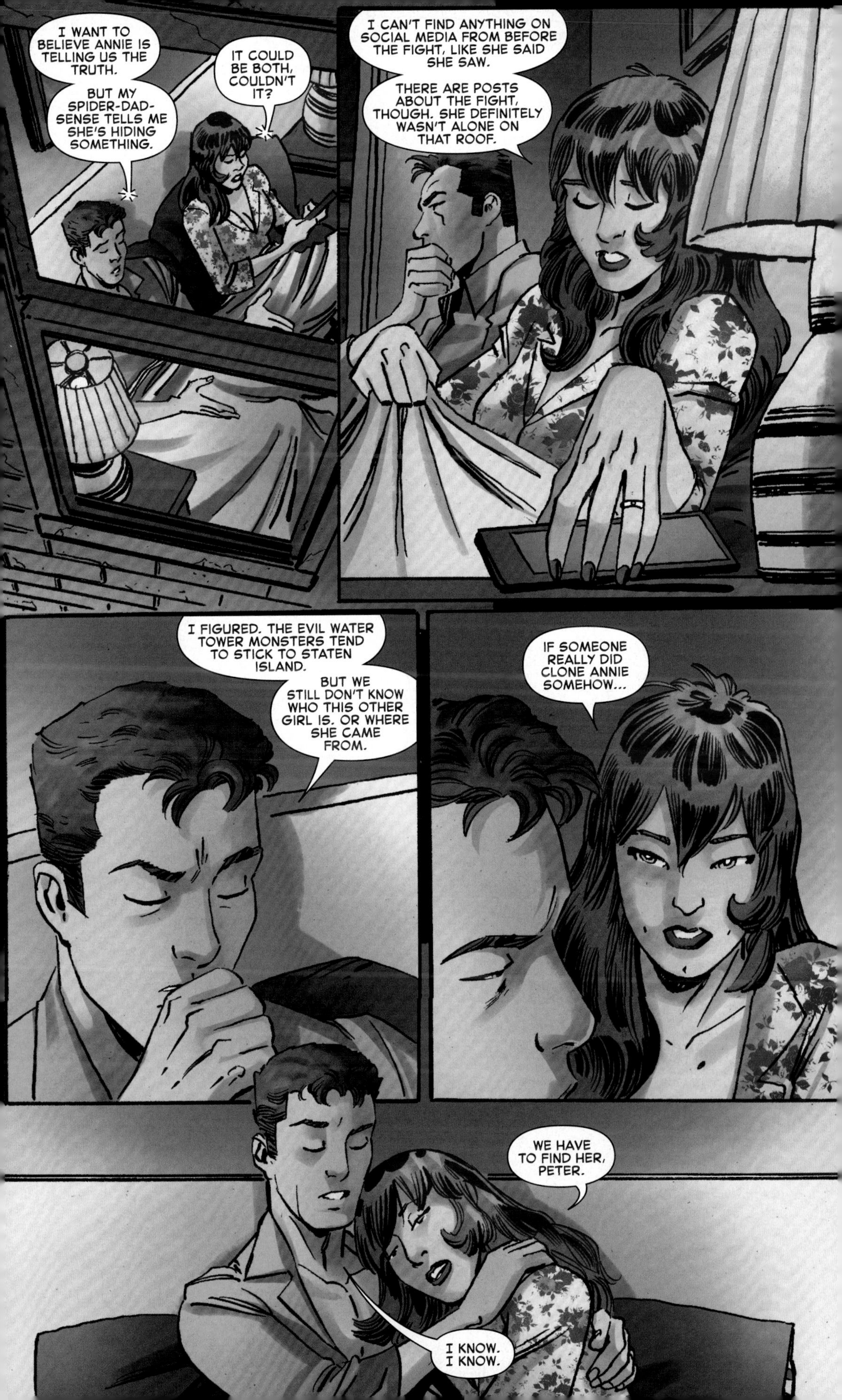
I WANT TO BELIEVE ANNIE IS TELLING US THE TRUTH.
BUT MY SPIDER-DAD-SENSE TELLS ME SHE'S HIDING SOMETHING.
IT COULD BE BOTH, COULDN'T IT?
I CAN'T FIND ANYTHING ON SOCIAL MEDIA FROM BEFORE THE FIGHT, LIKE SHE SAID SHE SAW.
THERE ARE POSTS ABOUT THE FIGHT, THOUGH. SHE DEFINITELY WASN'T ALONE ON THAT ROOF.
I FIGURED. THE EVIL WATER TOWER MONSTERS TEND TO STICK TO STATEN ISLAND.
BUT WE STILL DON'T KNOW WHO THIS OTHER GIRL IS. OR WHERE SHE CAME FROM.
IF SOMEONE REALLY DID CLONE ANNIE SOMEHOW...
WE HAVE TO FIND HER, PETER.
I KNOW. I KNOW.

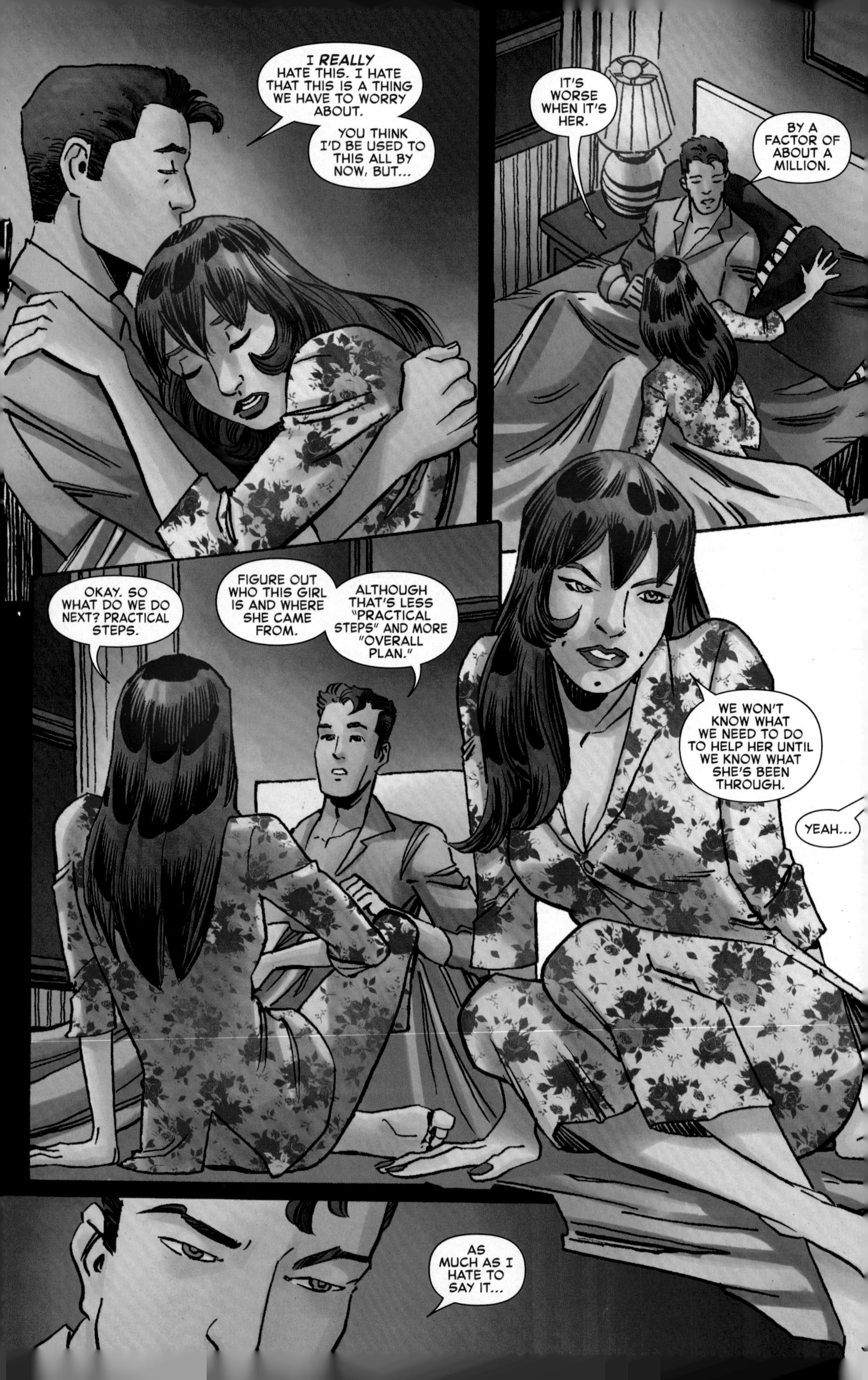
I *REALLY* HATE THIS. I HATE THAT THIS IS A THING WE HAVE TO WORRY ABOUT.
YOU THINK I'D BE USED TO THIS ALL BY NOW, BUT...
IT'S WORSE WHEN IT'S HER.
BY A FACTOR OF ABOUT A MILLION.
OKAY. SO WHAT DO WE DO NEXT? PRACTICAL STEPS.
FIGURE OUT WHO THIS GIRL IS AND WHERE SHE CAME FROM.
ALTHOUGH THAT'S LESS "PRACTICAL STEPS" AND MORE "OVERALL PLAN."
WE WON'T KNOW WHAT WE NEED TO DO TO HELP HER UNTIL WE KNOW WHAT SHE'S BEEN THROUGH.
YEAH...
AS MUCH AS I HATE TO SAY IT...

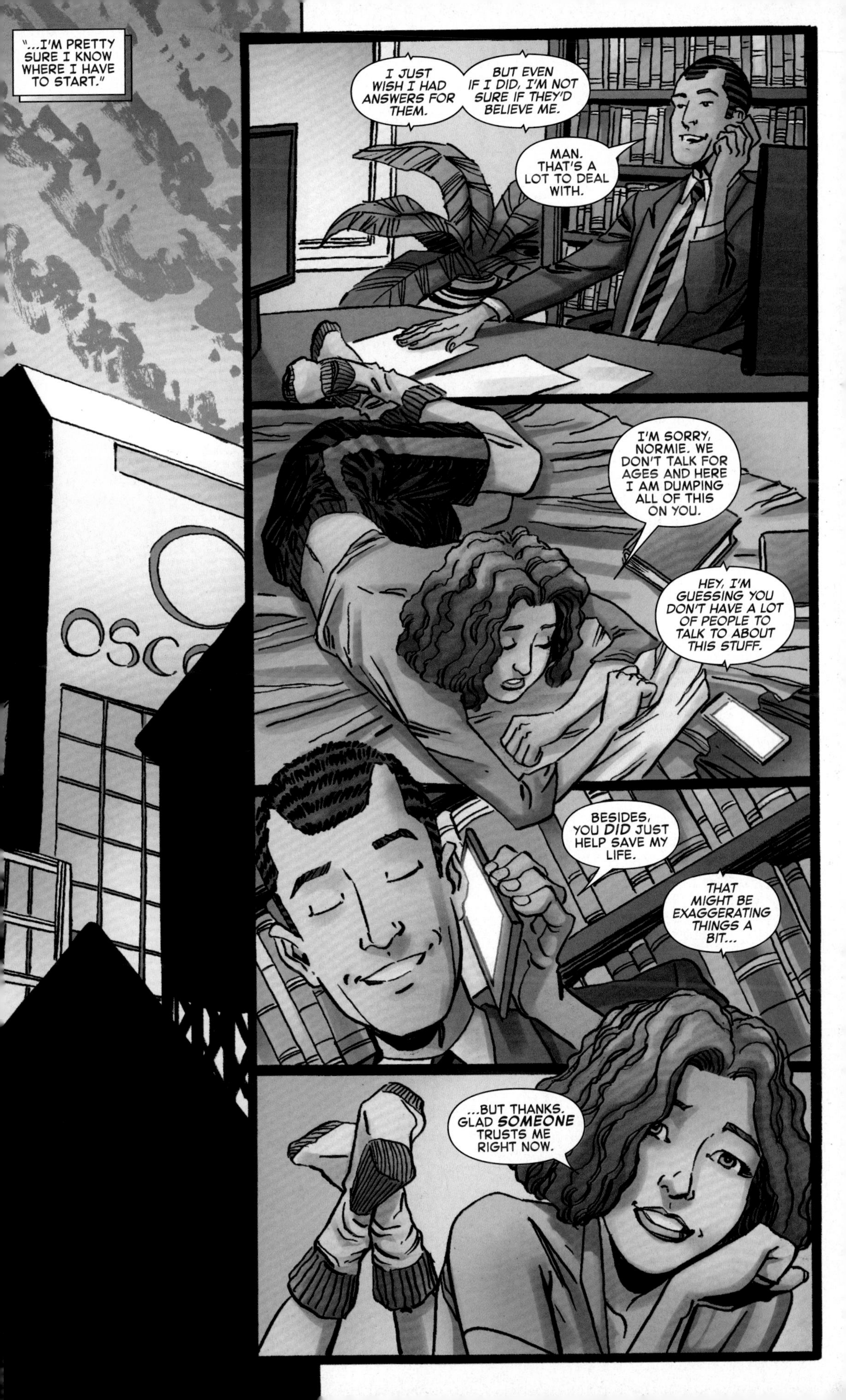
"...I'M PRETTY SURE I KNOW WHERE I HAVE TO START."
I JUST WISH I HAD ANSWERS FOR THEM.
BUT EVEN IF I DID, I'M NOT SURE IF THEY'D BELIEVE ME.
MAN. THAT'S A LOT TO DEAL WITH.
OSC
I'M SORRY, NORMIE. WE DON'T TALK FOR AGES AND HERE I AM DUMPING ALL OF THIS ON YOU.
HEY, I'M GUESSING YOU DON'T HAVE A LOT OF PEOPLE TO TALK TO ABOUT THIS STUFF.
BESIDES, YOU DID JUST HELP SAVE MY LIFE.
THAT MIGHT BE EXAGGERATING THINGS A BIT...
...BUT THANKS. GLAD SOMEONE TRUSTS ME RIGHT NOW.

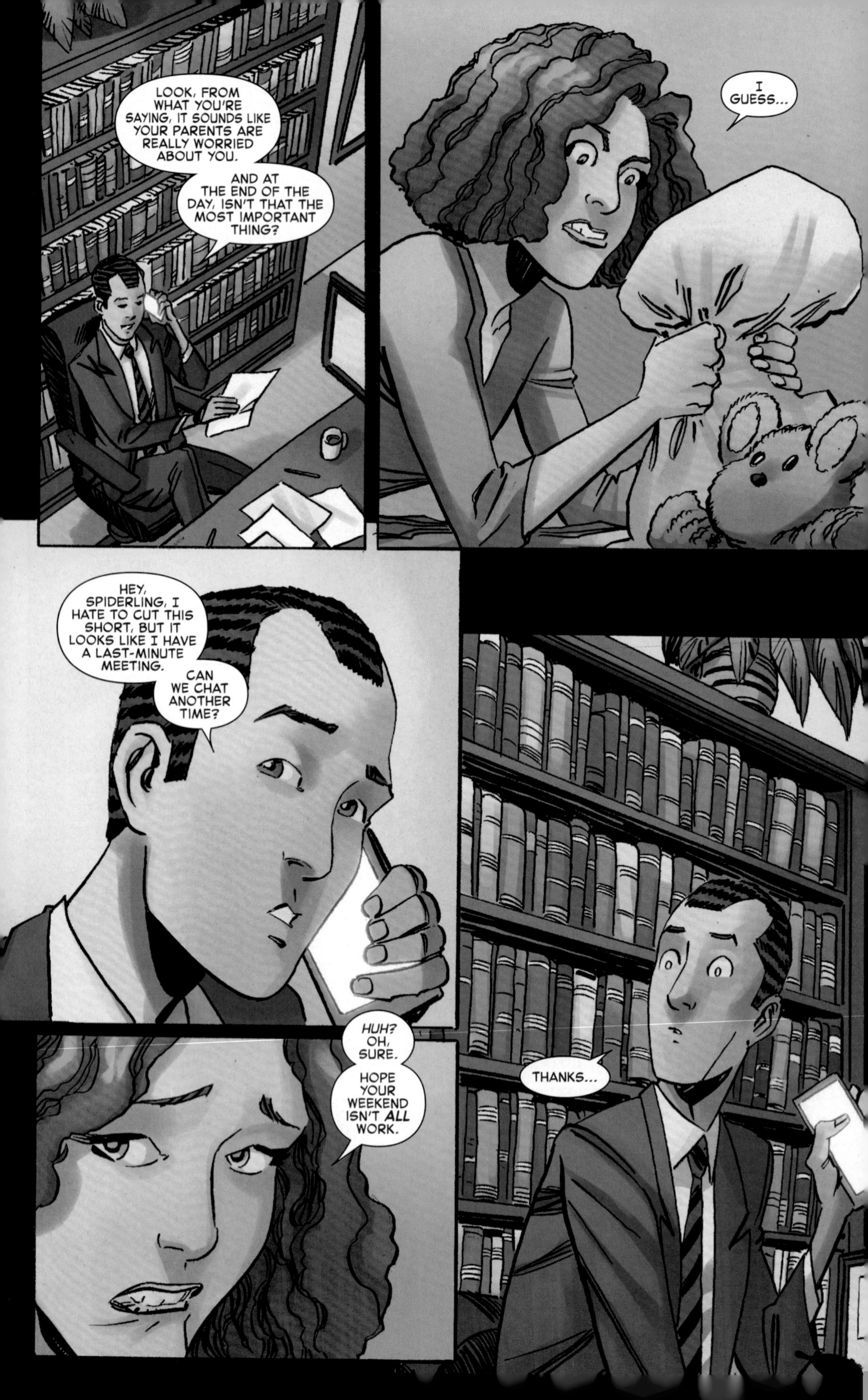
LOOK, FROM WHAT YOU'RE SAYING, IT SOUNDS LIKE YOUR PARENTS ARE REALLY WORRIED ABOUT YOU.
AND AT THE END OF THE DAY, ISN'T THAT THE MOST IMPORTANT THING?
I GUESS...
HEY, SPIDERLING, I HATE TO CUT THIS SHORT, BUT IT LOOKS LIKE I HAVE A LAST-MINUTE MEETING.
CAN WE CHAT ANOTHER TIME?
HUH? OH, SURE.
HOPE YOUR WEEKEND ISN'T *ALL* WORK.
THANKS...

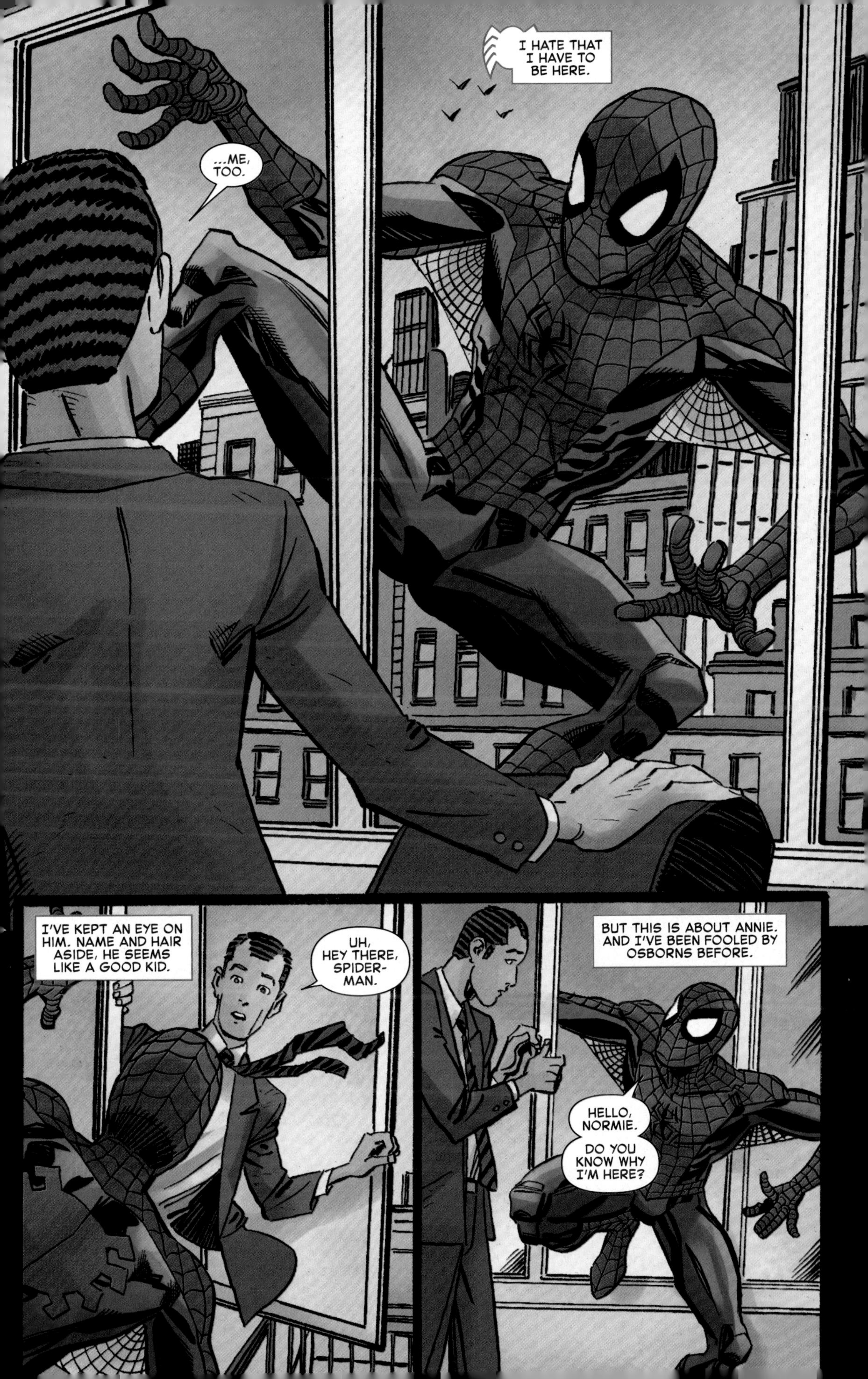
I HATE THAT I HAVE TO BE HERE.
...ME, TOO.
I'VE KEPT AN EYE ON HIM. NAME AND HAIR ASIDE, HE SEEMS LIKE A GOOD KID.
UH, HEY THERE, SPIDER-MAN.
BUT THIS IS ABOUT ANNIE. AND I'VE BEEN FOOLED BY OSBORNS BEFORE.
HELLO, NORMIE.
DO YOU KNOW WHY I'M HERE?

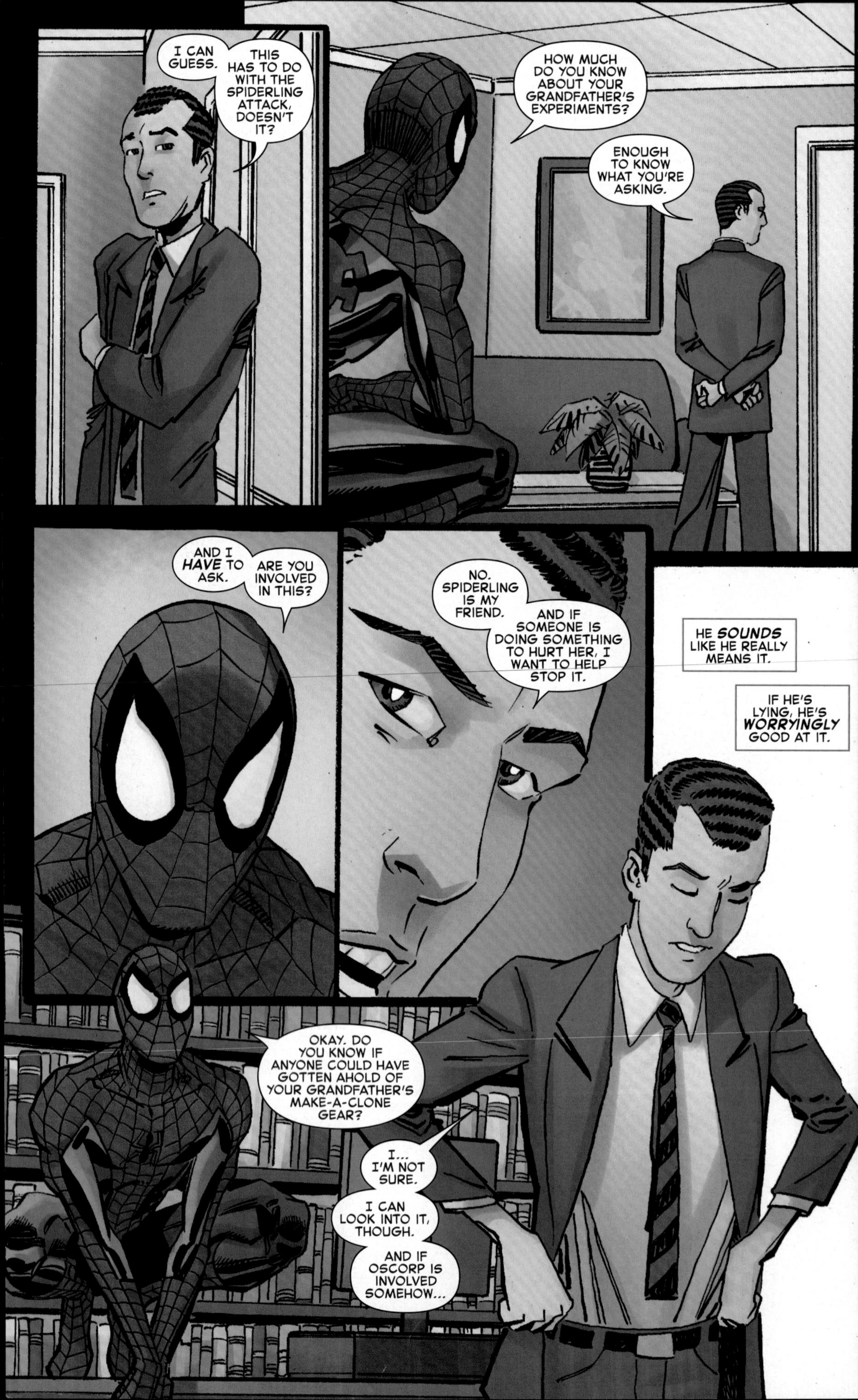
I CAN GUESS.
THIS HAS TO DO WITH THE SPIDERLING ATTACK, DOESN'T IT?
HOW MUCH DO YOU KNOW ABOUT YOUR GRANDFATHER'S EXPERIMENTS?
ENOUGH TO KNOW WHAT YOU'RE ASKING.
AND I HAVE TO ASK.
ARE YOU INVOLVED IN THIS?
NO. SPIDERLING IS MY FRIEND.
AND IF SOMEONE IS DOING SOMETHING TO HURT HER, I WANT TO HELP STOP IT.
HE SOUNDS LIKE HE REALLY MEANS IT.
IF HE'S LYING, HE'S WORRYINGLY GOOD AT IT.
OKAY. DO YOU KNOW IF ANYONE COULD HAVE GOTTEN AHOLD OF YOUR GRANDFATHER'S MAKE-A-CLONE GEAR?
I... I'M NOT SURE.
I CAN LOOK INTO IT, THOUGH.
AND IF OSCORP IS INVOLVED SOMEHOW...

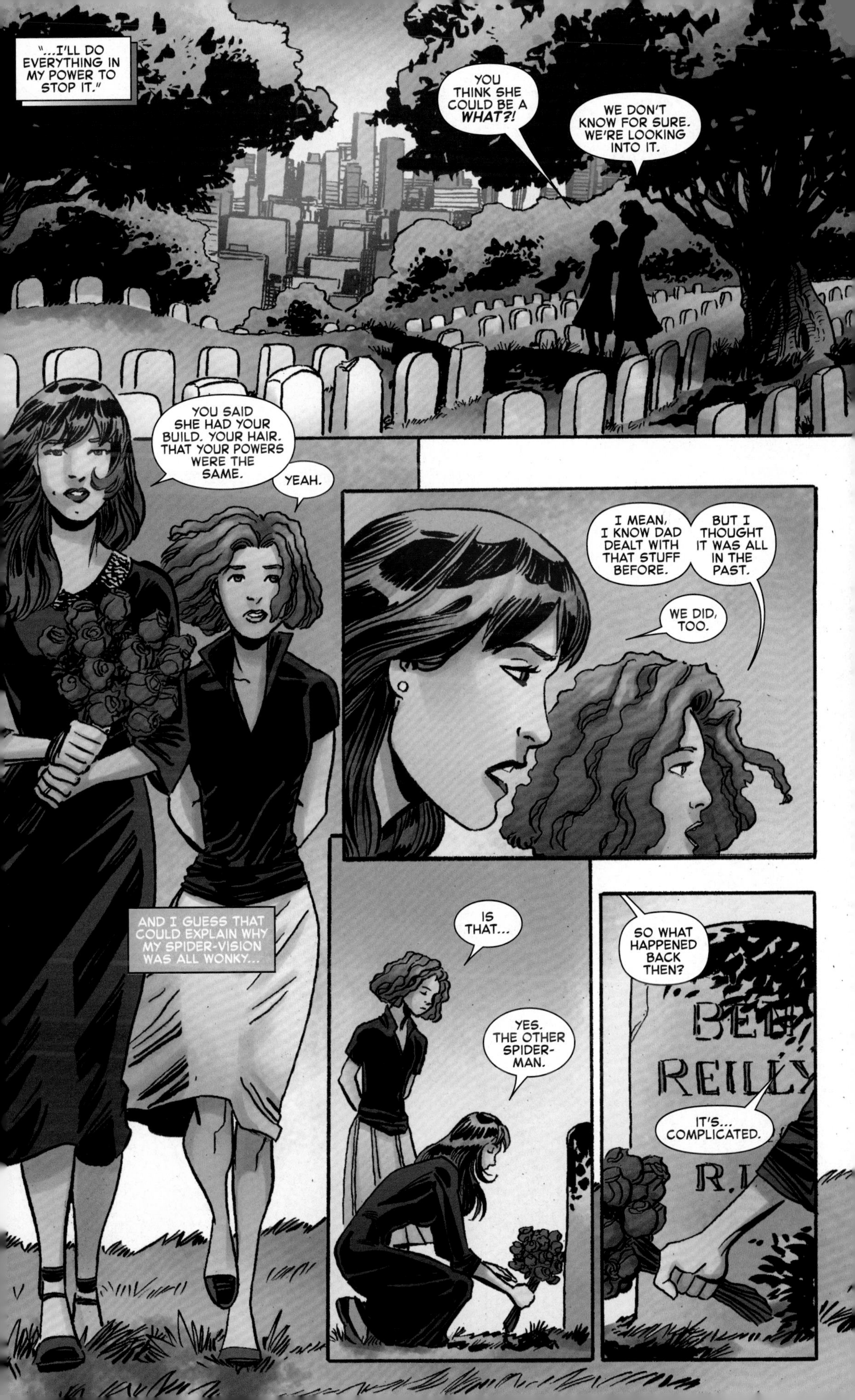
"...I'LL DO EVERYTHING IN MY POWER TO STOP IT."
YOU THINK SHE COULD BE A *WHAT?!*
WE DON'T KNOW FOR SURE. WE'RE LOOKING INTO IT.
YOU SAID SHE HAD YOUR BUILD. YOUR HAIR. THAT YOUR POWERS WERE THE SAME.
YEAH.
AND I GUESS THAT COULD EXPLAIN WHY MY SPIDER-VISION WAS ALL WONKY...
I MEAN, I KNOW DAD DEALT WITH THAT STUFF BEFORE.
BUT I THOUGHT IT WAS ALL IN THE PAST.
WE DID, TOO.
IS THAT...
YES. THE OTHER SPIDER-MAN.
SO WHAT HAPPENED BACK THEN?
REILLY
IT'S... COMPLICATED.

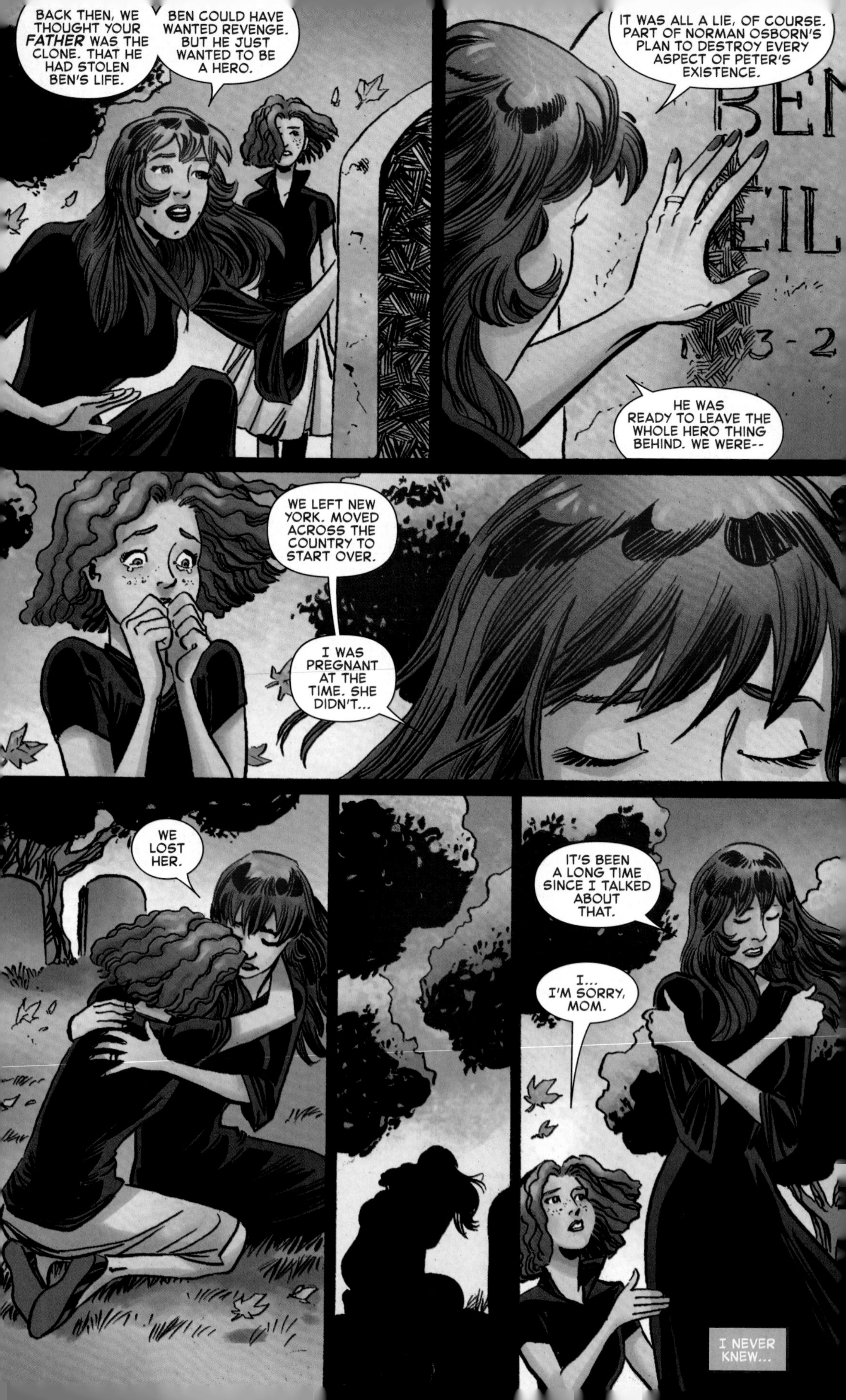
BACK THEN, WE THOUGHT YOUR FATHER WAS THE CLONE. THAT HE HAD STOLEN BEN'S LIFE.
BEN COULD HAVE WANTED REVENGE. BUT HE JUST WANTED TO BE A HERO.
IT WAS ALL A LIE, OF COURSE. PART OF NORMAN OSBORN'S PLAN TO DESTROY EVERY ASPECT OF PETER'S EXISTENCE.
HE WAS READY TO LEAVE THE WHOLE HERO THING BEHIND. WE WERE--
WE LEFT NEW YORK. MOVED ACROSS THE COUNTRY TO START OVER.
I WAS PREGNANT AT THE TIME. SHE DIDN'T...
WE LOST HER.
IT'S BEEN A LONG TIME SINCE I TALKED ABOUT THAT.
I... I'M SORRY, MOM.
I NEVER KNEW...

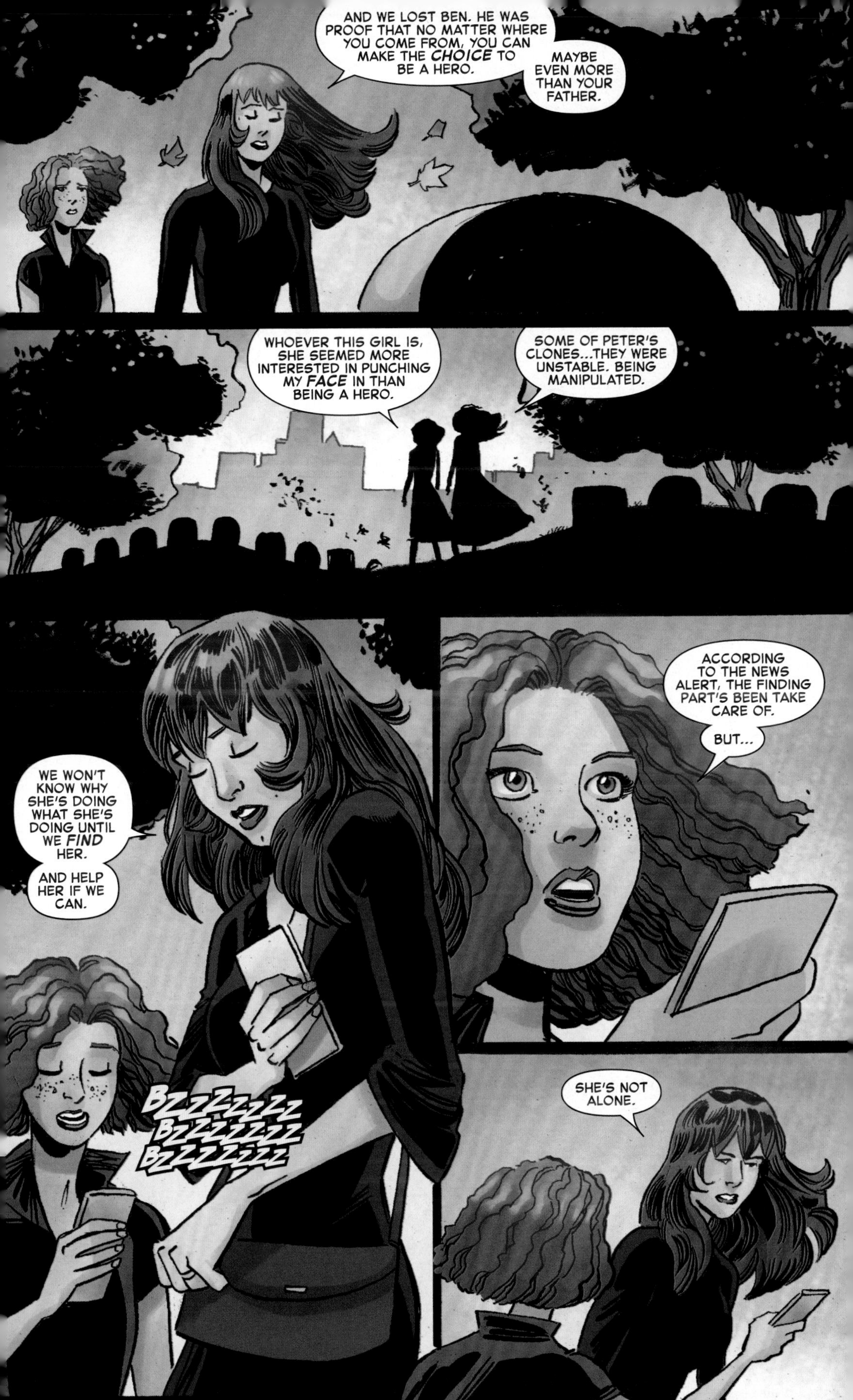
AND WE LOST BEN. HE WAS PROOF THAT NO MATTER WHERE YOU COME FROM, YOU CAN MAKE THE CHOICE TO BE A HERO.
MAYBE EVEN MORE THAN YOUR FATHER.
WHOEVER THIS GIRL IS, SHE SEEMED MORE INTERESTED IN PUNCHING MY FACE IN THAN BEING A HERO.
SOME OF PETER'S CLONES...THEY WERE UNSTABLE. BEING MANIPULATED.
WE WON'T KNOW WHY SHE'S DOING WHAT SHE'S DOING UNTIL WE FIND HER.
AND HELP HER IF WE CAN.
BZZZZZZZ
BZZZZZZZZ
BZZZZZZZ
ACCORDING TO THE NEWS ALERT, THE FINDING PART'S BEEN TAKE CARE OF.
BUT...
SHE'S NOT ALONE.

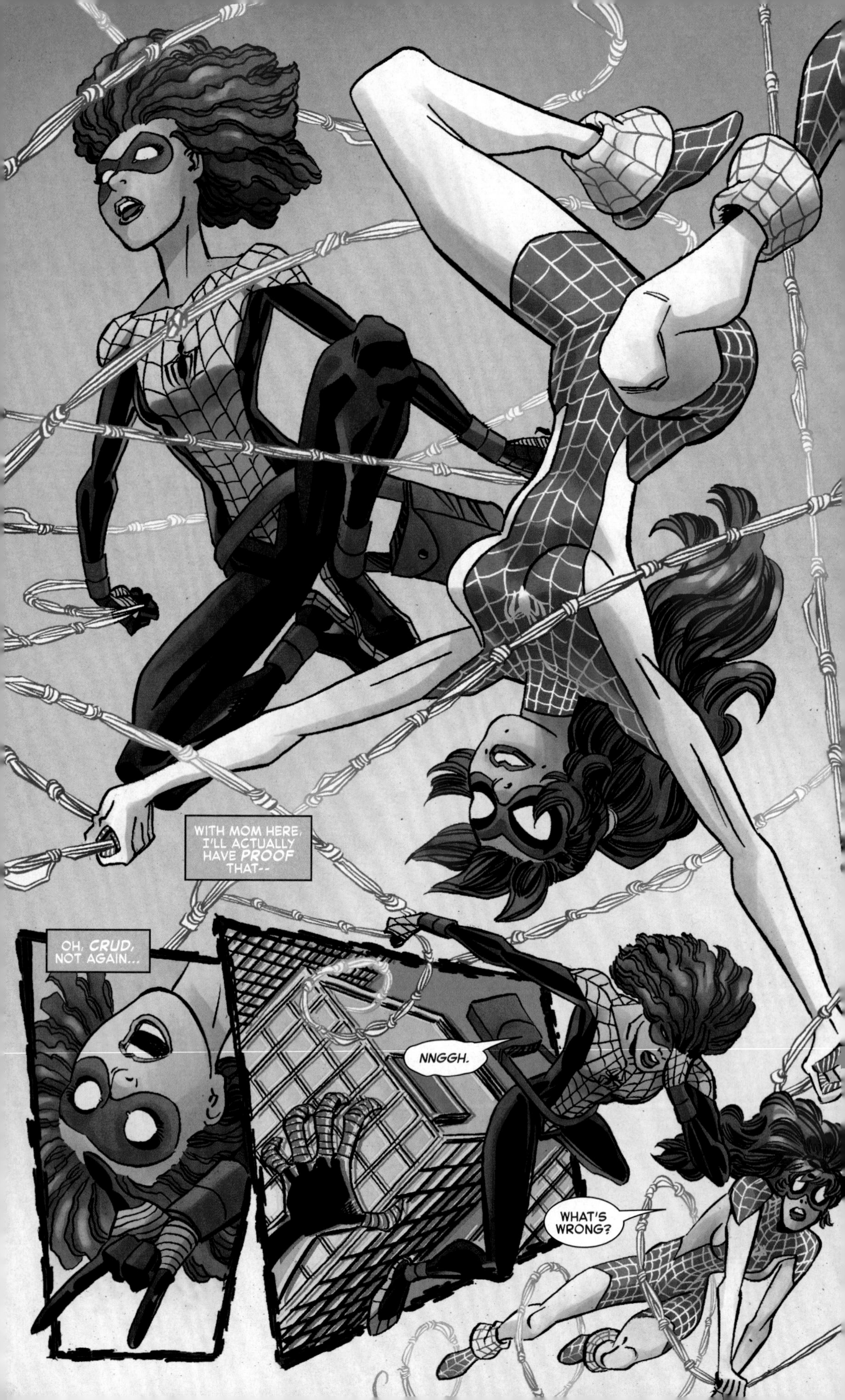
WITH MOM HERE, I'LL ACTUALLY HAVE PROOF THAT--
OH, CRUD, NOT AGAIN...
NNGGH.
WHAT'S WRONG?

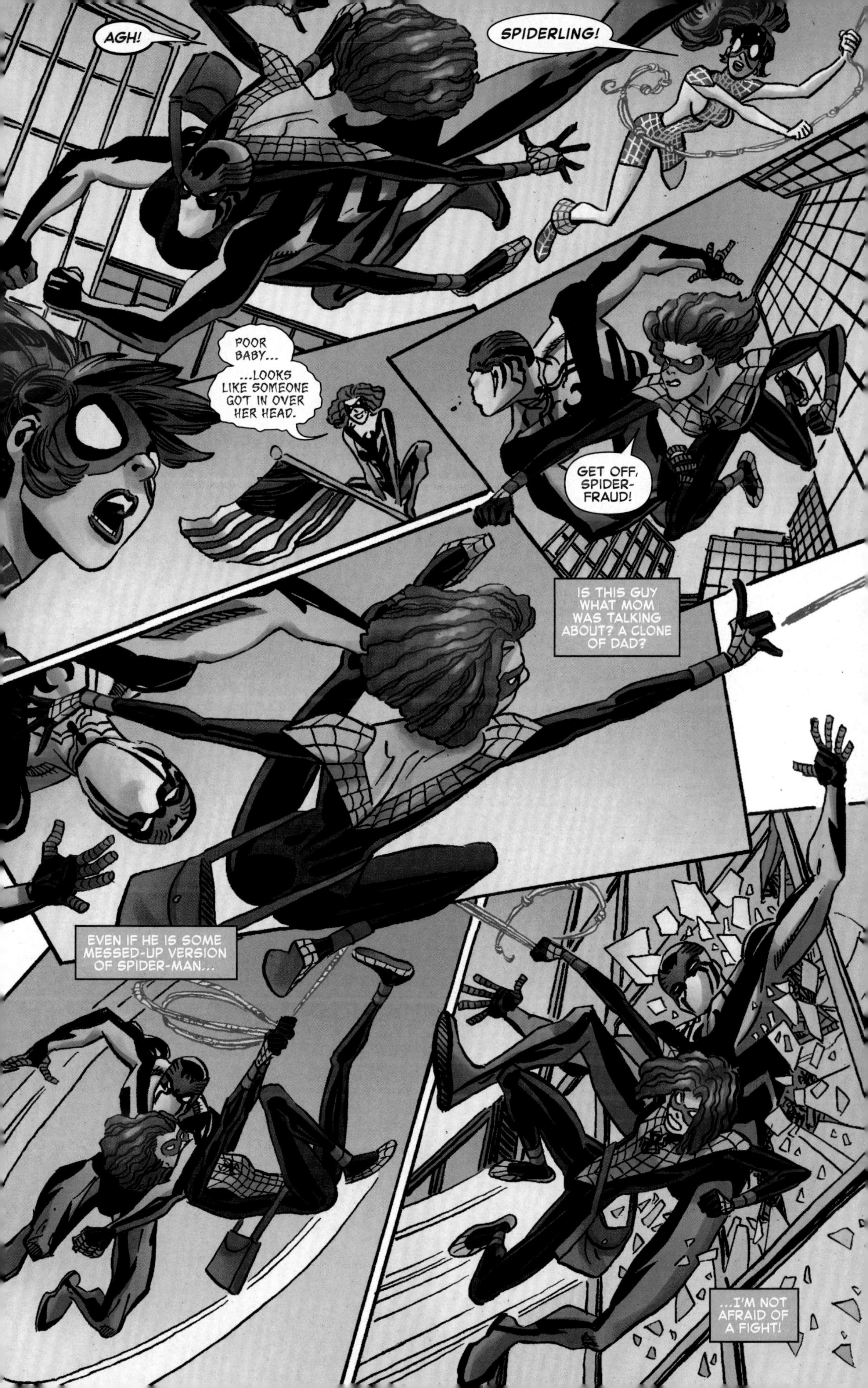
AGH!
SPIDERLING!
POOR BABY... ...LOOKS LIKE SOMEONE GOT IN OVER HER HEAD.
GET OFF, SPIDER-FRAUD!
IS THIS GUY WHAT MOM WAS TALKING ABOUT? A CLONE OF DAD?
EVEN IF HE IS SOME MESSED-UP VERSION OF SPIDER-MAN...
...I'M NOT AFRAID OF A FIGHT!

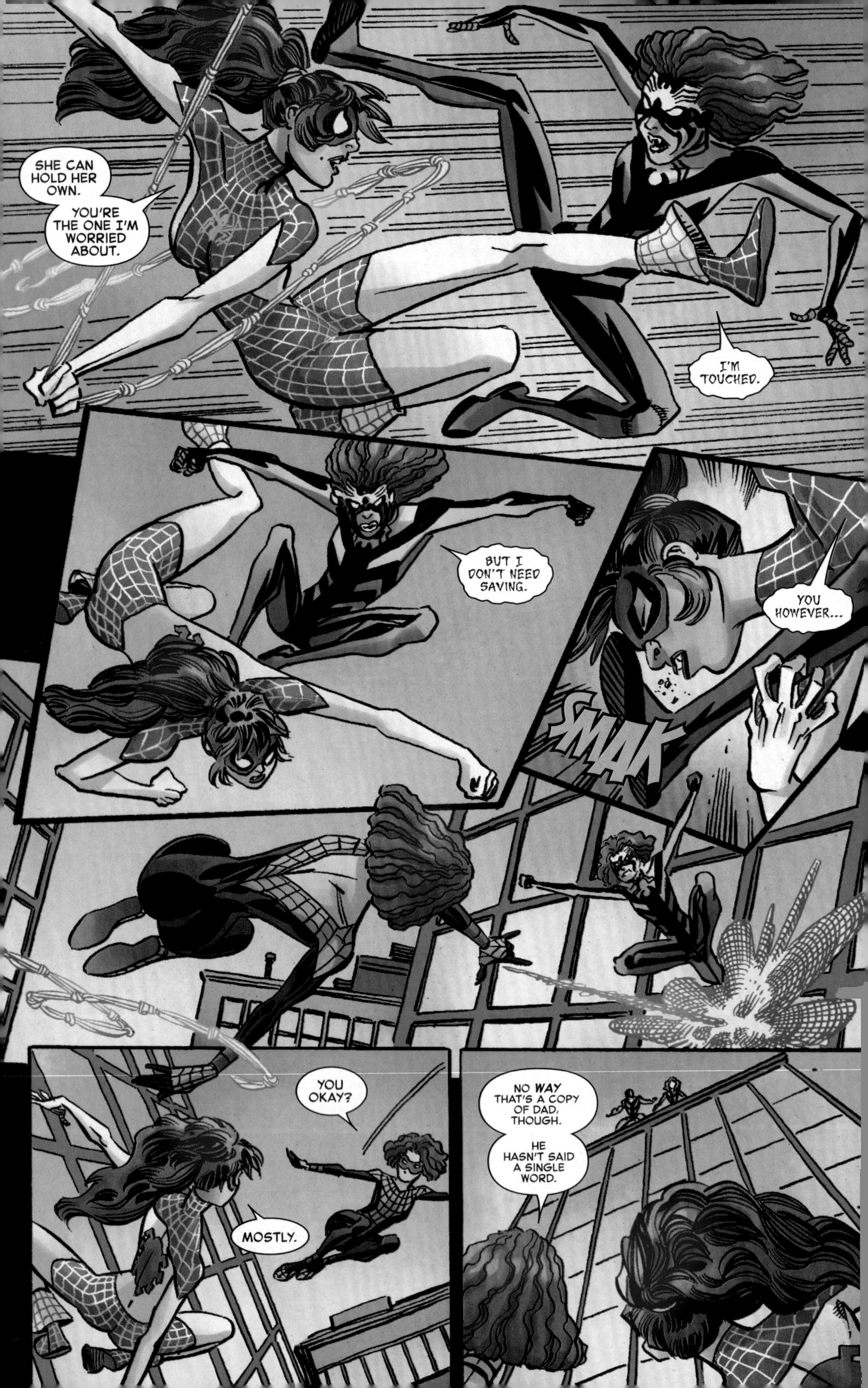
SHE CAN HOLD HER OWN.
YOU'RE THE ONE I'M WORRIED ABOUT.
I'M TOUCHED.
BUT I DON'T NEED SAVING.
YOU HOWEVER...
SMAK
YOU OKAY?
MOSTLY.
NO WAY THAT'S A COPY OF DAD, THOUGH.
HE HASN'T SAID A SINGLE WORD.

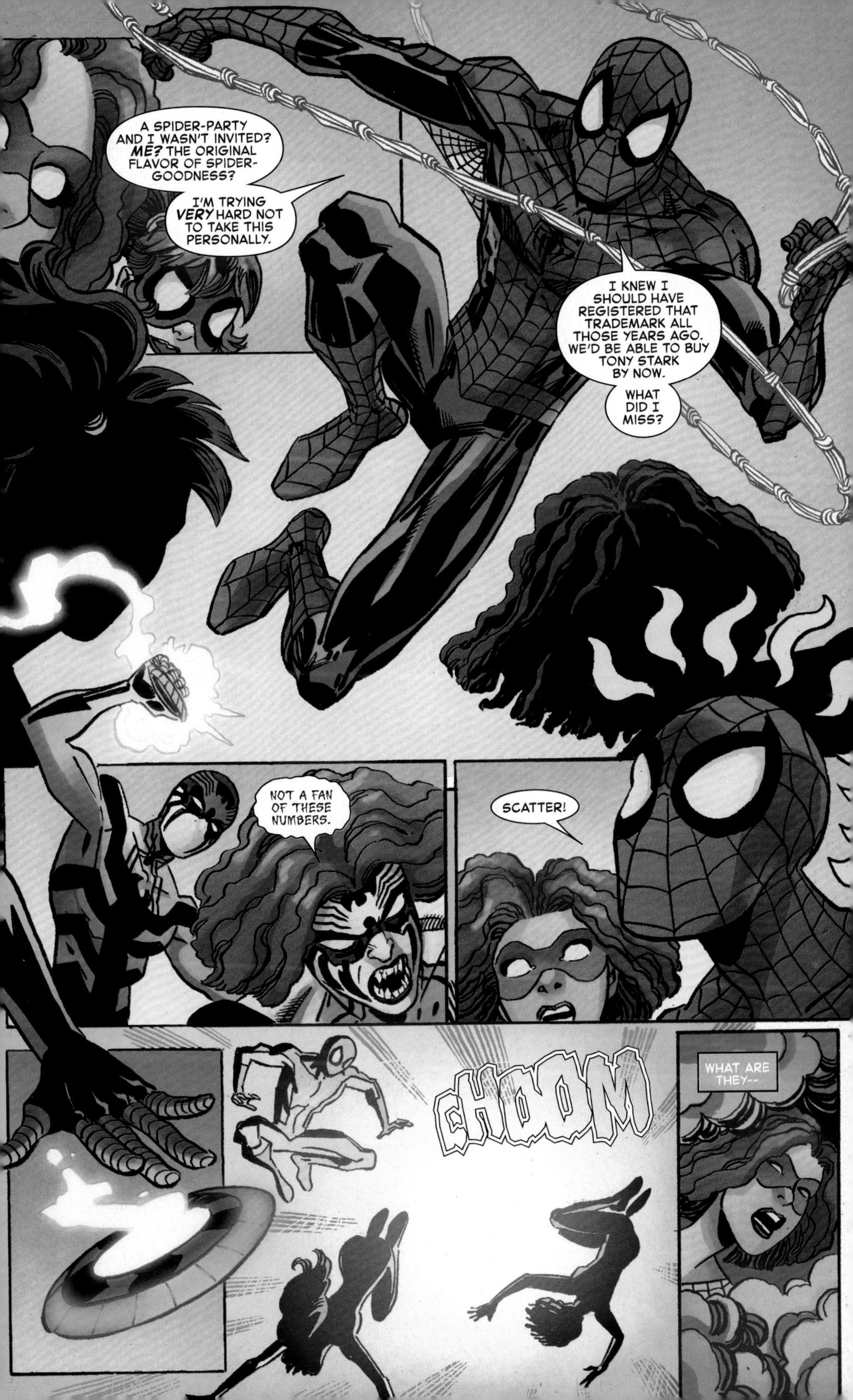

A SPIDER-PARTY AND I WASN'T INVITED? ME? THE ORIGINAL FLAVOR OF SPIDER-GOODNESS?
I'M TRYING VERY HARD NOT TO TAKE THIS PERSONALLY.
I KNEW I SHOULD HAVE REGISTERED THAT TRADEMARK ALL THOSE YEARS AGO. WE'D BE ABLE TO BUY TONY STARK BY NOW.
WHAT DID I MISS?
NOT A FAN OF THESE NUMBERS.
SCATTER!
CHOOM
WHAT ARE THEY--

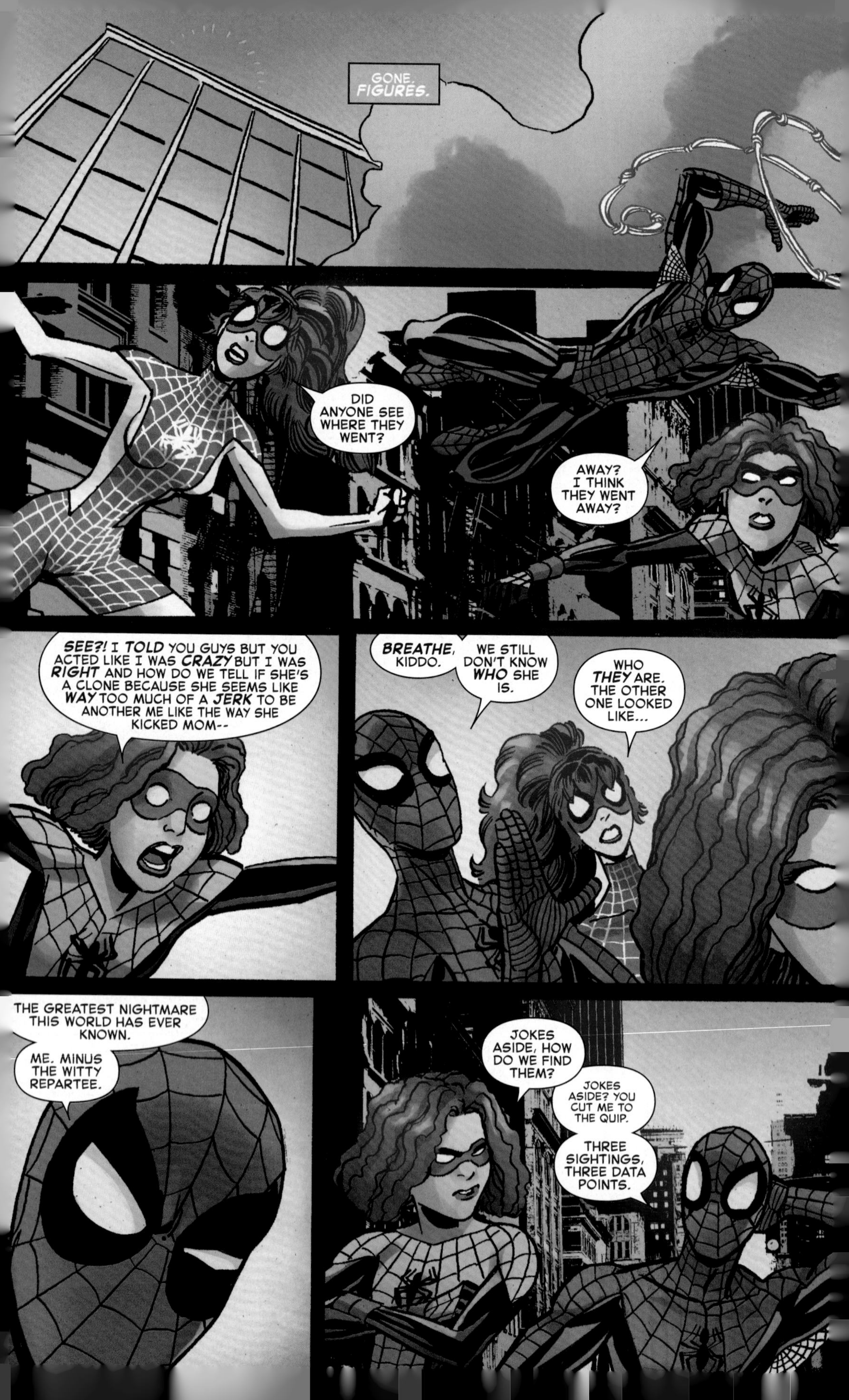
GONE. FIGURES.
DID ANYONE SEE WHERE THEY WENT?
AWAY? I THINK THEY WENT AWAY?
SEE?! I TOLD YOU GUYS BUT YOU ACTED LIKE I WAS CRAZY BUT I WAS RIGHT AND HOW DO WE TELL IF SHE'S A CLONE BECAUSE SHE SEEMS LIKE WAY TOO MUCH OF A JERK TO BE ANOTHER ME LIKE THE WAY SHE KICKED MOM--
BREATHE, KIDDO.
WE STILL DON'T KNOW WHO SHE IS.
WHO THEY ARE. THE OTHER ONE LOOKED LIKE...
THE GREATEST NIGHTMARE THIS WORLD HAS EVER KNOWN.
ME. MINUS THE WITTY REPARTEE.
JOKES ASIDE, HOW DO WE FIND THEM?
JOKES ASIDE? YOU CUT ME TO THE QUIP.
THREE SIGHTINGS, THREE DATA POINTS.

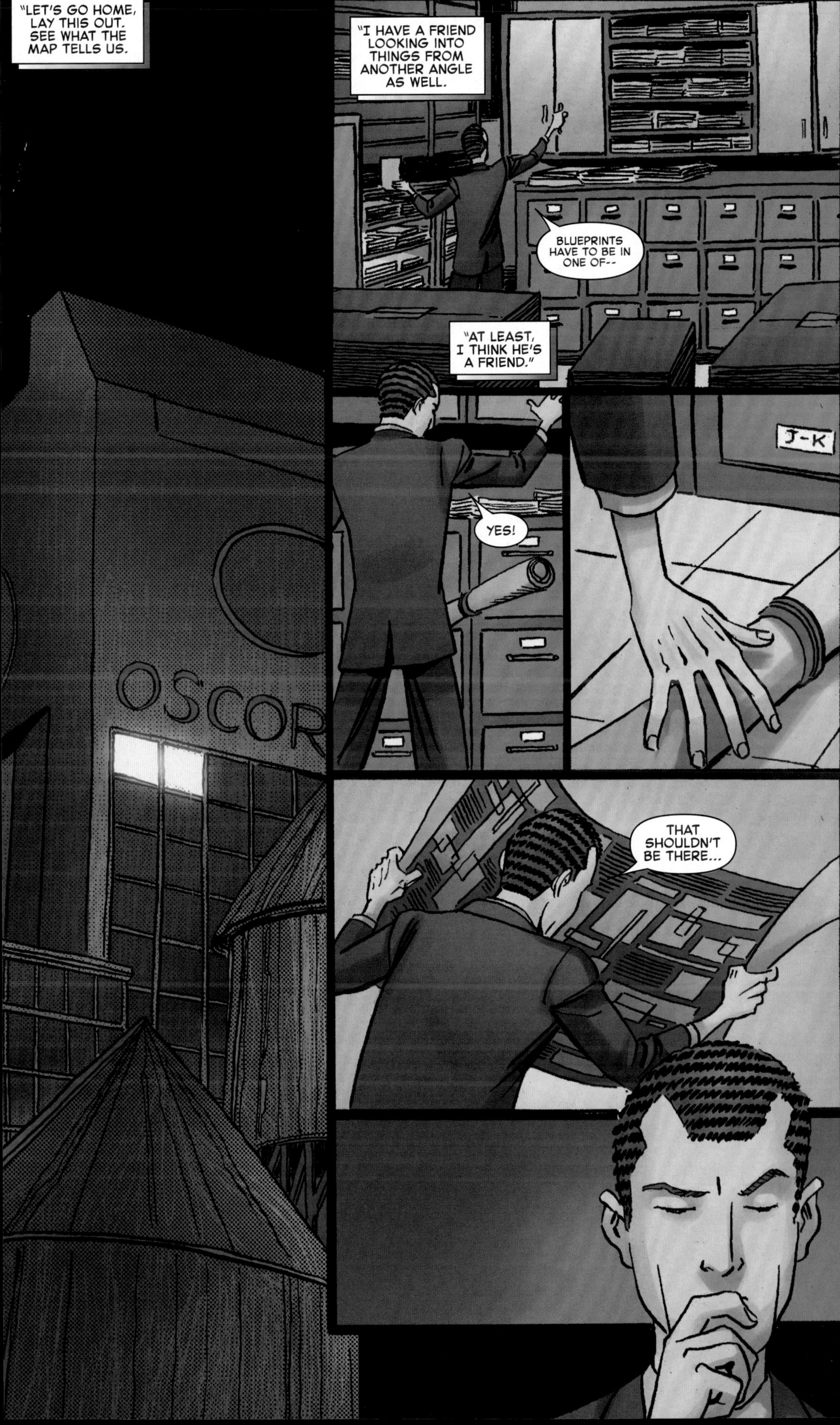
"LET'S GO HOME, LAY THIS OUT. SEE WHAT THE MAP TELLS US.
OSCOR
"I HAVE A FRIEND LOOKING INTO THINGS FROM ANOTHER ANGLE AS WELL.
BLUEPRINTS HAVE TO BE IN ONE OF--
"AT LEAST, I THINK HE'S A FRIEND."
YES!
J-K
THAT SHOULDN'T BE THERE...

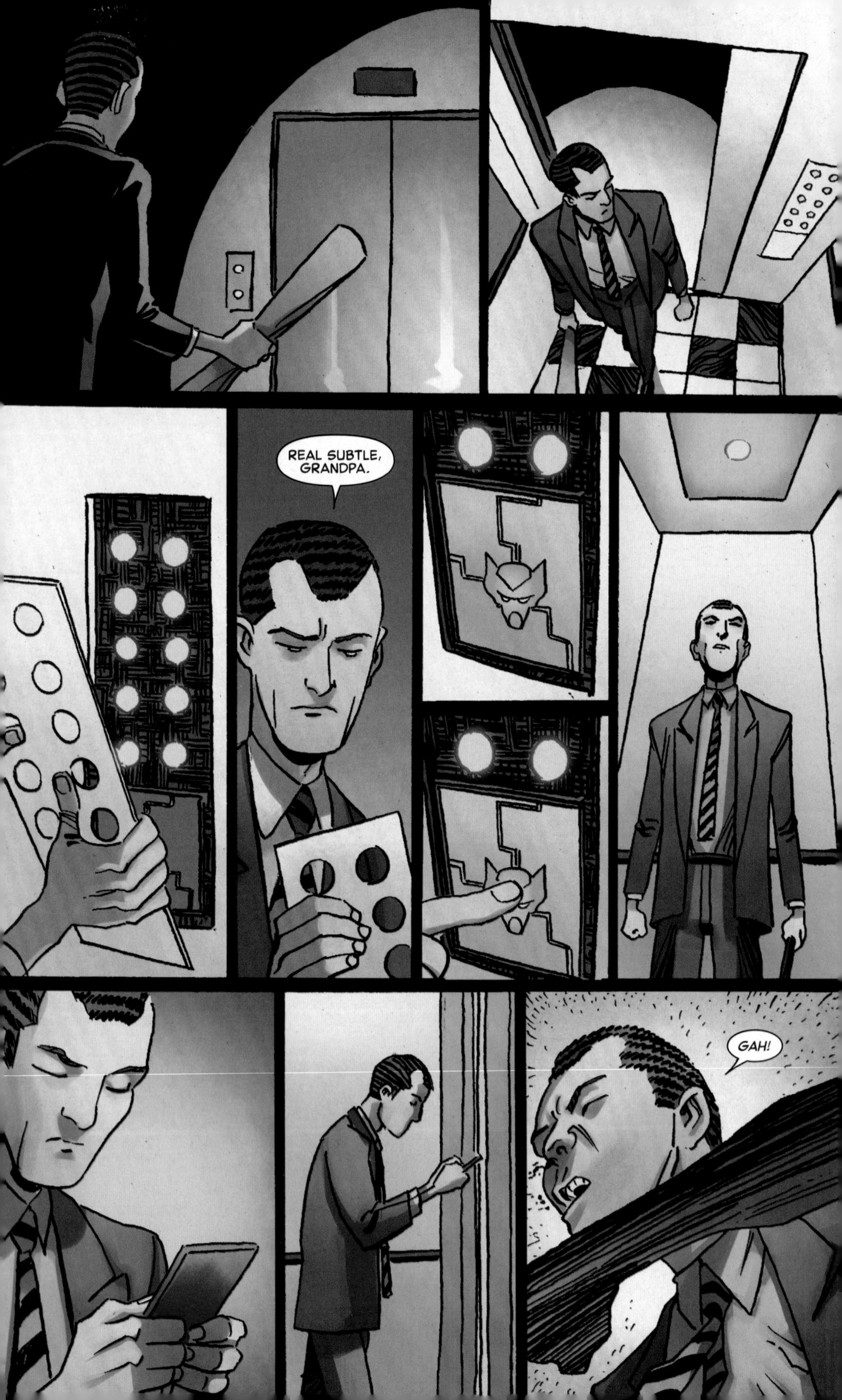
REAL SUBTLE, GRANDPA.
GAH!

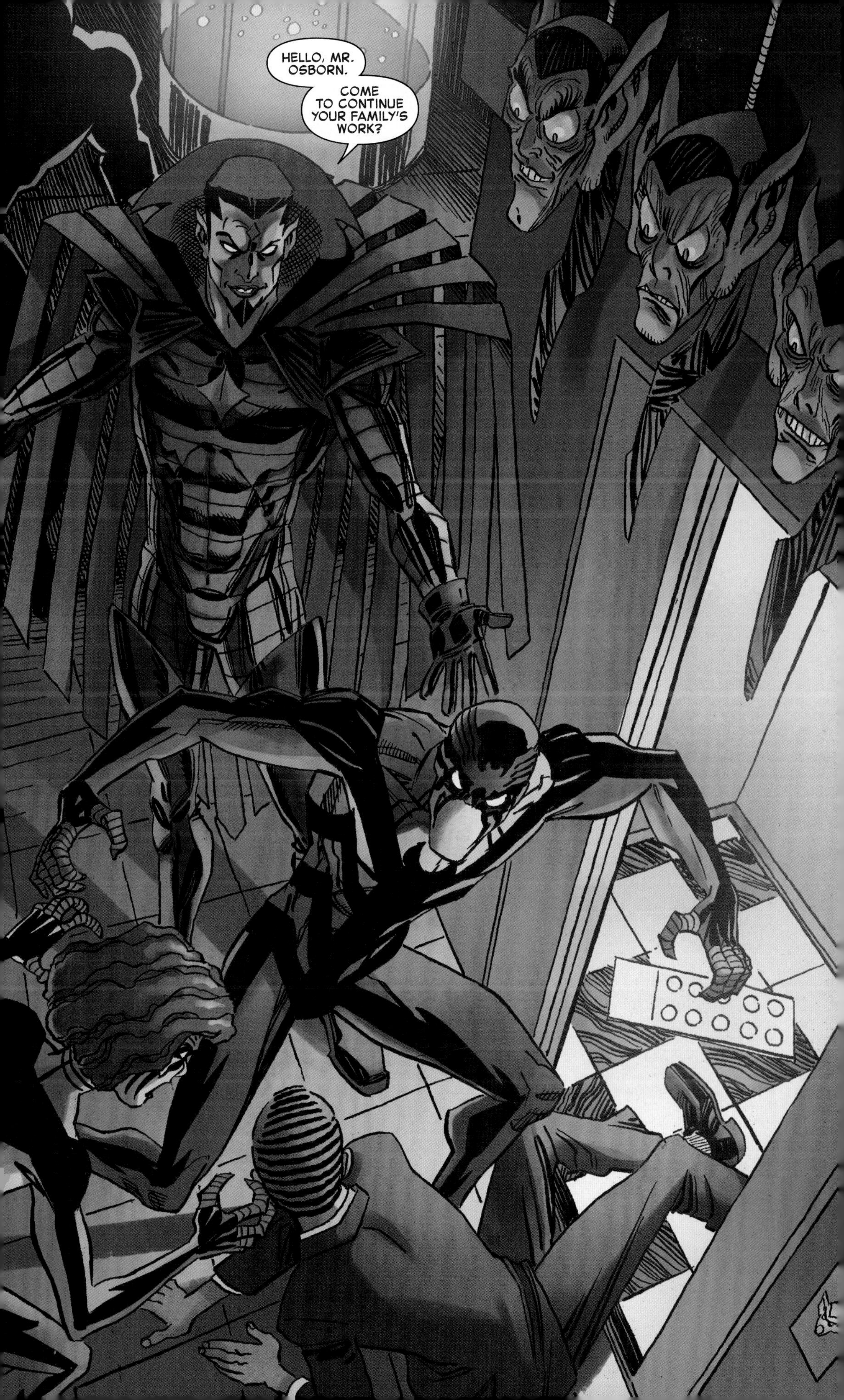
HELLO, MR. OSBORN.
COME TO CONTINUE YOUR FAMILY'S WORK?

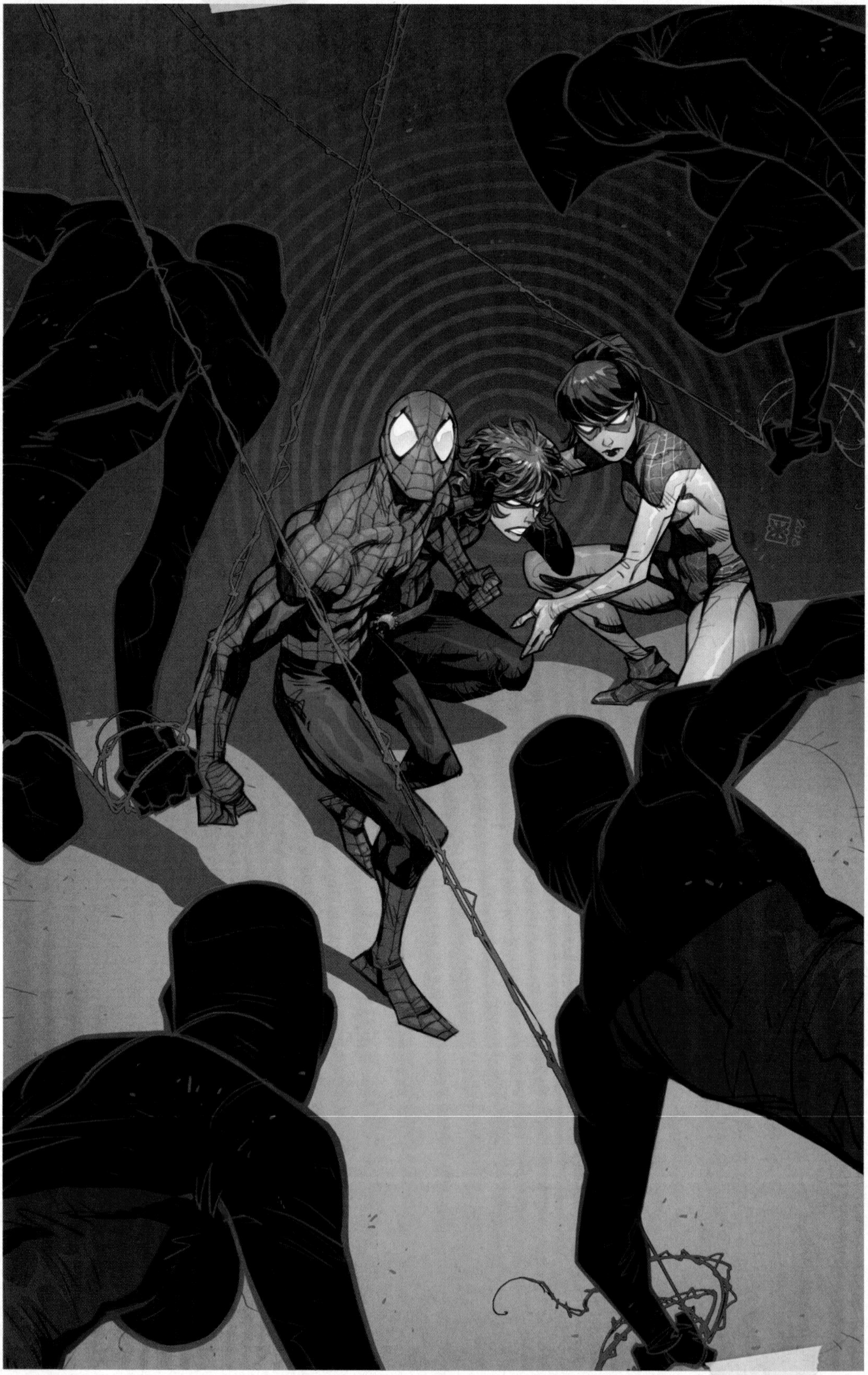

22: WEIRD SCIENCE — PART 3

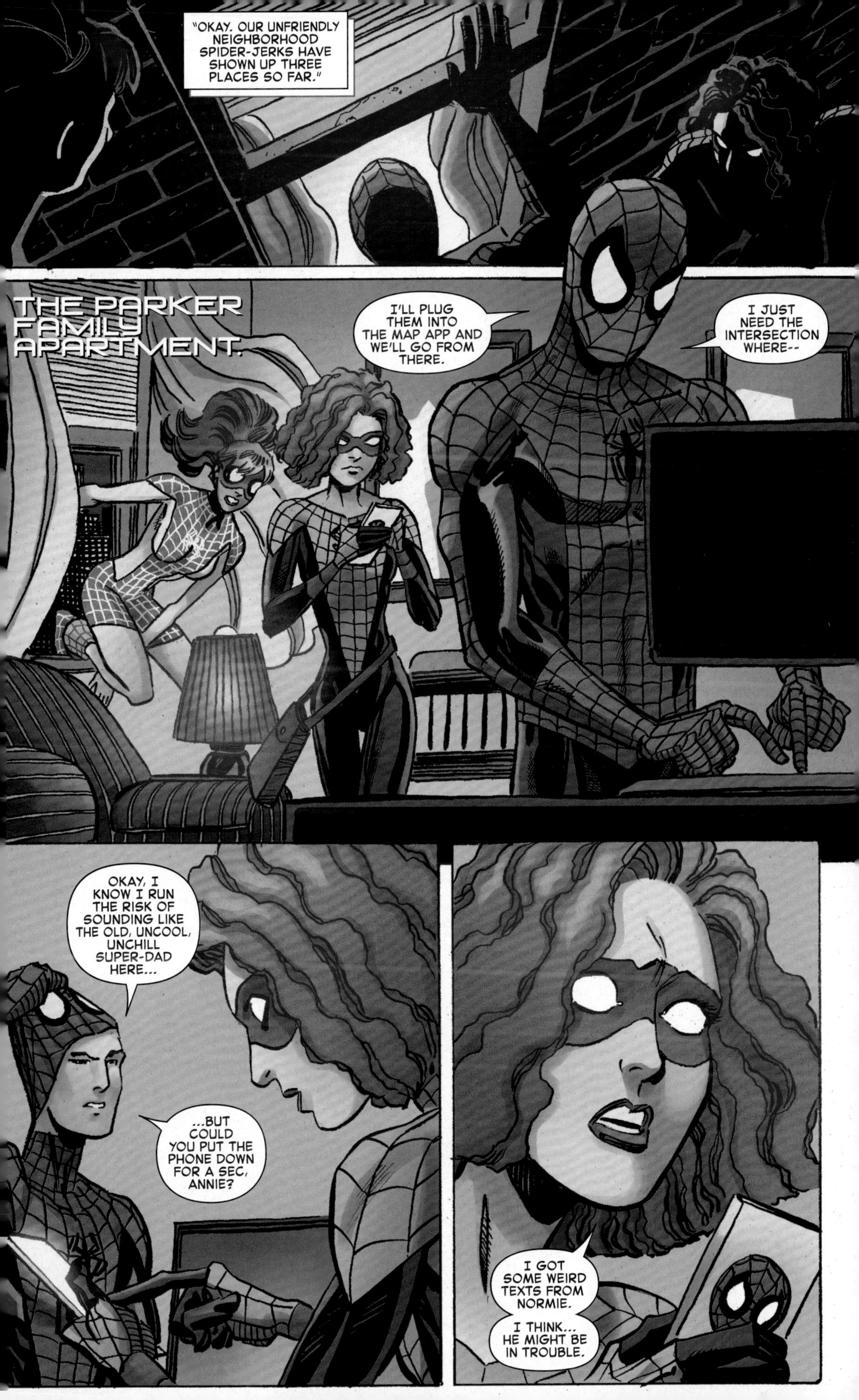
"OKAY. OUR UNFRIENDLY NEIGHBORHOOD SPIDER-JERKS HAVE SHOWN UP THREE PLACES SO FAR."
THE PARKER FAMILY APARTMENT.
I'LL PLUG THEM INTO THE MAP APP AND WE'LL GO FROM THERE.
I JUST NEED THE INTERSECTION WHERE--
OKAY, I KNOW I RUN THE RISK OF SOUNDING LIKE THE OLD, UNCOOL, UNCHILL SUPER-DAD HERE...
...BUT COULD YOU PUT THE PHONE DOWN FOR A SEC, ANNIE?
I GOT SOME WEIRD TEXTS FROM NORMIE.
I THINK... HE MIGHT BE IN TROUBLE.

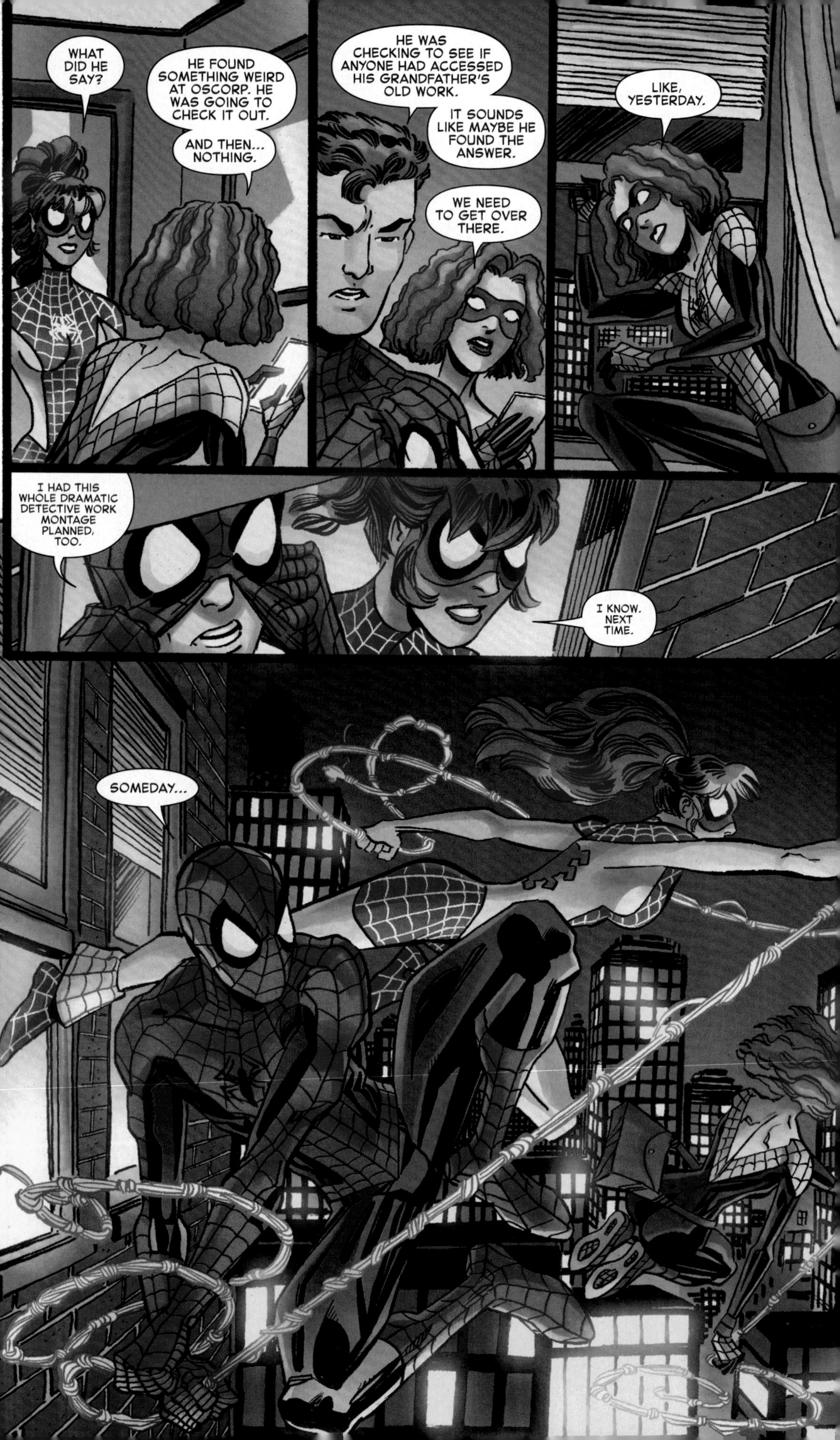
WHAT DID HE SAY?
HE FOUND SOMETHING WEIRD AT OSCORP. HE WAS GOING TO CHECK IT OUT.
AND THEN... NOTHING.
HE WAS CHECKING TO SEE IF ANYONE HAD ACCESSED HIS GRANDFATHER'S OLD WORK.
IT SOUNDS LIKE MAYBE HE FOUND THE ANSWER.
WE NEED TO GET OVER THERE.
LIKE, YESTERDAY.
I HAD THIS WHOLE DRAMATIC DETECTIVE WORK MONTAGE PLANNED, TOO.
I KNOW. NEXT TIME.
SOMEDAY...

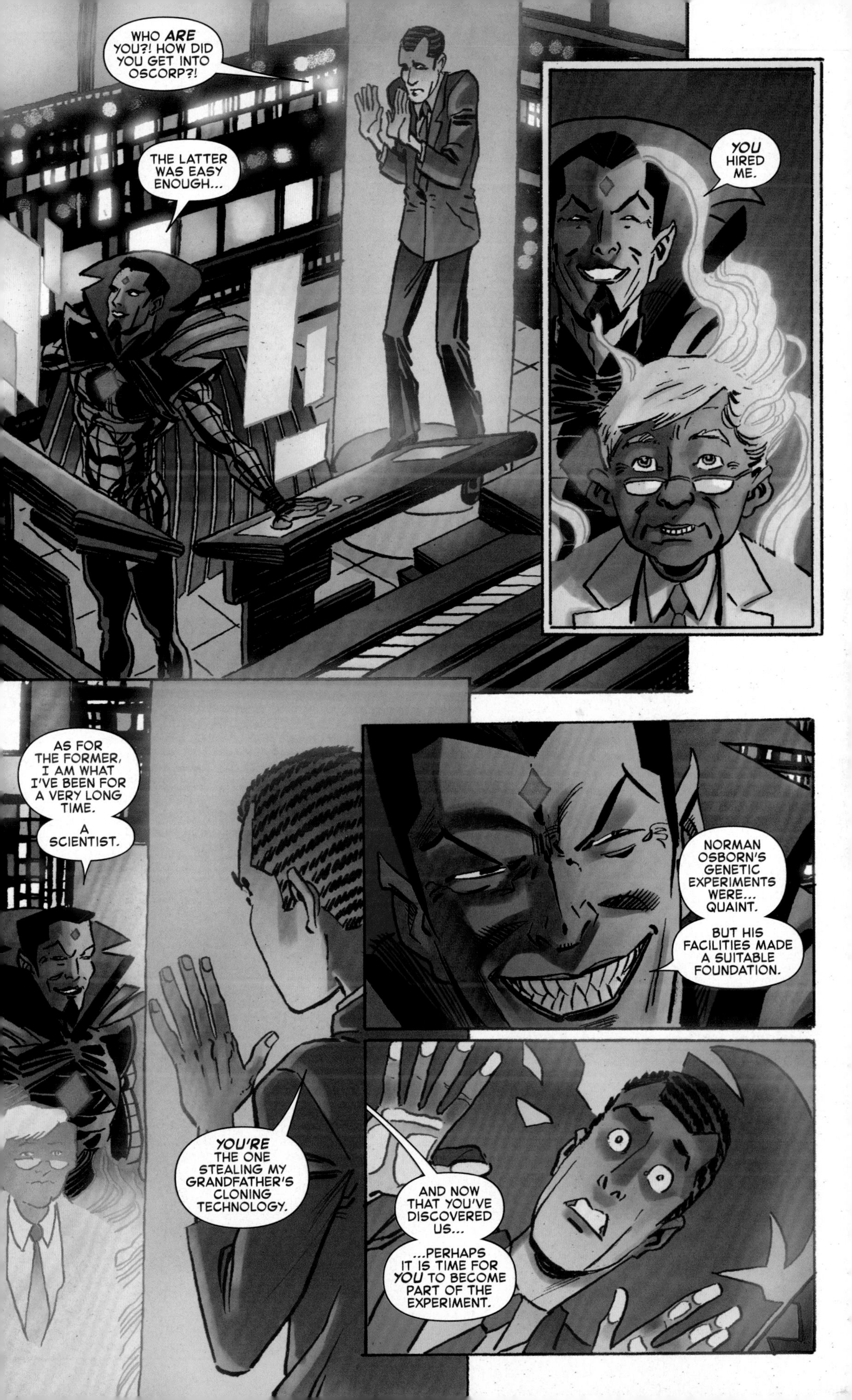
WHO ARE YOU?! HOW DID YOU GET INTO OSCORP?!
THE LATTER WAS EASY ENOUGH...
YOU HIRED ME.
AS FOR THE FORMER, I AM WHAT I'VE BEEN FOR A VERY LONG TIME.
A SCIENTIST.
NORMAN OSBORN'S GENETIC EXPERIMENTS WERE... QUAINT.
BUT HIS FACILITIES MADE A SUITABLE FOUNDATION.
YOU'RE THE ONE STEALING MY GRANDFATHER'S CLONING TECHNOLOGY.
AND NOW THAT YOU'VE DISCOVERED US...
...PERHAPS IT IS TIME FOR YOU TO BECOME PART OF THE EXPERIMENT.

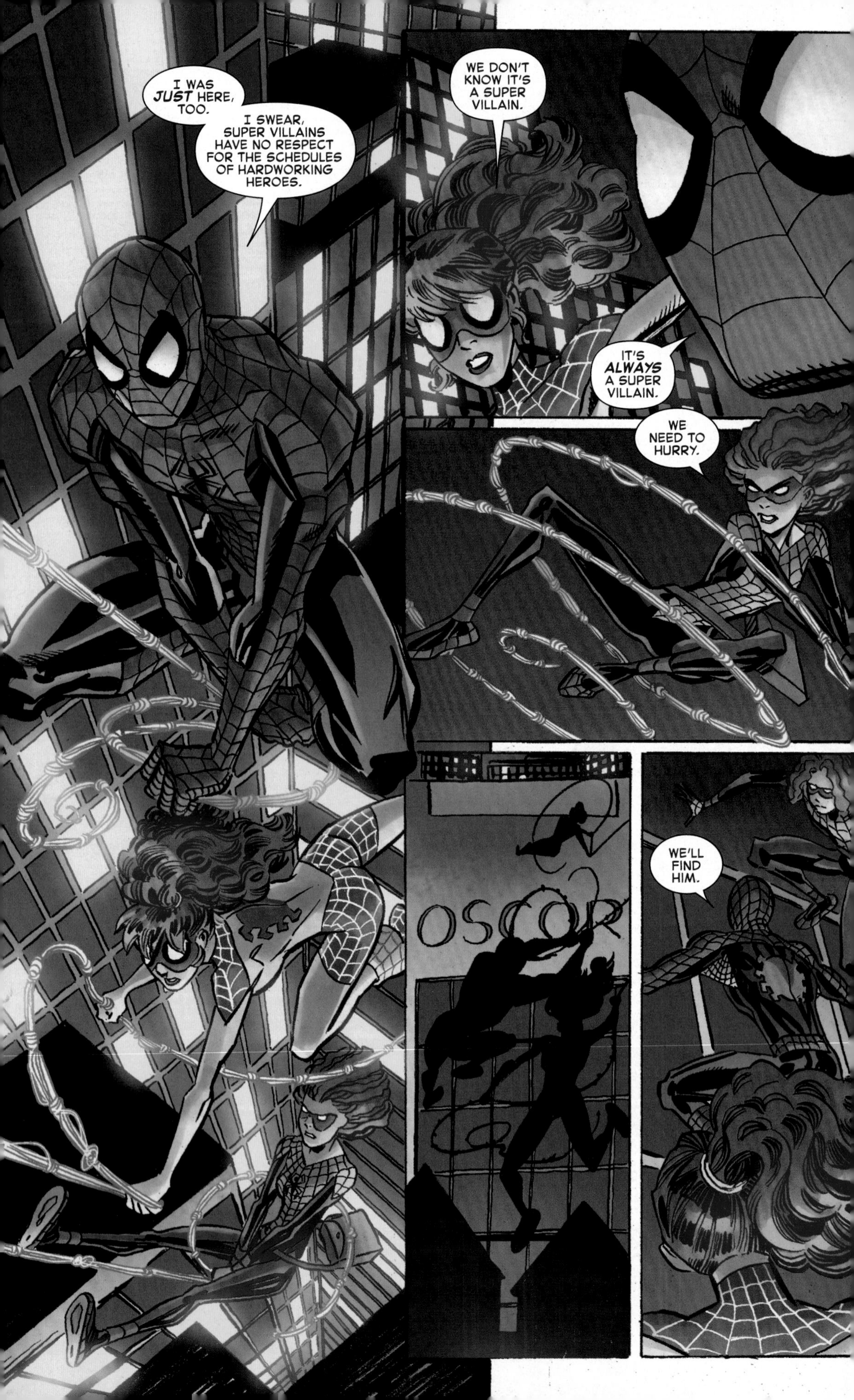

I WAS JUST HERE, TOO.
I SWEAR, SUPER VILLAINS HAVE NO RESPECT FOR THE SCHEDULES OF HARDWORKING HEROES.
WE DON'T KNOW IT'S A SUPER VILLAIN.
IT'S ALWAYS A SUPER VILLAIN.
WE NEED TO HURRY.
OSCOR
WE'LL FIND HIM.

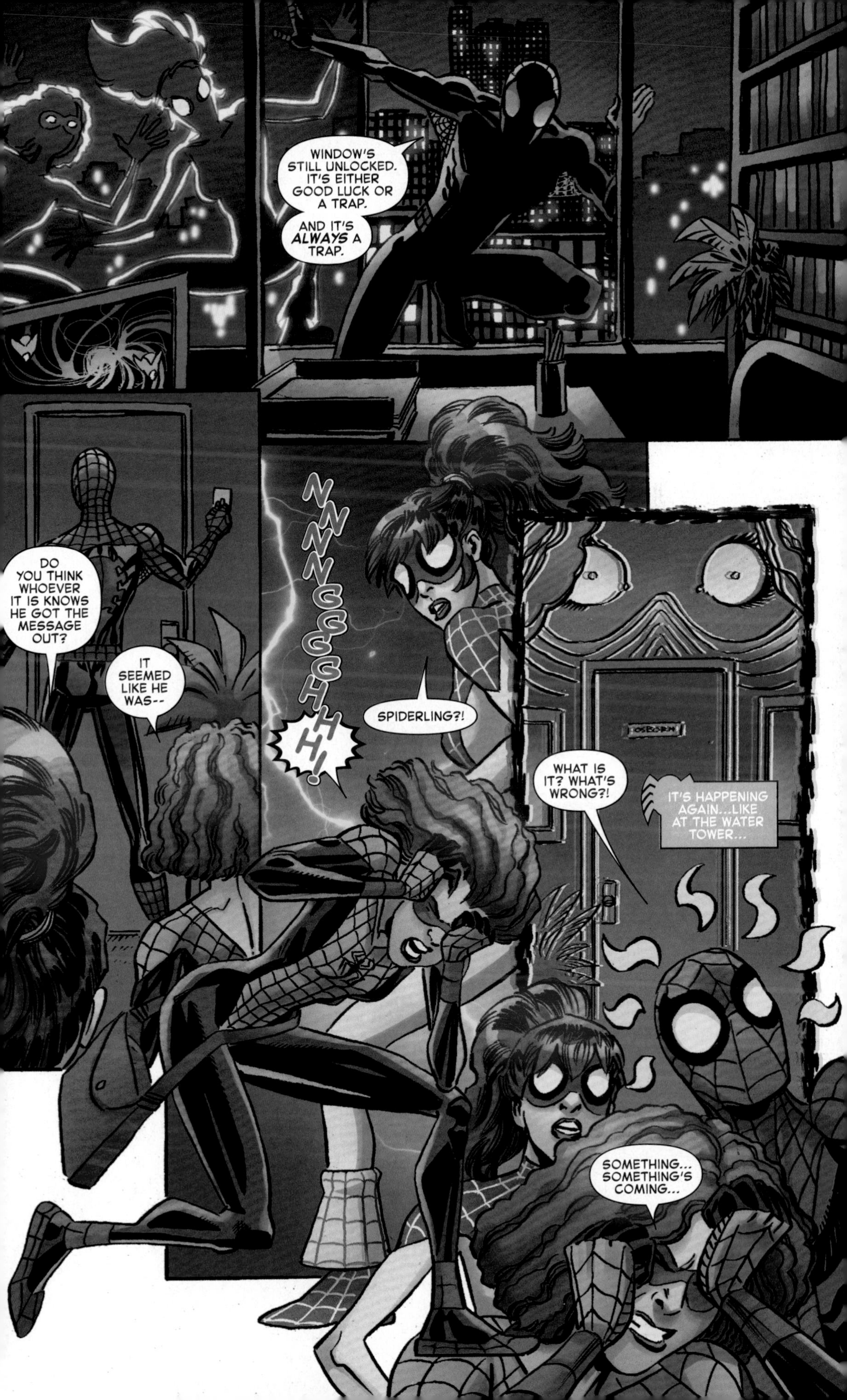
WINDOW'S STILL UNLOCKED. IT'S EITHER GOOD LUCK OR A TRAP.
AND IT'S *ALWAYS* A TRAP.
DO YOU THINK WHOEVER IT IS KNOWS HE GOT THE MESSAGE OUT?
IT SEEMED LIKE HE WAS--
NNNNGGGHHH!
SPIDERLING?!
OSBORN
WHAT IS IT? WHAT'S WRONG?!
IT'S HAPPENING AGAIN...LIKE AT THE WATER TOWER...
SOMETHING... SOMETHING'S COMING...

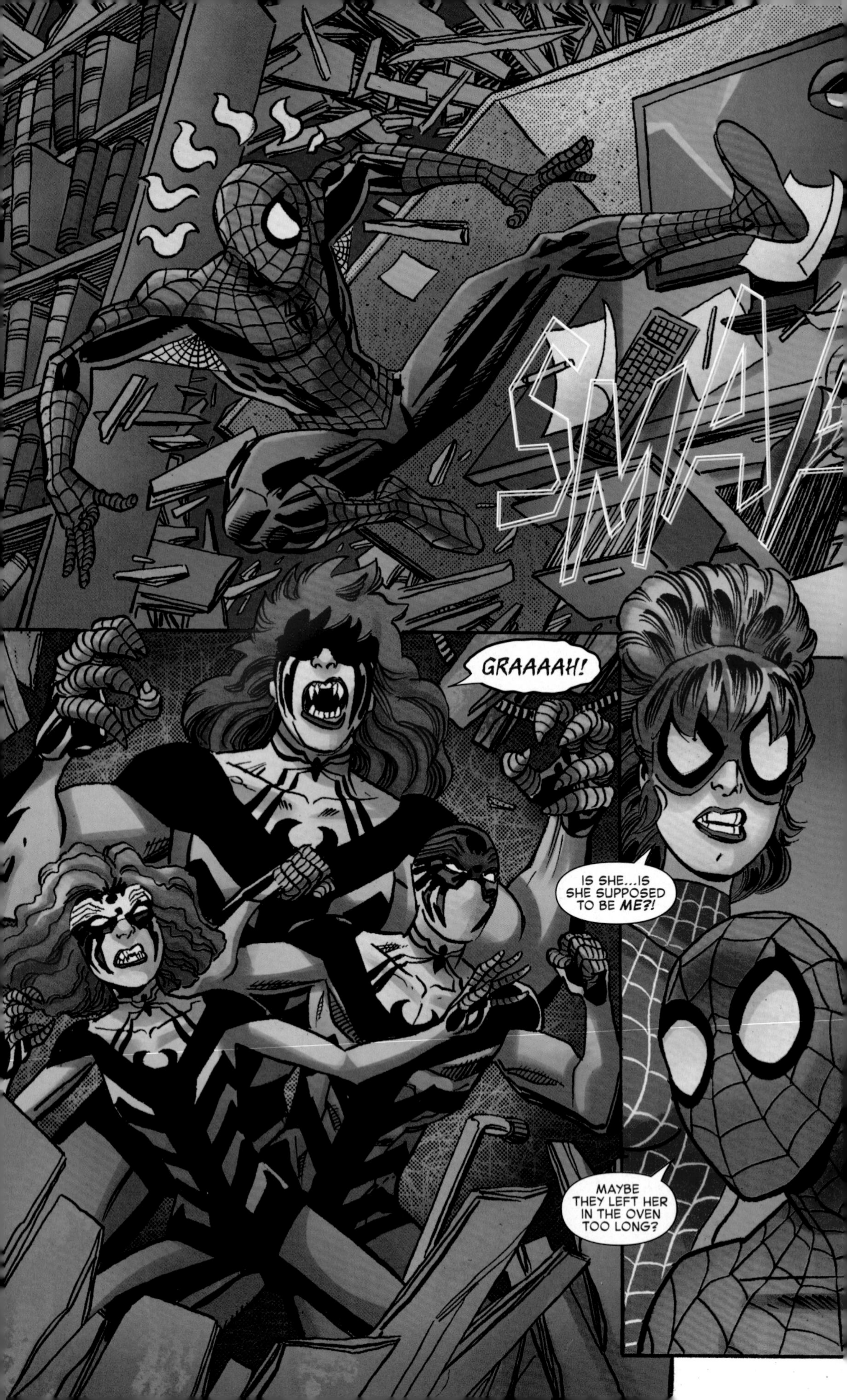
SMAA
GRAAAAH!
IS SHE...IS SHE SUPPOSED TO BE ME?!
MAYBE THEY LEFT HER IN THE OVEN TOO LONG?

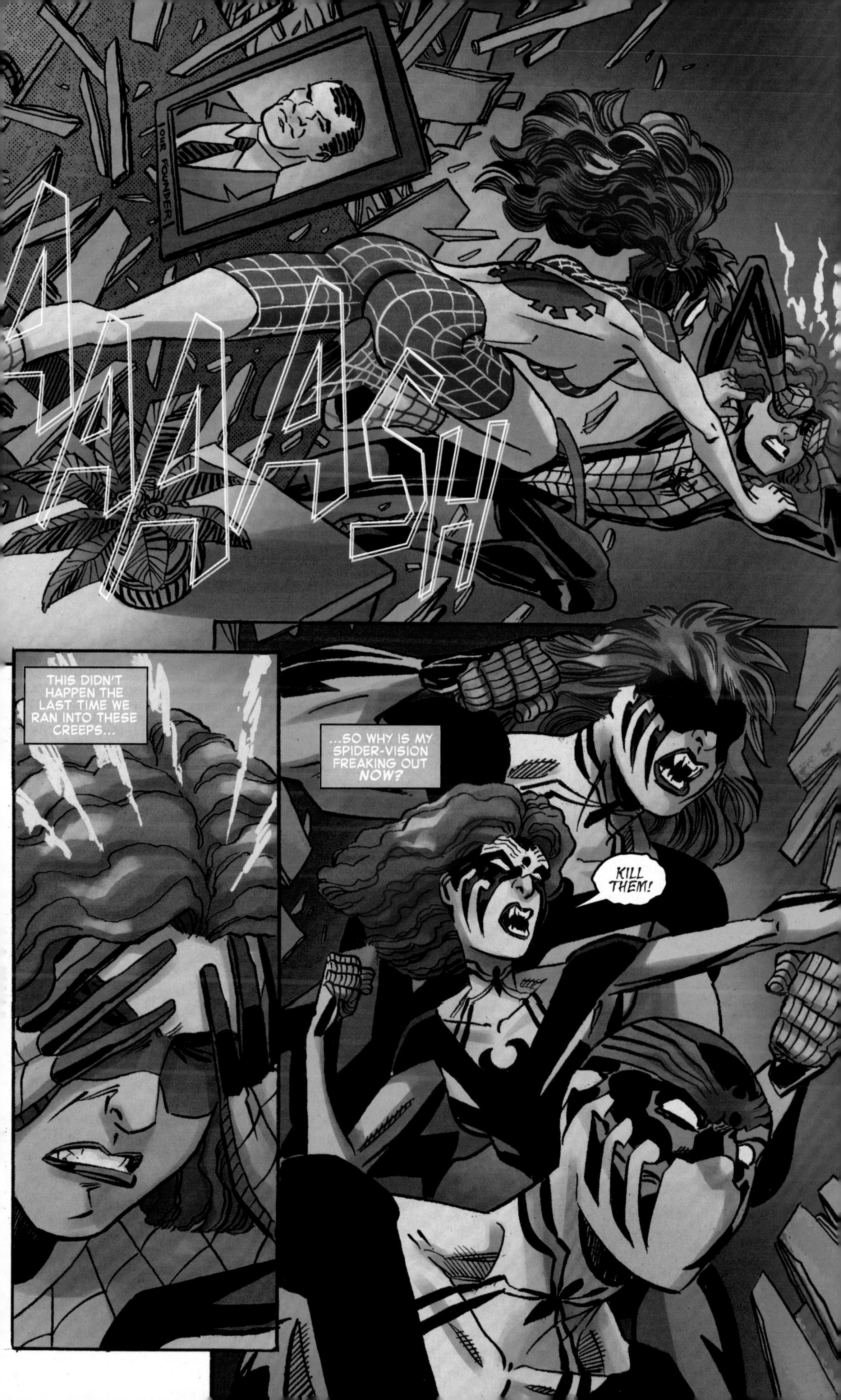
OUR FOUNDER
SMAASH
THIS DIDN'T HAPPEN THE LAST TIME WE RAN INTO THESE CREEPS...
...SO WHY IS MY SPIDER-VISION FREAKING OUT NOW?
KILL THEM!

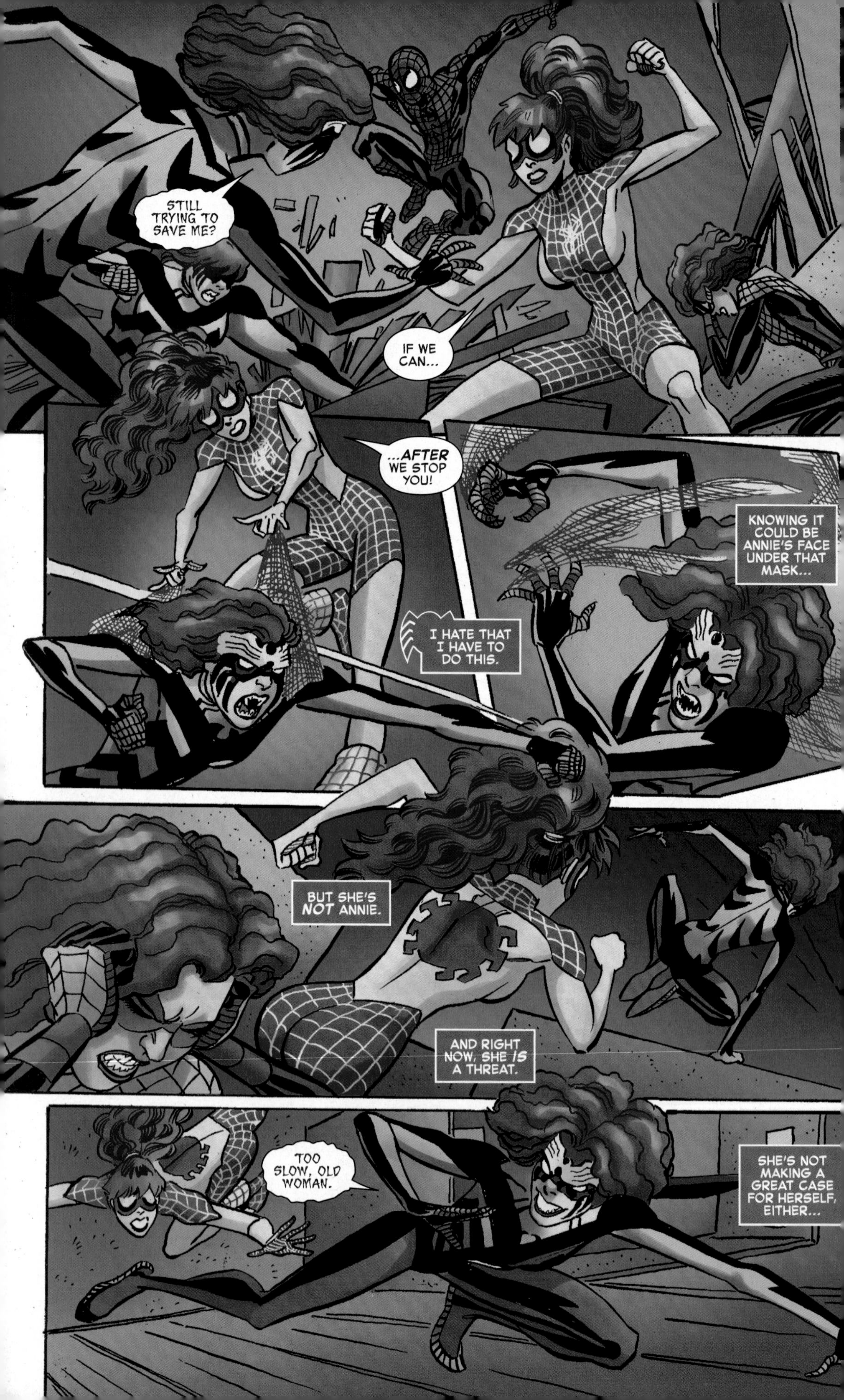
STILL TRYING TO SAVE ME?
IF WE CAN...
...AFTER WE STOP YOU!
KNOWING IT COULD BE ANNIE'S FACE UNDER THAT MASK...
I HATE THAT I HAVE TO DO THIS.
BUT SHE'S NOT ANNIE.
AND RIGHT NOW, SHE IS A THREAT.
TOO SLOW, OLD WOMAN.
SHE'S NOT MAKING A GREAT CASE FOR HERSELF, EITHER...

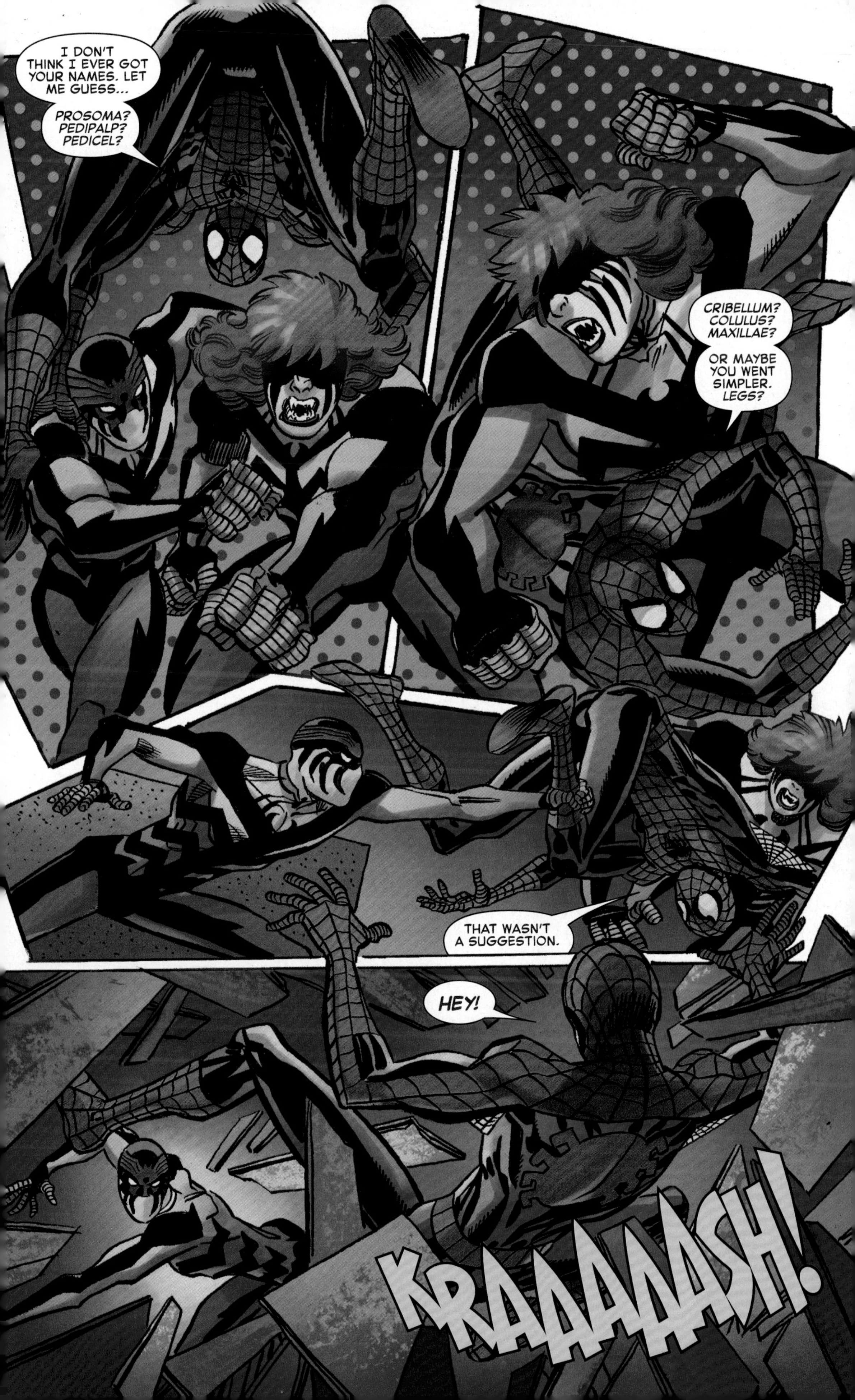
I DON'T THINK I EVER GOT YOUR NAMES. LET ME GUESS...
PROSOMA? PEDIPALP? PEDICEL?
CRIBELLUM? COLULUS? MAXILLAE?
OR MAYBE YOU WENT SIMPLER. LEGS?
THAT WASN'T A SUGGESTION.
HEY!
KRAAAAASH!

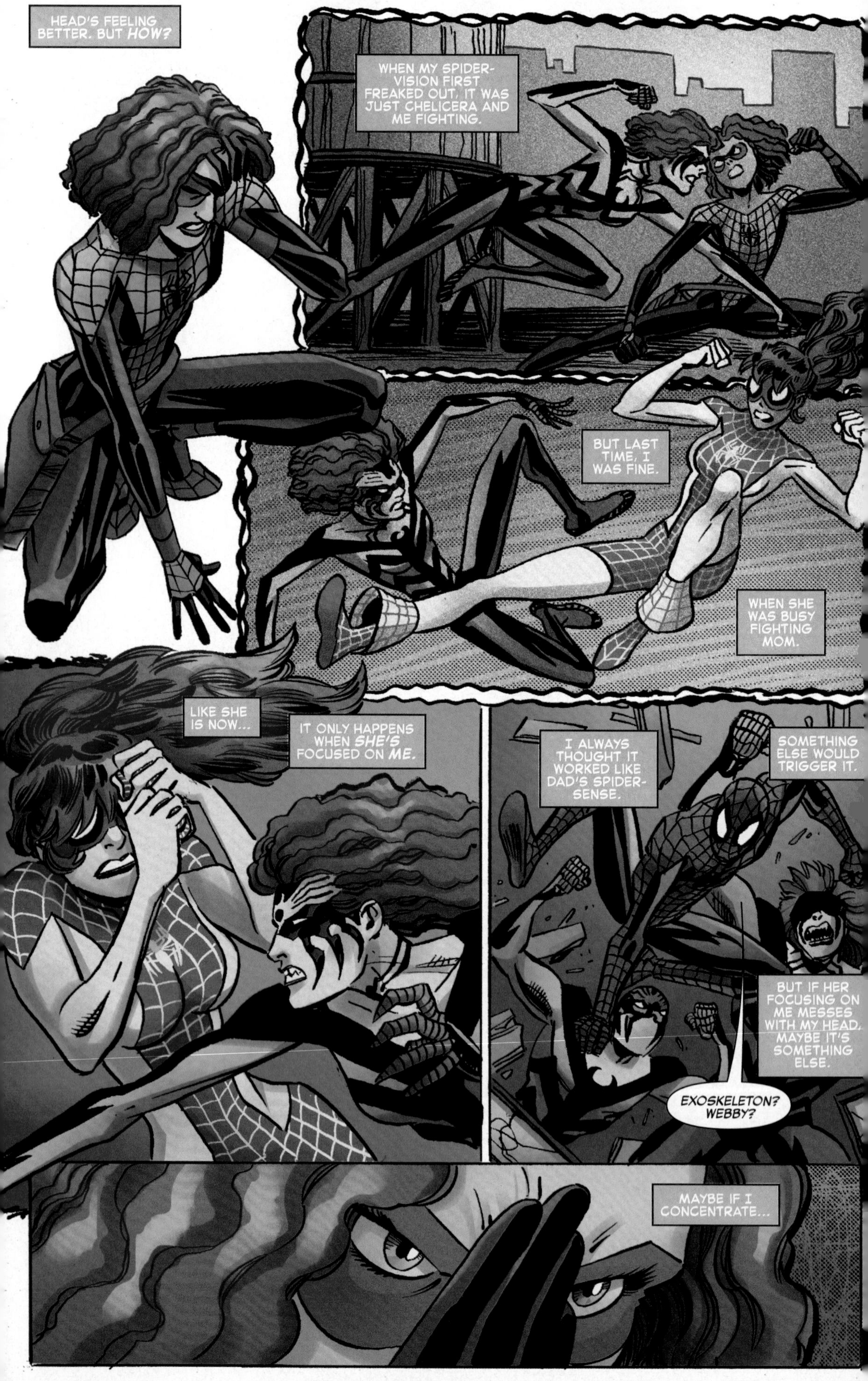
HEAD'S FEELING BETTER. BUT HOW?
WHEN MY SPIDER-VISION FIRST FREAKED OUT, IT WAS JUST CHELICERA AND ME FIGHTING.
BUT LAST TIME, I WAS FINE.
WHEN SHE WAS BUSY FIGHTING MOM.
LIKE SHE IS NOW...
IT ONLY HAPPENS WHEN SHE'S FOCUSED ON ME.
I ALWAYS THOUGHT IT WORKED LIKE DAD'S SPIDER-SENSE.
SOMETHING ELSE WOULD TRIGGER IT.
BUT IF HER FOCUSING ON ME MESSES WITH MY HEAD, MAYBE IT'S SOMETHING ELSE.
EXOSKELETON? WEBBY?
MAYBE IF I CONCENTRATE...

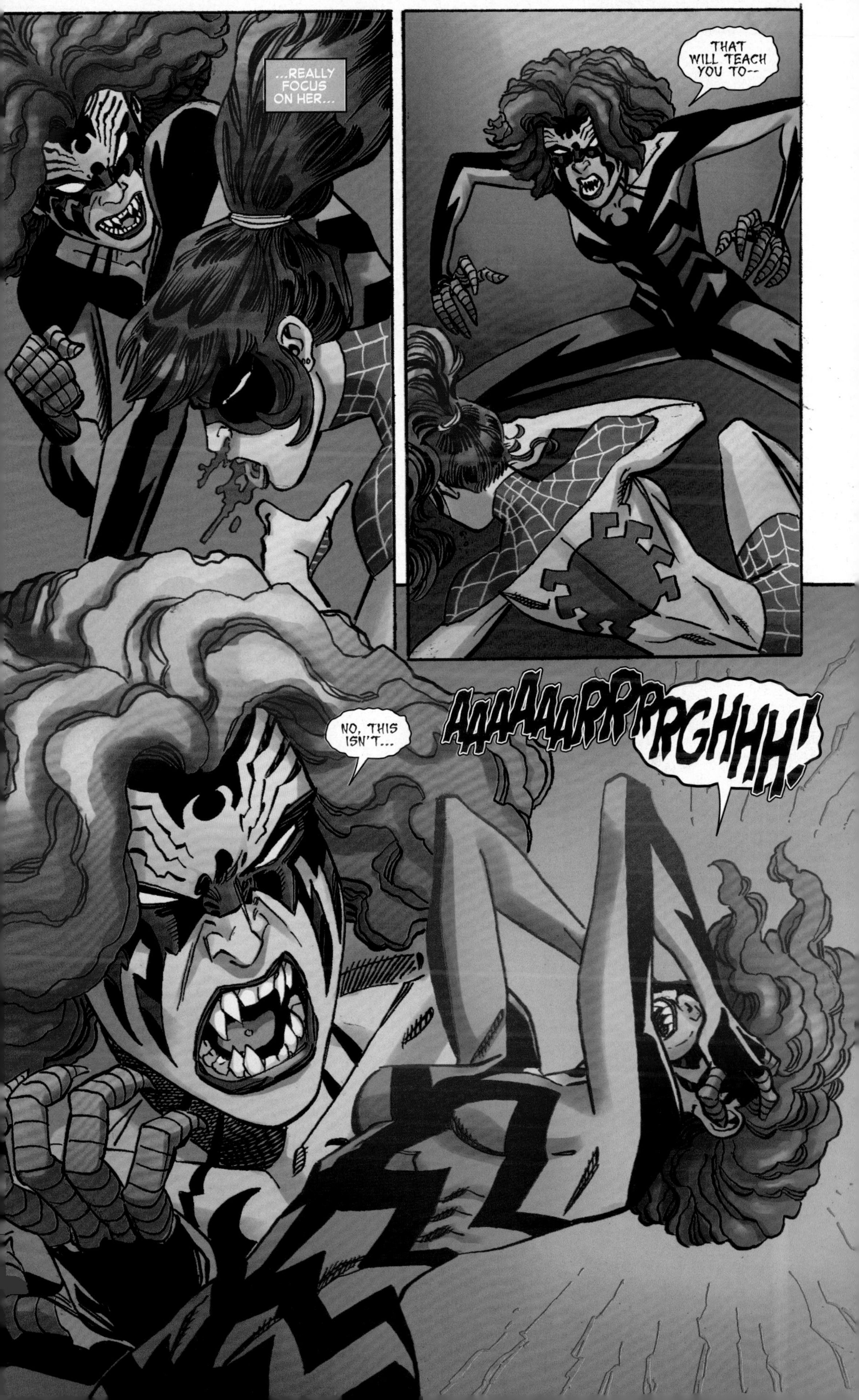
...REALLY FOCUS ON HER...
THAT WILL TEACH YOU TO--
NO, THIS ISN'T...
AAAAAARRRRGHHH!

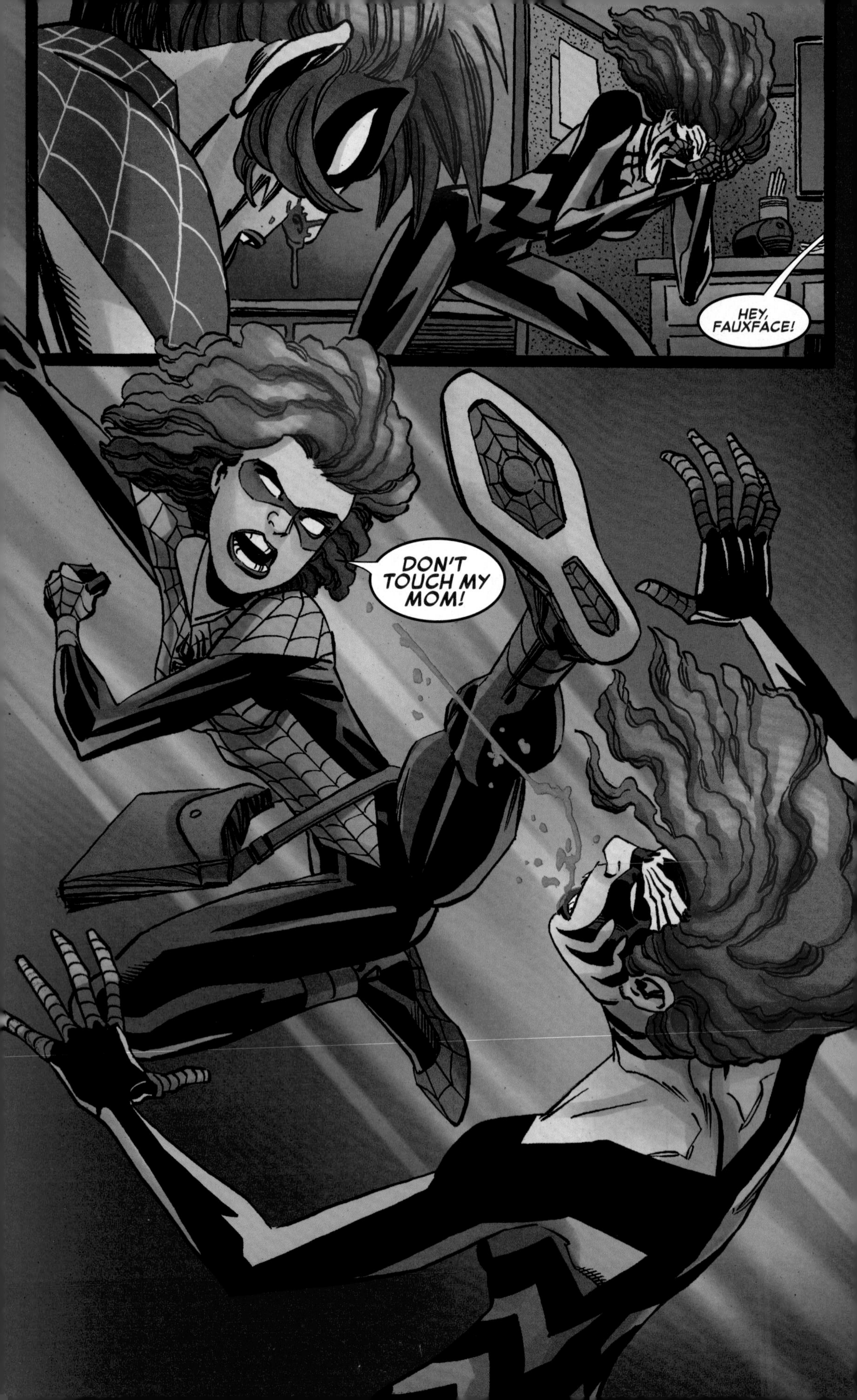
HEY, FAUXFACE!
DON'T TOUCH MY MOM!

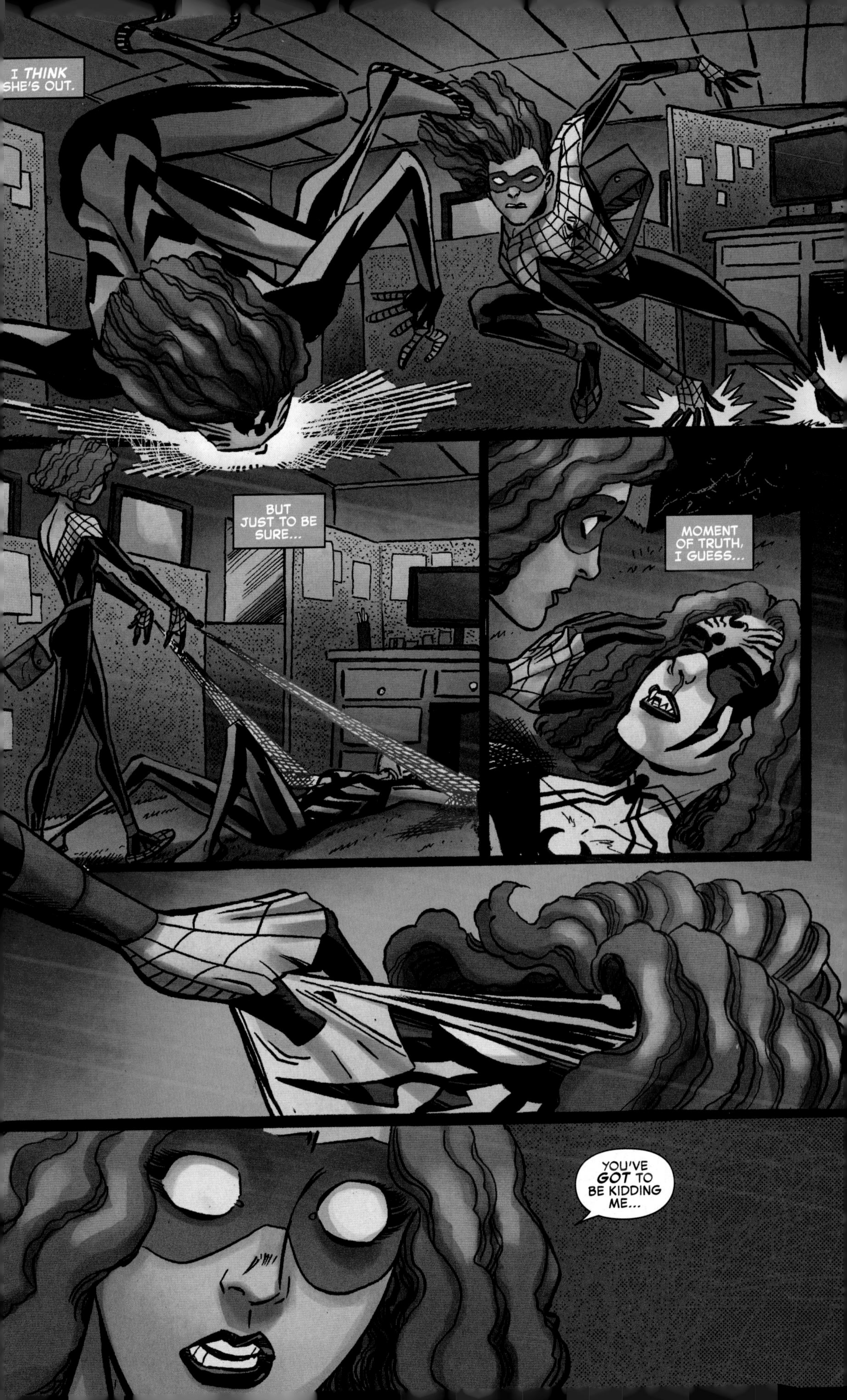
I THINK SHE'S OUT.
BUT JUST TO BE SURE...
MOMENT OF TRUTH, I GUESS...
YOU'VE GOT TO BE KIDDING ME...

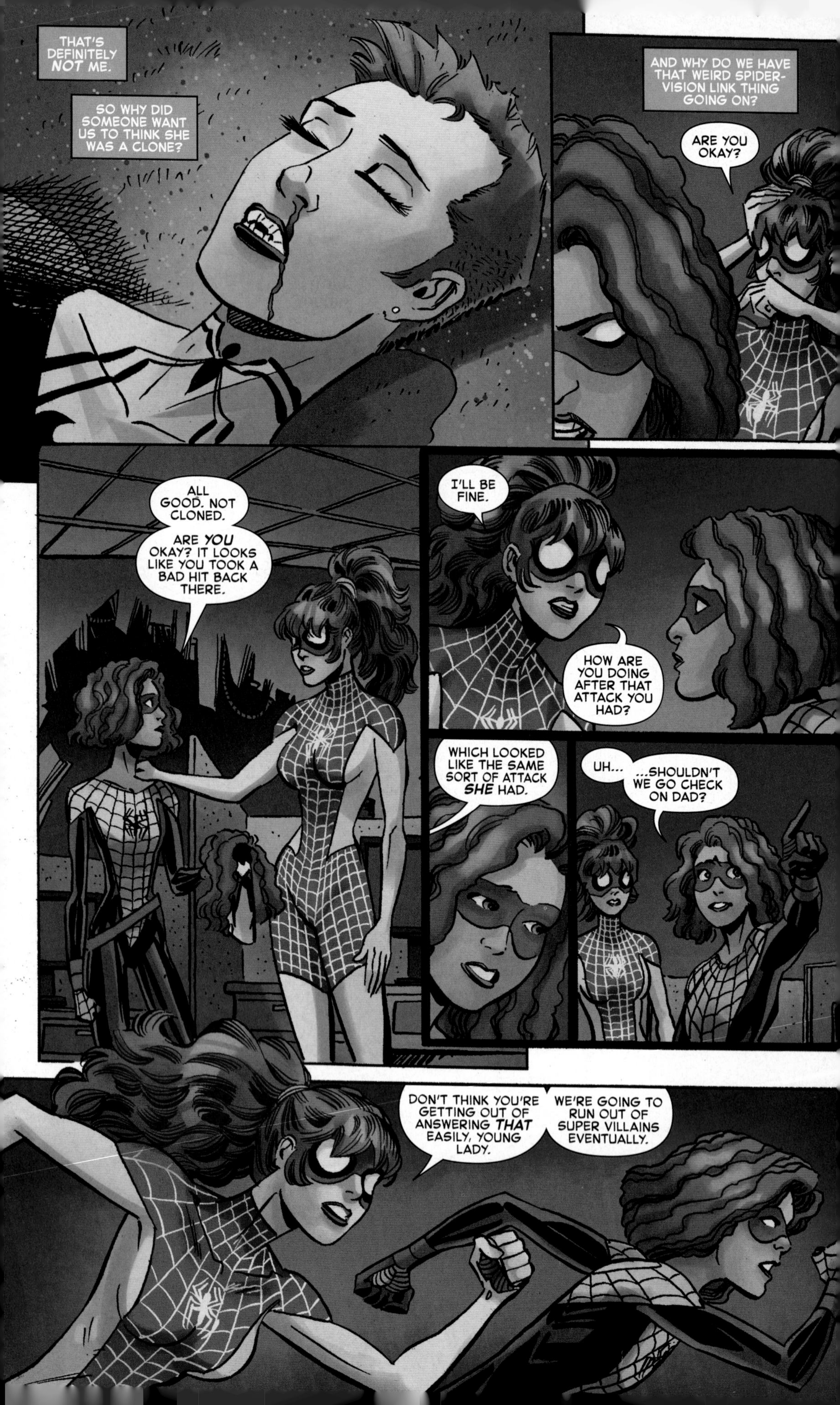
THAT'S DEFINITELY NOT ME.
SO WHY DID SOMEONE WANT US TO THINK SHE WAS A CLONE?
AND WHY DO WE HAVE THAT WEIRD SPIDER-VISION LINK THING GOING ON?
ARE YOU OKAY?
ALL GOOD. NOT CLONED.
ARE YOU OKAY? IT LOOKS LIKE YOU TOOK A BAD HIT BACK THERE.
I'LL BE FINE.
HOW ARE YOU DOING AFTER THAT ATTACK YOU HAD?
WHICH LOOKED LIKE THE SAME SORT OF ATTACK SHE HAD.
UH...
...SHOULDN'T WE GO CHECK ON DAD?
DON'T THINK YOU'RE GETTING OUT OF ANSWERING THAT EASILY, YOUNG LADY.
WE'RE GOING TO RUN OUT OF SUPER VILLAINS EVENTUALLY.

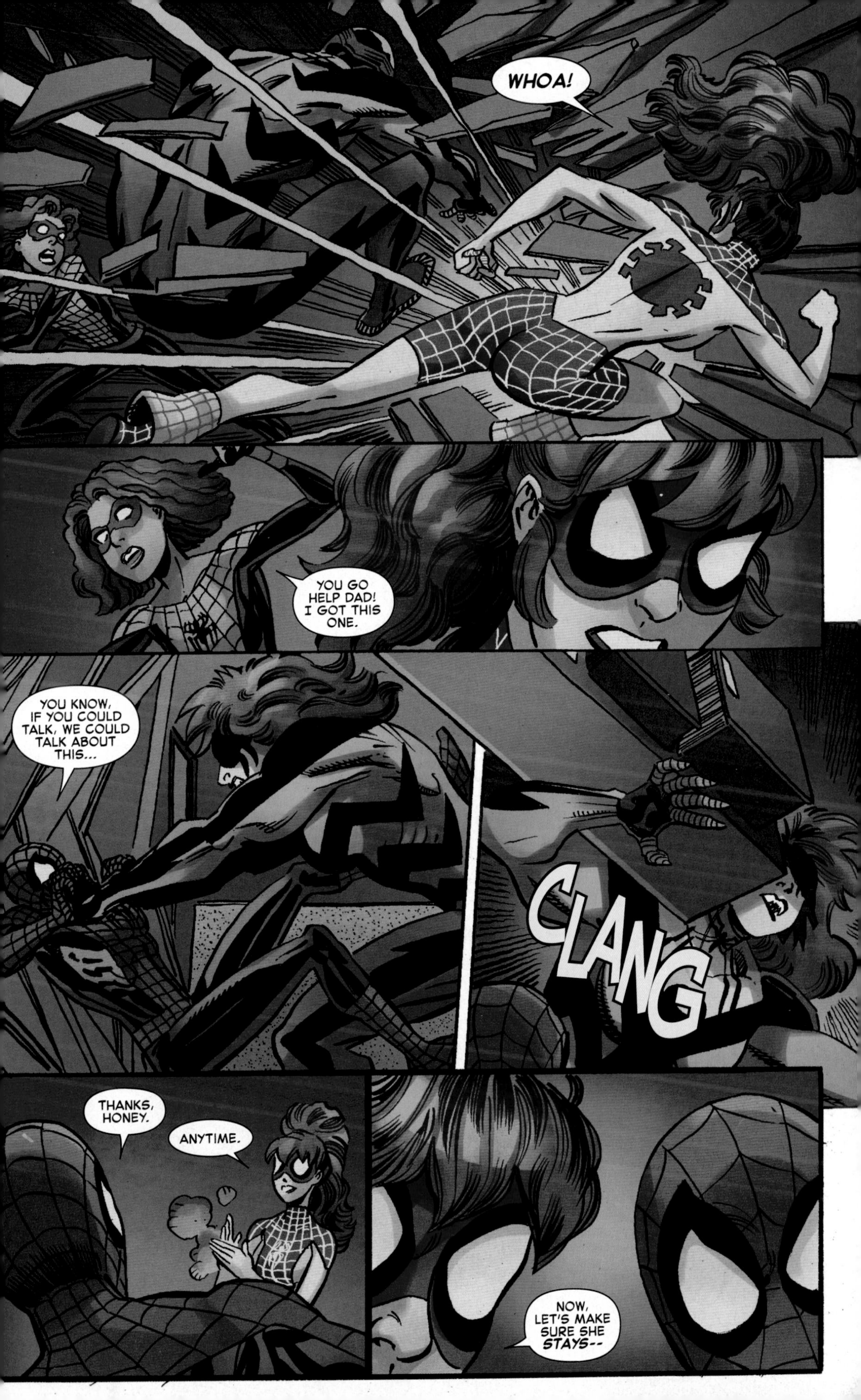
WHOA!
YOU GO HELP DAD! I GOT THIS ONE.
YOU KNOW, IF YOU COULD TALK, WE COULD TALK ABOUT THIS...
CLANG!!
THANKS, HONEY.
ANYTIME.
NOW, LET'S MAKE SURE SHE *STAYS*--

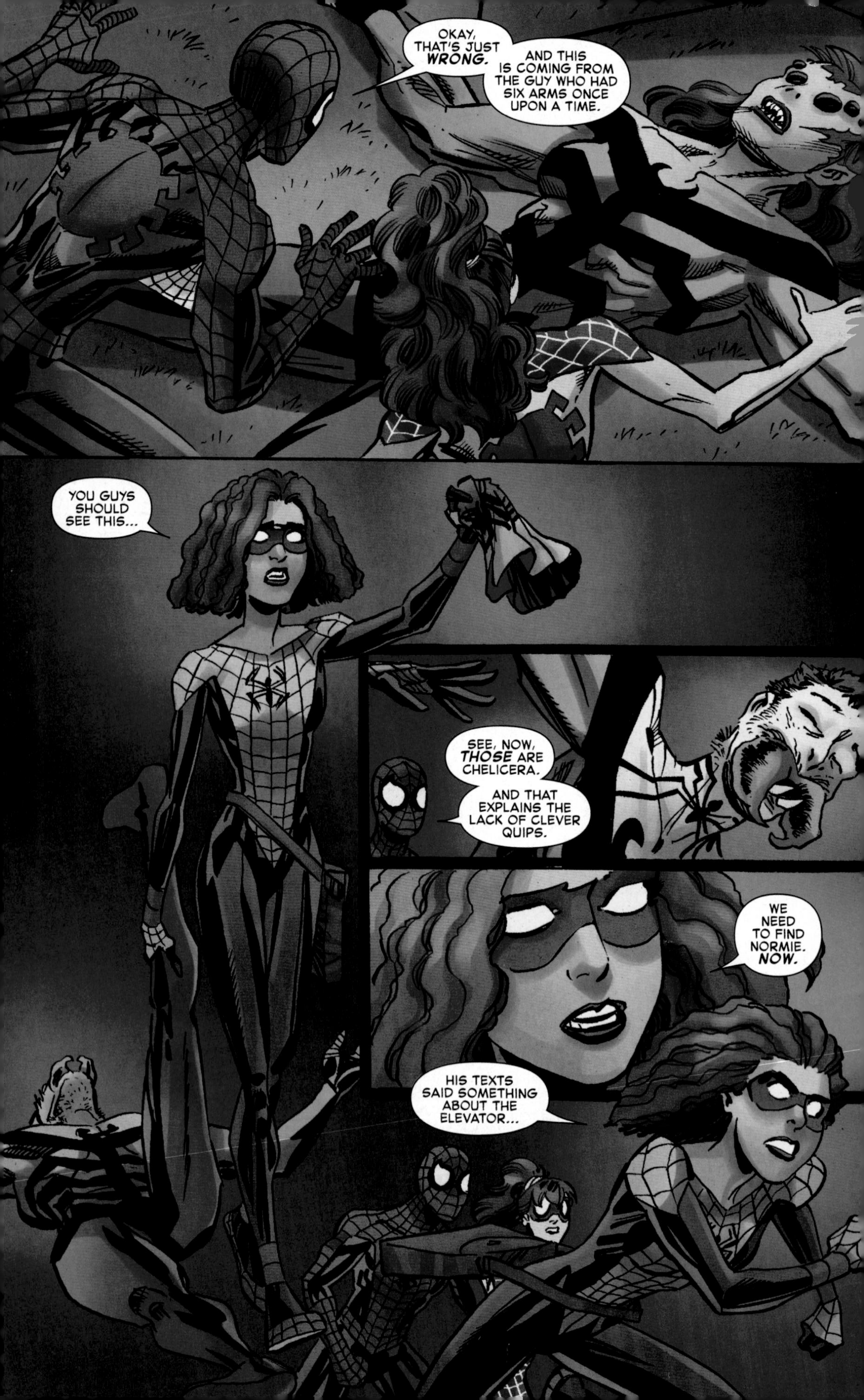
OKAY, THAT'S JUST WRONG.
AND THIS IS COMING FROM THE GUY WHO HAD SIX ARMS ONCE UPON A TIME.
YOU GUYS SHOULD SEE THIS...
SEE, NOW, THOSE ARE CHELICERA.
AND THAT EXPLAINS THE LACK OF CLEVER QUIPS.
WE NEED TO FIND NORMIE. NOW.
HIS TEXTS SAID SOMETHING ABOUT THE ELEVATOR...

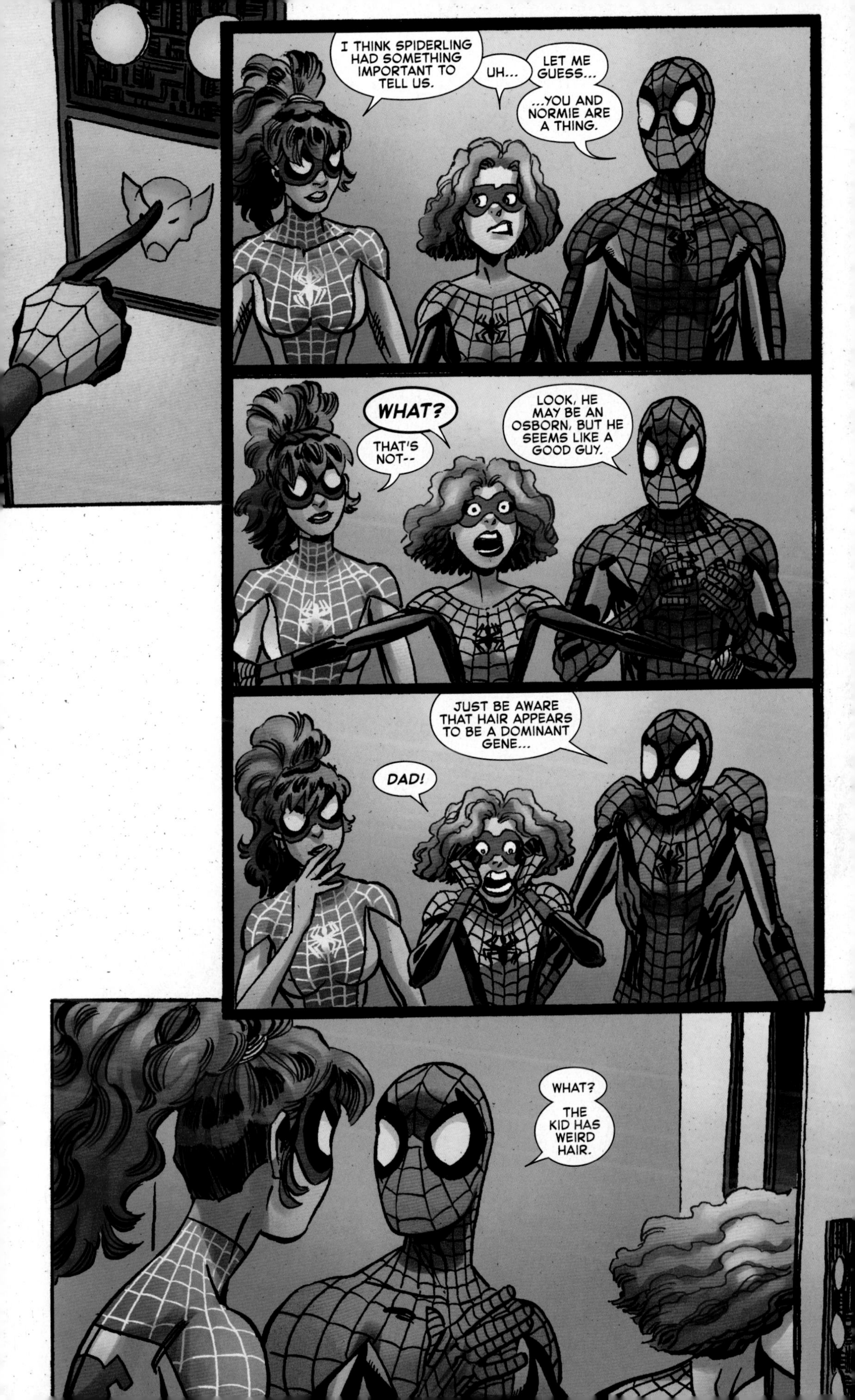
I THINK SPIDERLING HAD SOMETHING IMPORTANT TO TELL US.
UH...
LET ME GUESS...
...YOU AND NORMIE ARE A THING.
WHAT?
THAT'S NOT--
LOOK, HE MAY BE AN OSBORN, BUT HE SEEMS LIKE A GOOD GUY.
JUST BE AWARE THAT HAIR APPEARS TO BE A DOMINANT GENE...
DAD!
WHAT?
THE KID HAS WEIRD HAIR.

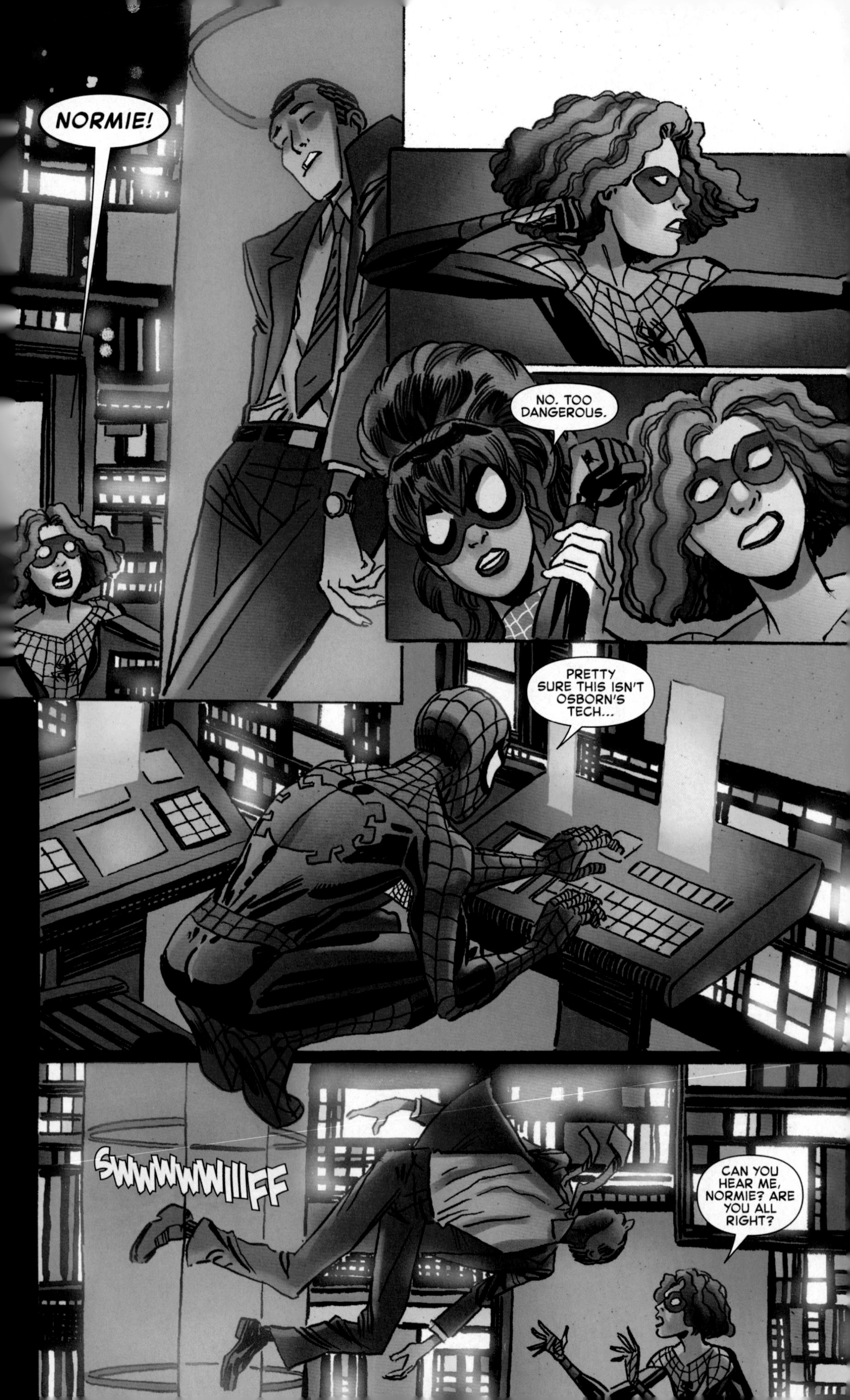
NORMIE!
NO. TOO DANGEROUS.
PRETTY SURE THIS ISN'T OSBORN'S TECH...
SWWWWWIIIIFF
CAN YOU HEAR ME, NORMIE? ARE YOU ALL RIGHT?

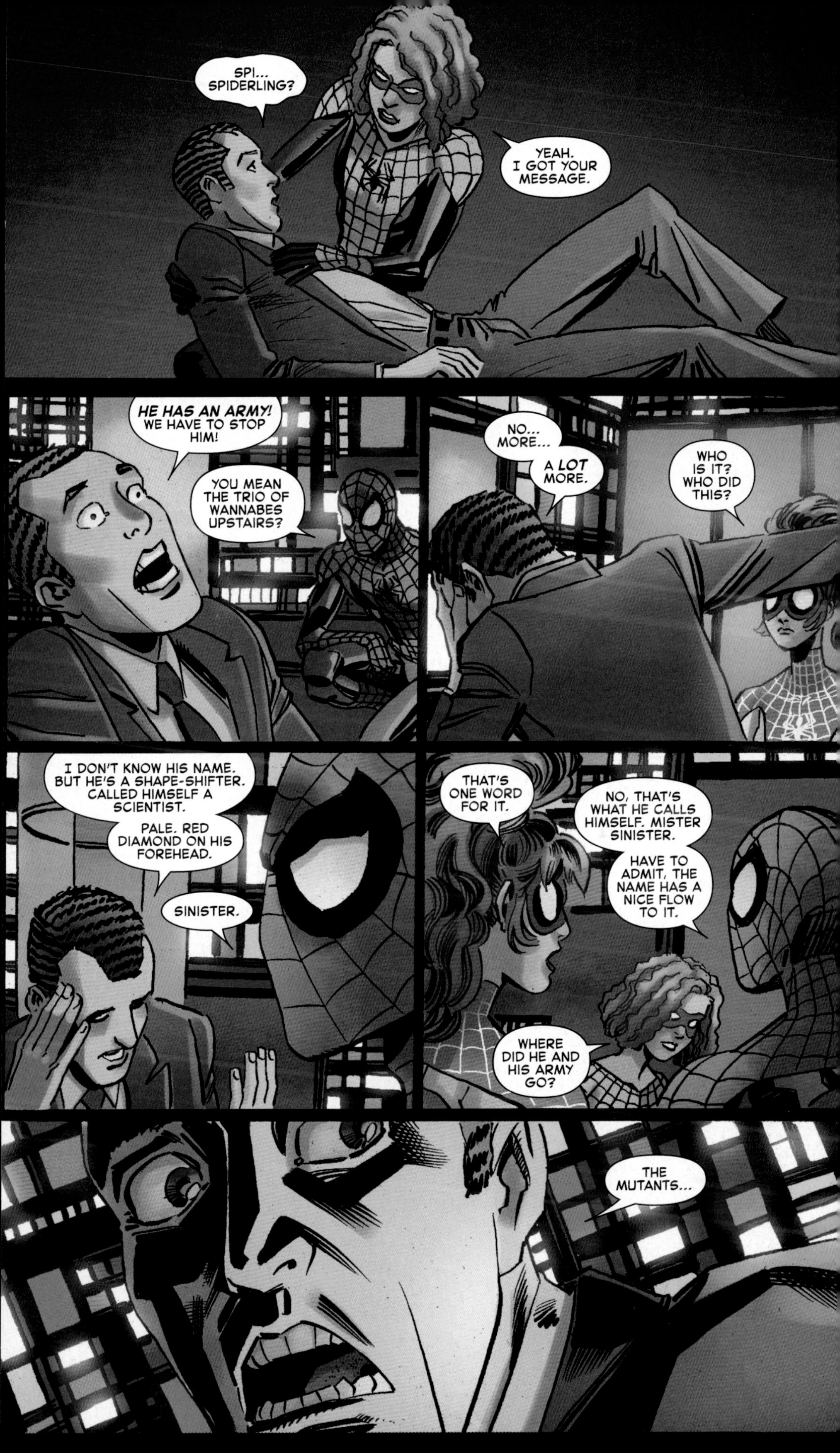
SPI... SPIDERLING?
YEAH. I GOT YOUR MESSAGE.
HE HAS AN ARMY! WE HAVE TO STOP HIM!
YOU MEAN THE TRIO OF WANNABES UPSTAIRS?
NO... MORE...
A **LOT** MORE.
WHO IS IT? WHO DID THIS?
I DON'T KNOW HIS NAME. BUT HE'S A SHAPE-SHIFTER. CALLED HIMSELF A SCIENTIST.
PALE. RED DIAMOND ON HIS FOREHEAD.
SINISTER.
THAT'S ONE WORD FOR IT.
NO, THAT'S WHAT HE CALLS HIMSELF. MISTER SINISTER.
HAVE TO ADMIT, THE NAME HAS A NICE FLOW TO IT.
WHERE DID HE AND HIS ARMY GO?
THE MUTANTS...

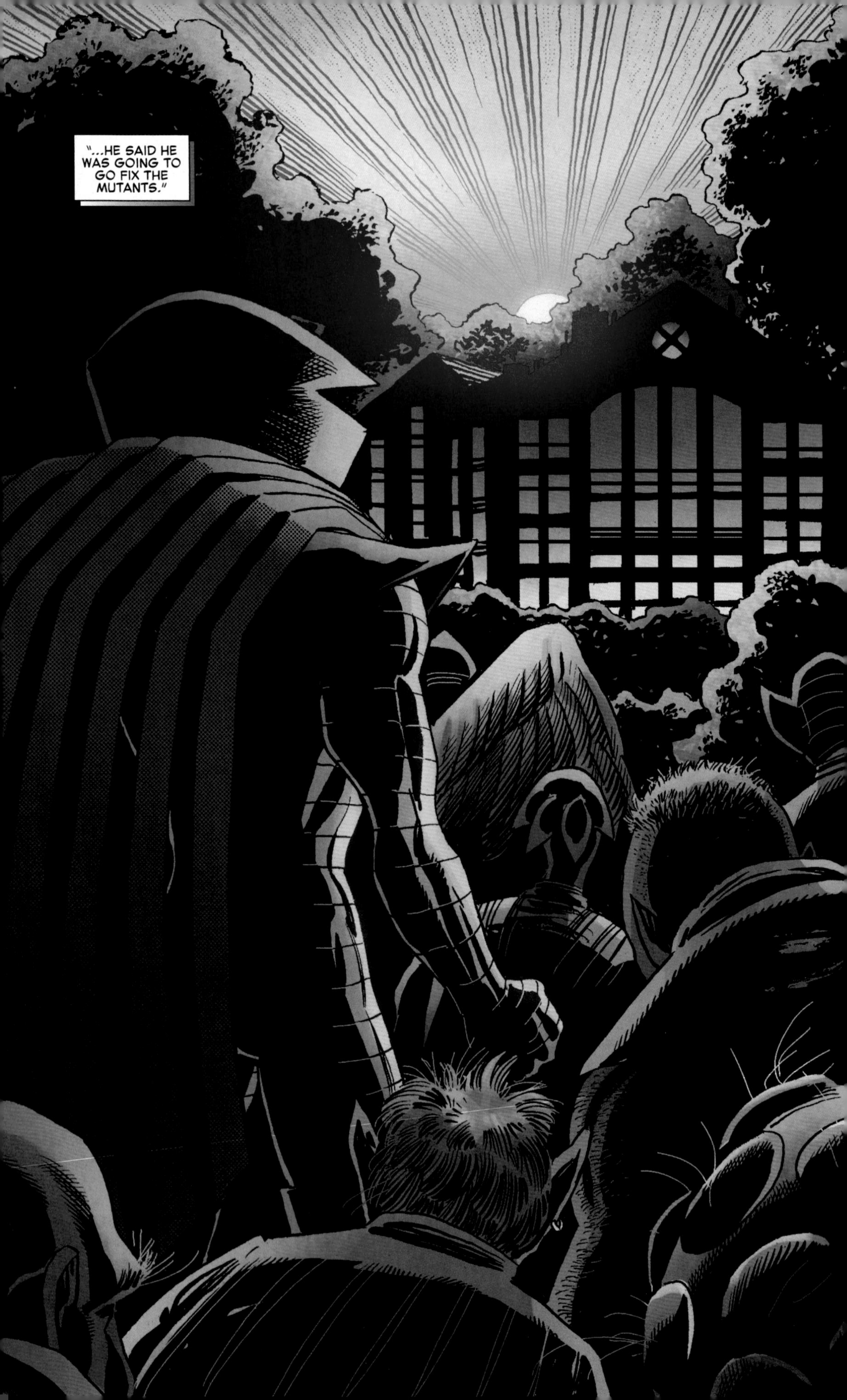
"...HE SAID HE WAS GOING TO GO FIX THE MUTANTS."

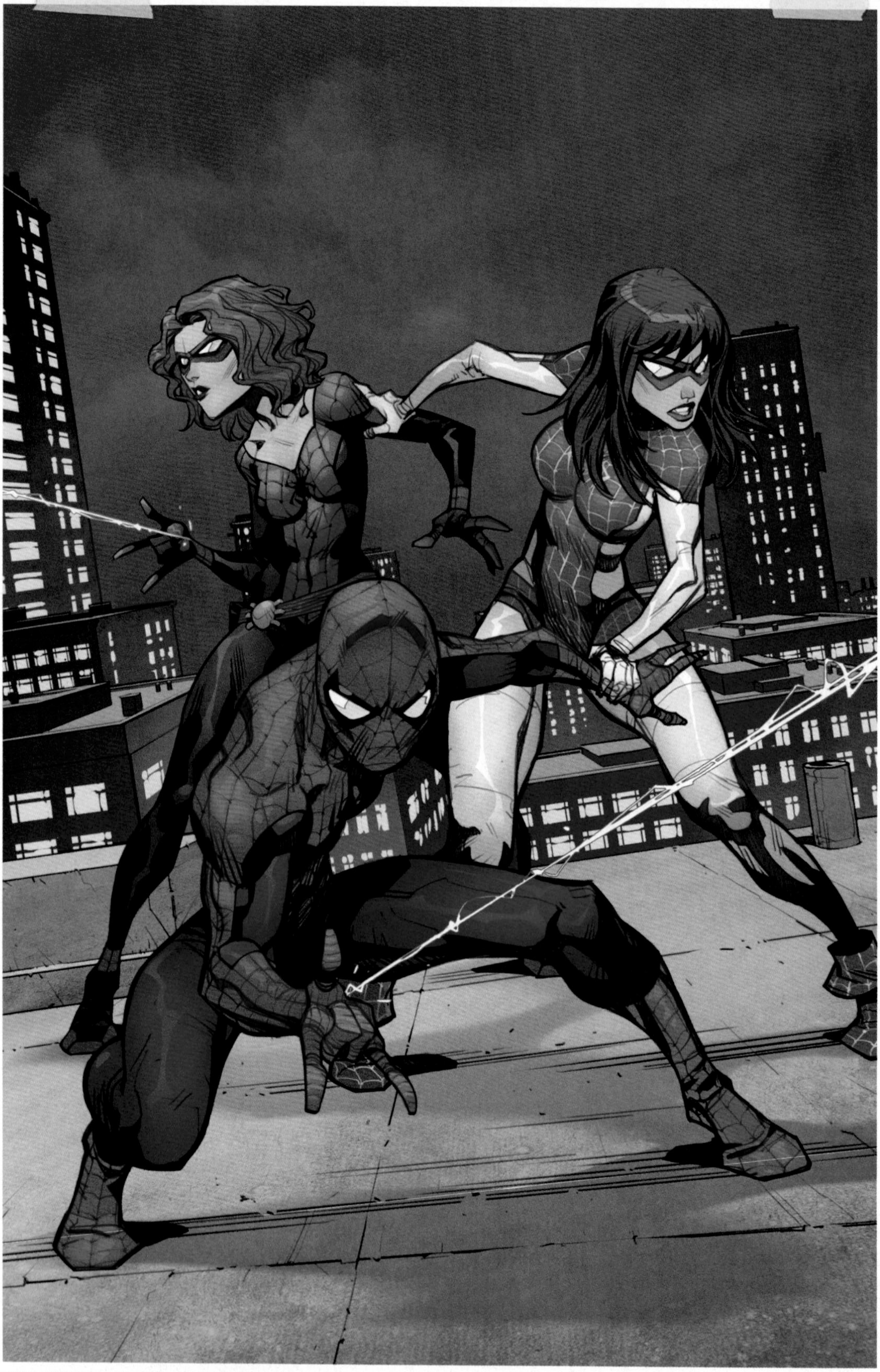

23: WEIRD SCIENCE — PART 4

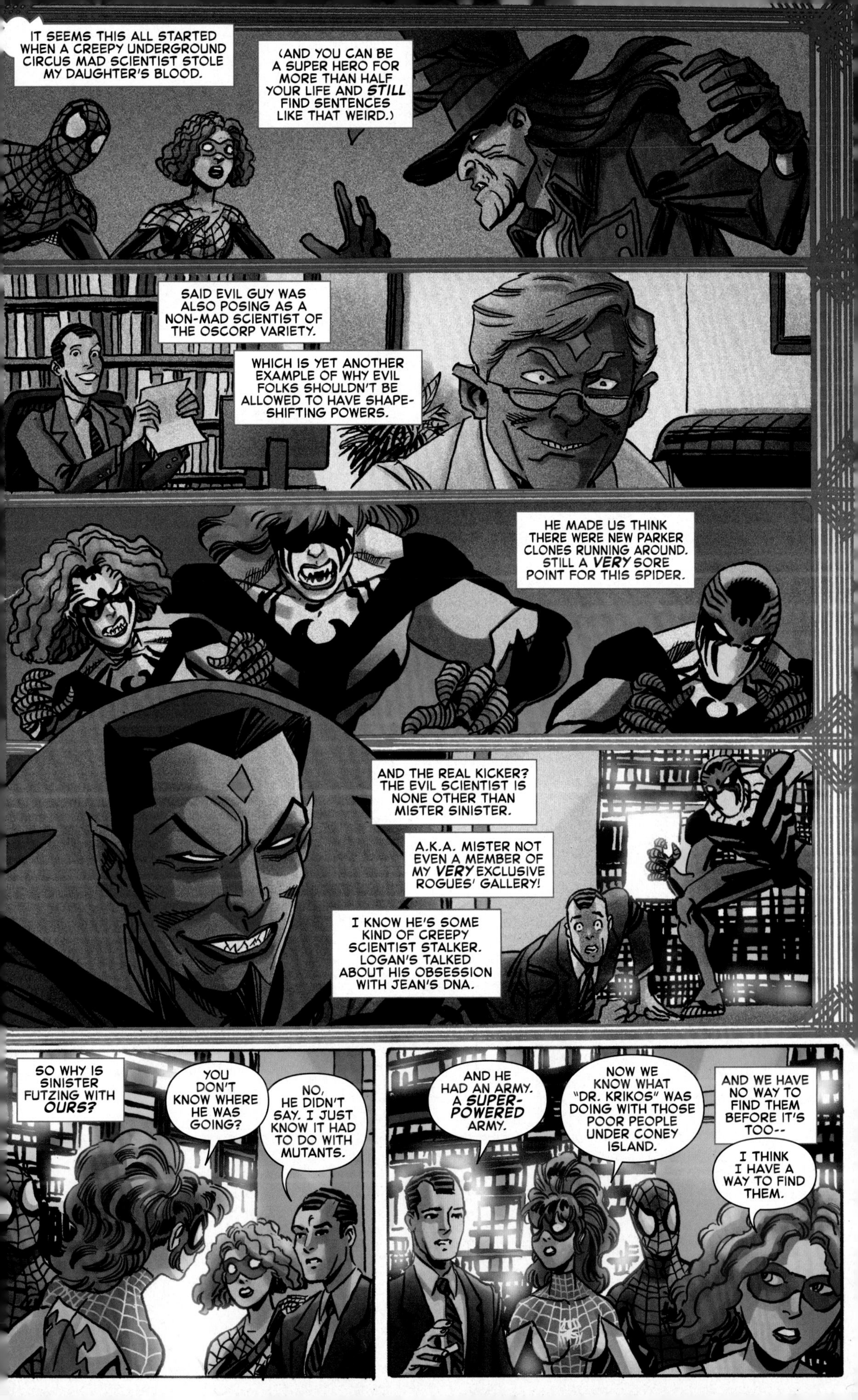

IT SEEMS THIS ALL STARTED WHEN A CREEPY UNDERGROUND CIRCUS MAD SCIENTIST STOLE MY DAUGHTER'S BLOOD.
(AND YOU CAN BE A SUPER HERO FOR MORE THAN HALF YOUR LIFE AND STILL FIND SENTENCES LIKE THAT WEIRD.)
SAID EVIL GUY WAS ALSO POSING AS A NON-MAD SCIENTIST OF THE OSCORP VARIETY.
WHICH IS YET ANOTHER EXAMPLE OF WHY EVIL FOLKS SHOULDN'T BE ALLOWED TO HAVE SHAPE-SHIFTING POWERS.
HE MADE US THINK THERE WERE NEW PARKER CLONES RUNNING AROUND. STILL A VERY SORE POINT FOR THIS SPIDER.
AND THE REAL KICKER? THE EVIL SCIENTIST IS NONE OTHER THAN MISTER SINISTER.
A.K.A. MISTER NOT EVEN A MEMBER OF MY VERY EXCLUSIVE ROGUES' GALLERY!
I KNOW HE'S SOME KIND OF CREEPY SCIENTIST STALKER. LOGAN'S TALKED ABOUT HIS OBSESSION WITH JEAN'S DNA.
SO WHY IS SINISTER FUTZING WITH OURS?
YOU DON'T KNOW WHERE HE WAS GOING?
NO, HE DIDN'T SAY. I JUST KNOW IT HAD TO DO WITH MUTANTS.
AND HE HAD AN ARMY. A SUPER-POWERED ARMY.
NOW WE KNOW WHAT "DR. KRIKOS" WAS DOING WITH THOSE POOR PEOPLE UNDER CONEY ISLAND.
AND WE HAVE NO WAY TO FIND THEM BEFORE IT'S TOO--
I THINK I HAVE A WAY TO FIND THEM.

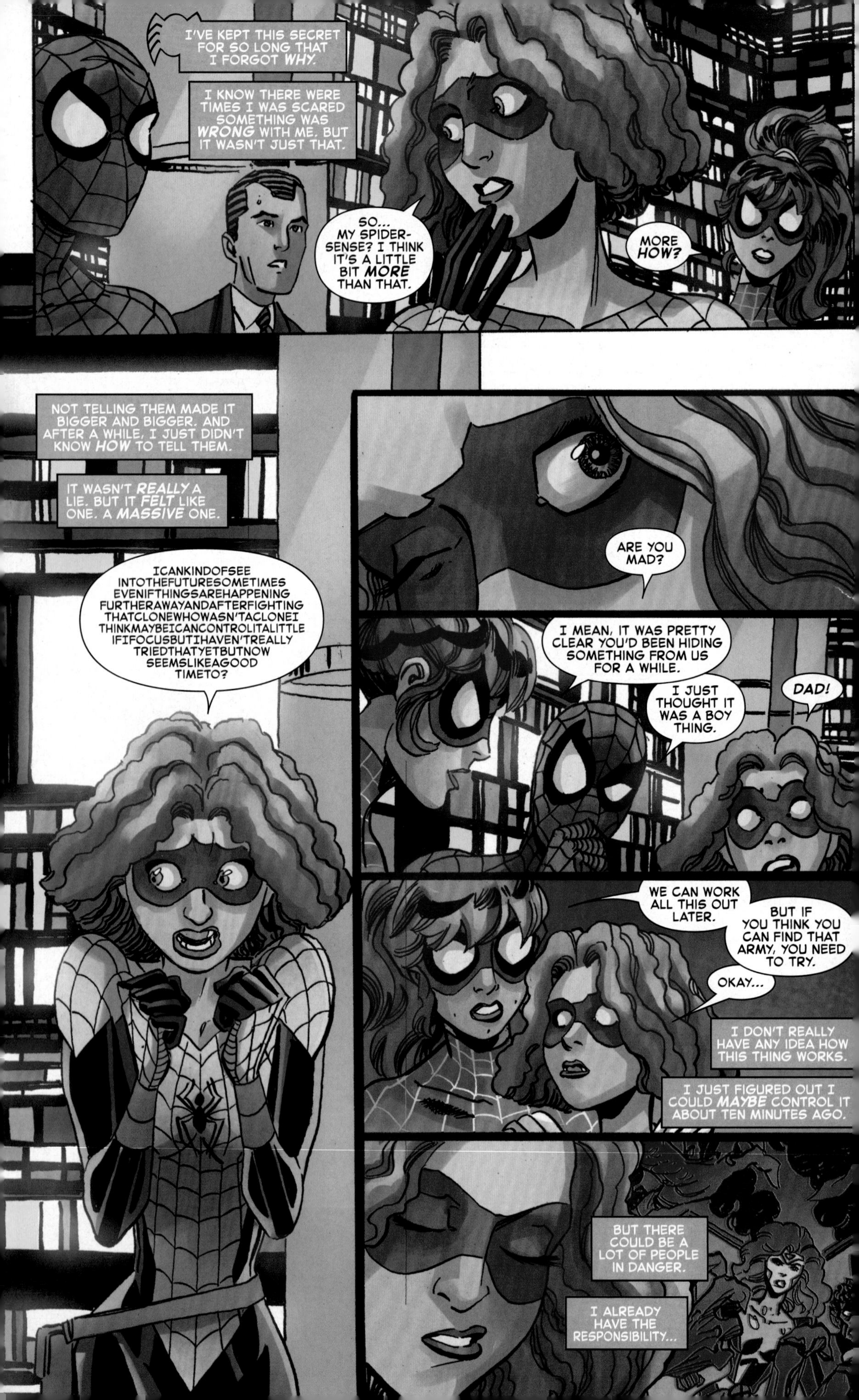

I'VE KEPT THIS SECRET FOR SO LONG THAT I FORGOT *WHY.*
I KNOW THERE WERE TIMES I WAS SCARED SOMETHING WAS *WRONG* WITH ME. BUT IT WASN'T JUST THAT.
SO... MY SPIDER-SENSE? I THINK IT'S A LITTLE BIT *MORE* THAN THAT.
MORE *HOW?*
NOT TELLING THEM MADE IT BIGGER AND BIGGER. AND AFTER A WHILE, I JUST DIDN'T KNOW *HOW* TO TELL THEM.
IT WASN'T *REALLY* A LIE. BUT IT *FELT* LIKE ONE. A *MASSIVE* ONE.
ICANKINDOFSEE INTOTHEFUTURESOMETIMES EVENIFTHINGSAREHAPPENING FURTHERAWAYANDAFTERFIGHTING THATCLONEWHOWASN'TACLONEI THINKMAYBEICANCONTROLITALITTLE IFIFOCUSBUTIHAVEN'TREALLY TRIEDTHATYETBUTNOW SEEMSLIKEAGOOD TIMETO?
ARE YOU MAD?
I MEAN, IT WAS PRETTY CLEAR YOU'D BEEN HIDING SOMETHING FROM US FOR A WHILE.
I JUST THOUGHT IT WAS A BOY THING.
DAD!
WE CAN WORK ALL THIS OUT LATER.
BUT IF YOU THINK YOU CAN FIND THAT ARMY, YOU NEED TO TRY.
OKAY...
I DON'T REALLY HAVE ANY IDEA HOW THIS THING WORKS.
I JUST FIGURED OUT I COULD *MAYBE* CONTROL IT ABOUT TEN MINUTES AGO.
BUT THERE COULD BE A LOT OF PEOPLE IN DANGER.
I ALREADY HAVE THE RESPONSIBILITY...

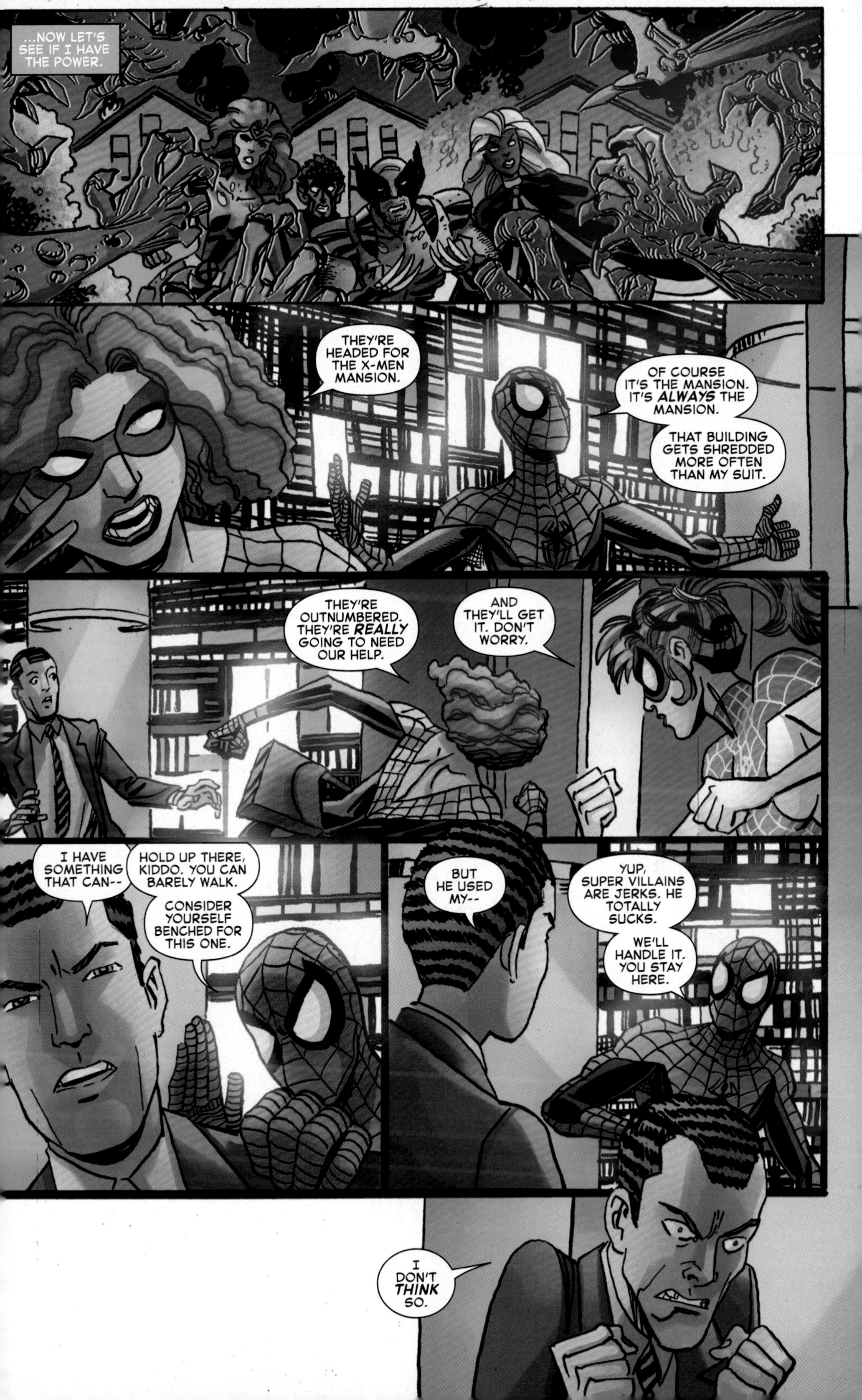
...NOW LET'S SEE IF I HAVE THE POWER.
THEY'RE HEADED FOR THE X-MEN MANSION.
OF COURSE IT'S THE MANSION. IT'S ALWAYS THE MANSION.
THAT BUILDING GETS SHREDDED MORE OFTEN THAN MY SUIT.
THEY'RE OUTNUMBERED. THEY'RE REALLY GOING TO NEED OUR HELP.
AND THEY'LL GET IT. DON'T WORRY.
I HAVE SOMETHING THAT CAN--
HOLD UP THERE, KIDDO. YOU CAN BARELY WALK.
CONSIDER YOURSELF BENCHED FOR THIS ONE.
BUT HE USED MY--
YUP, SUPER VILLAINS ARE JERKS. HE TOTALLY SUCKS.
WE'LL HANDLE IT. YOU STAY HERE.
I DON'T THINK SO.

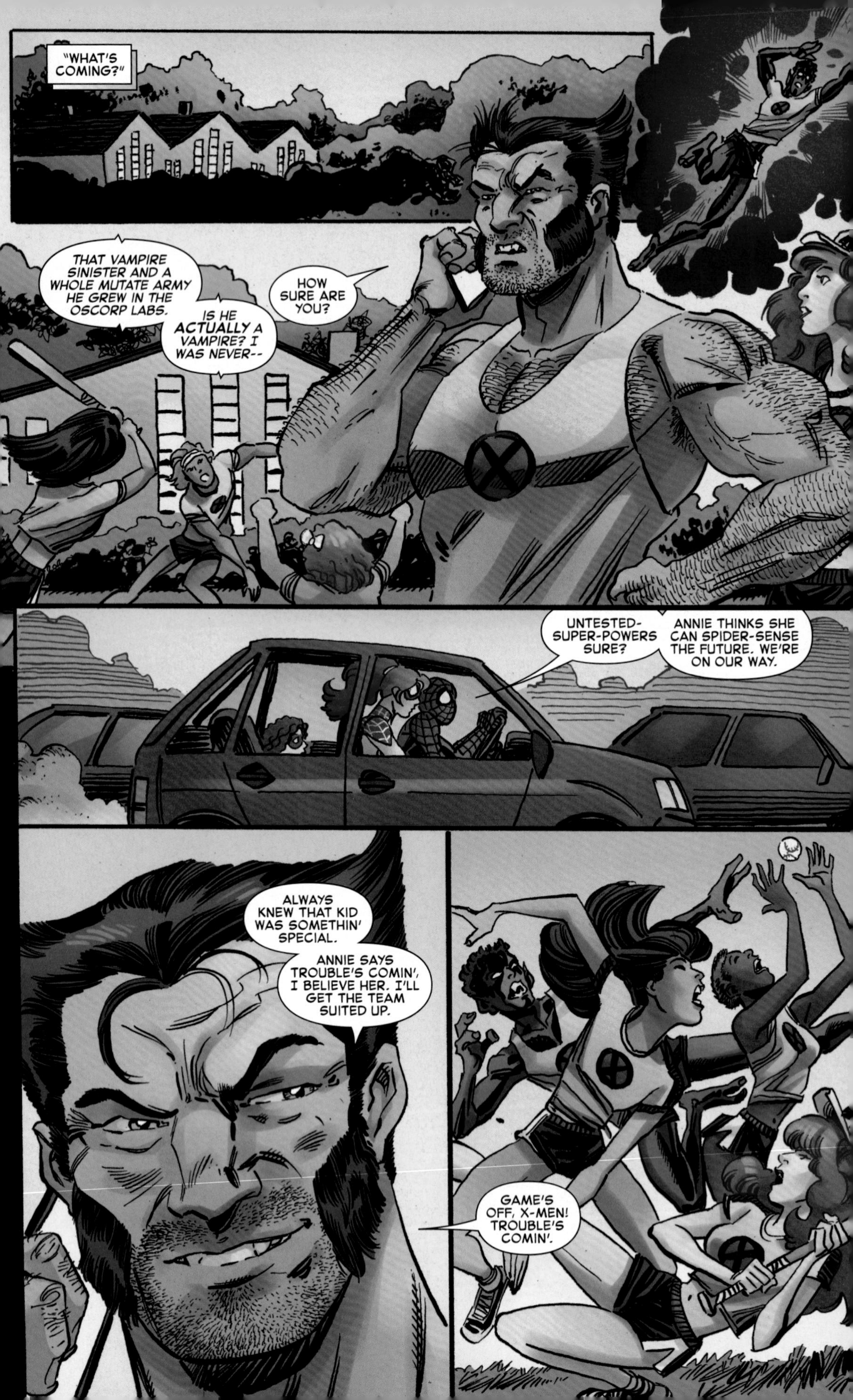
"WHAT'S COMING?"
THAT VAMPIRE SINISTER AND A WHOLE MUTATE ARMY HE GREW IN THE OSCORP LABS.
IS HE ACTUALLY A VAMPIRE? I WAS NEVER--
HOW SURE ARE YOU?
UNTESTED-SUPER-POWERS SURE?
ANNIE THINKS SHE CAN SPIDER-SENSE THE FUTURE. WE'RE ON OUR WAY.
ALWAYS KNEW THAT KID WAS SOMETHIN' SPECIAL.
ANNIE SAYS TROUBLE'S COMIN', I BELIEVE HER. I'LL GET THE TEAM SUITED UP.
GAME'S OFF, X-MEN! TROUBLE'S COMIN'.

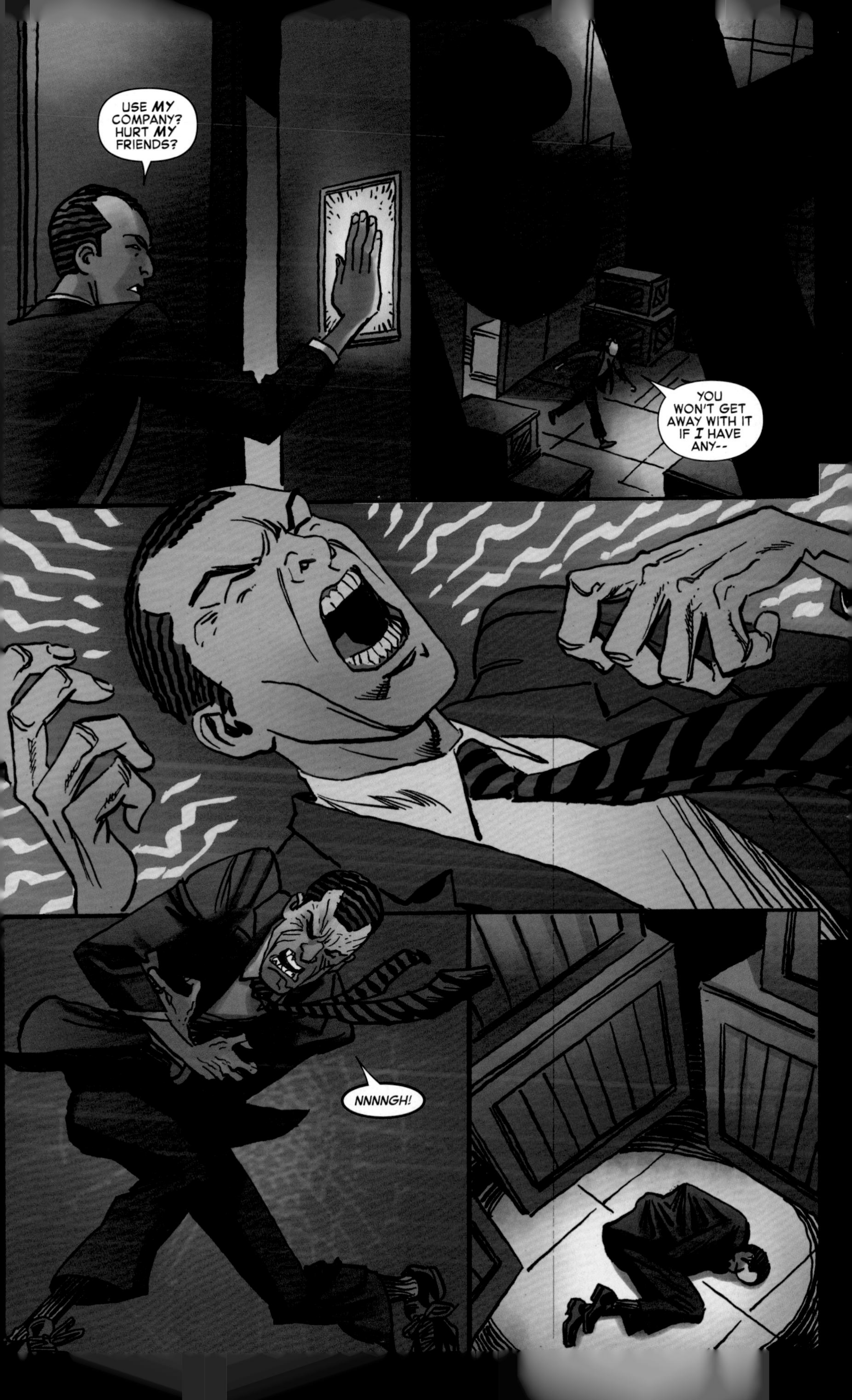
USE MY COMPANY? HURT MY FRIENDS?
YOU WON'T GET AWAY WITH IT IF I HAVE ANY--
NNNNGH!

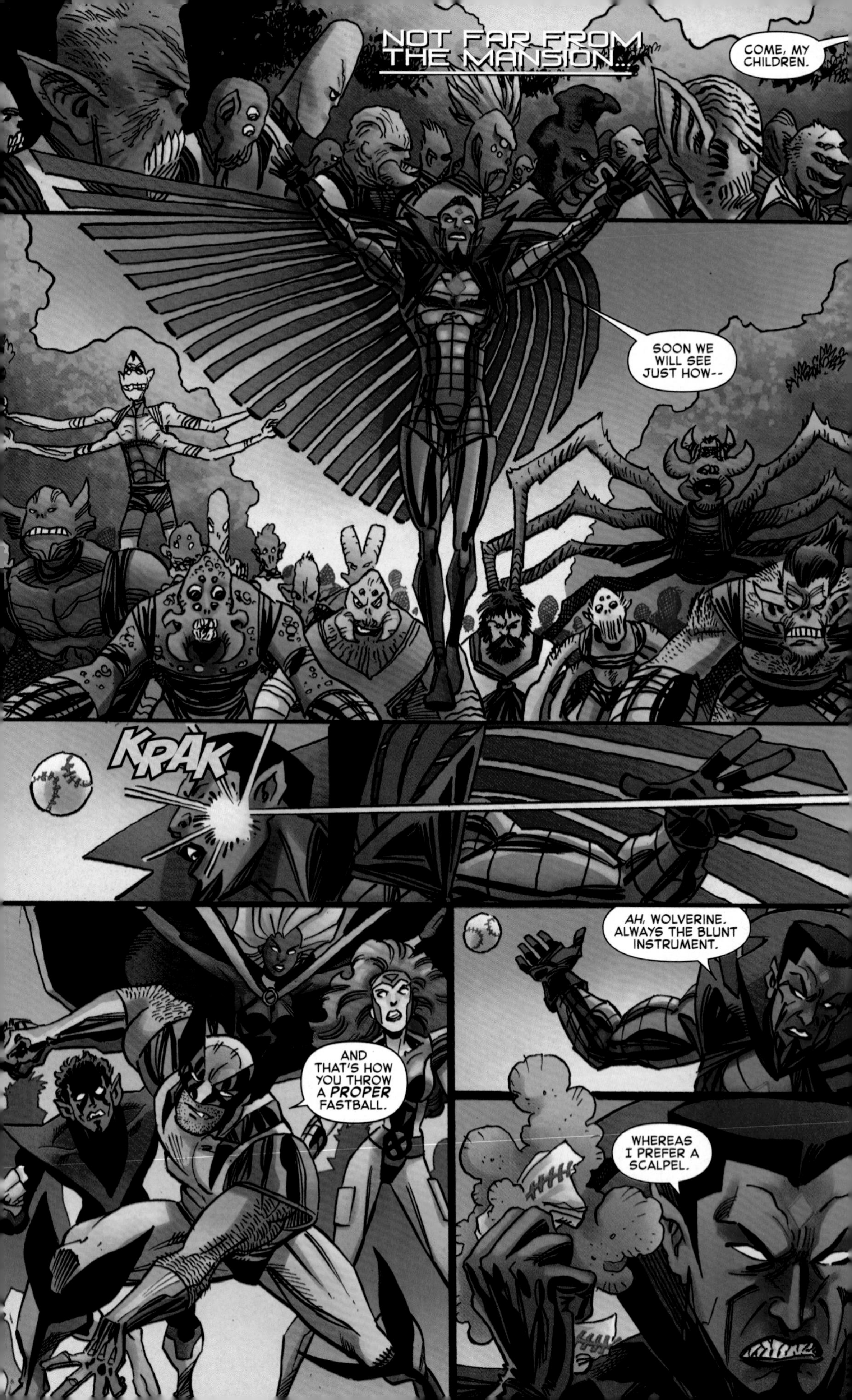
NOT FAR FROM THE MANSION...
COME, MY CHILDREN.
SOON WE WILL SEE JUST HOW--
KRAK
AND THAT'S HOW YOU THROW A PROPER FASTBALL.
AH, WOLVERINE. ALWAYS THE BLUNT INSTRUMENT.
WHEREAS I PREFER A SCALPEL.

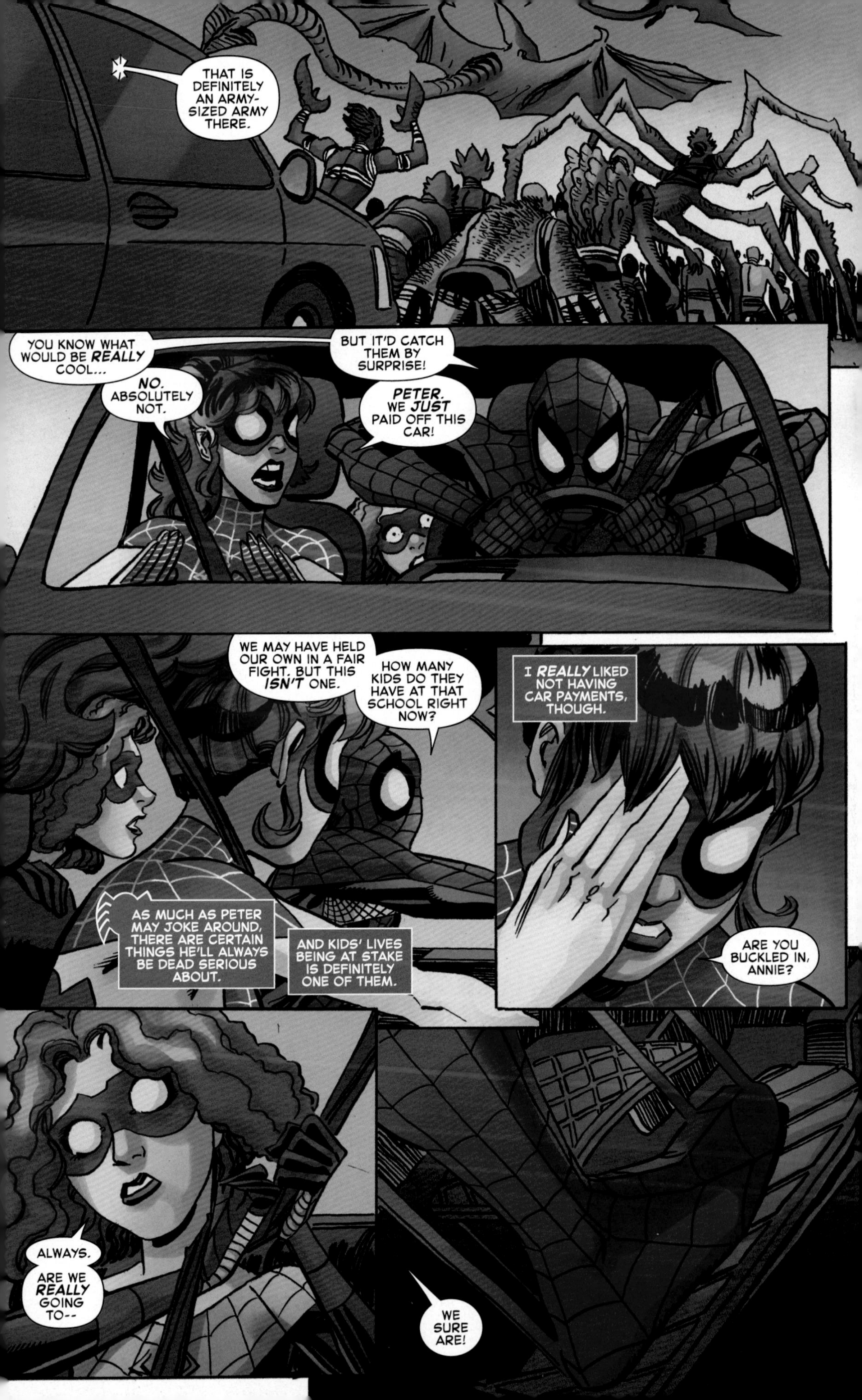
THAT IS DEFINITELY AN ARMY-SIZED ARMY THERE.
YOU KNOW WHAT WOULD BE REALLY COOL...
NO. ABSOLUTELY NOT.
BUT IT'D CATCH THEM BY SURPRISE!
PETER. WE JUST PAID OFF THIS CAR!
WE MAY HAVE HELD OUR OWN IN A FAIR FIGHT. BUT THIS ISN'T ONE.
HOW MANY KIDS DO THEY HAVE AT THAT SCHOOL RIGHT NOW?
AS MUCH AS PETER MAY JOKE AROUND, THERE ARE CERTAIN THINGS HE'LL ALWAYS BE DEAD SERIOUS ABOUT.
AND KIDS' LIVES BEING AT STAKE IS DEFINITELY ONE OF THEM.
I REALLY LIKED NOT HAVING CAR PAYMENTS, THOUGH.
ARE YOU BUCKLED IN, ANNIE?
ALWAYS.
ARE WE REALLY GOING TO--
WE SURE ARE!

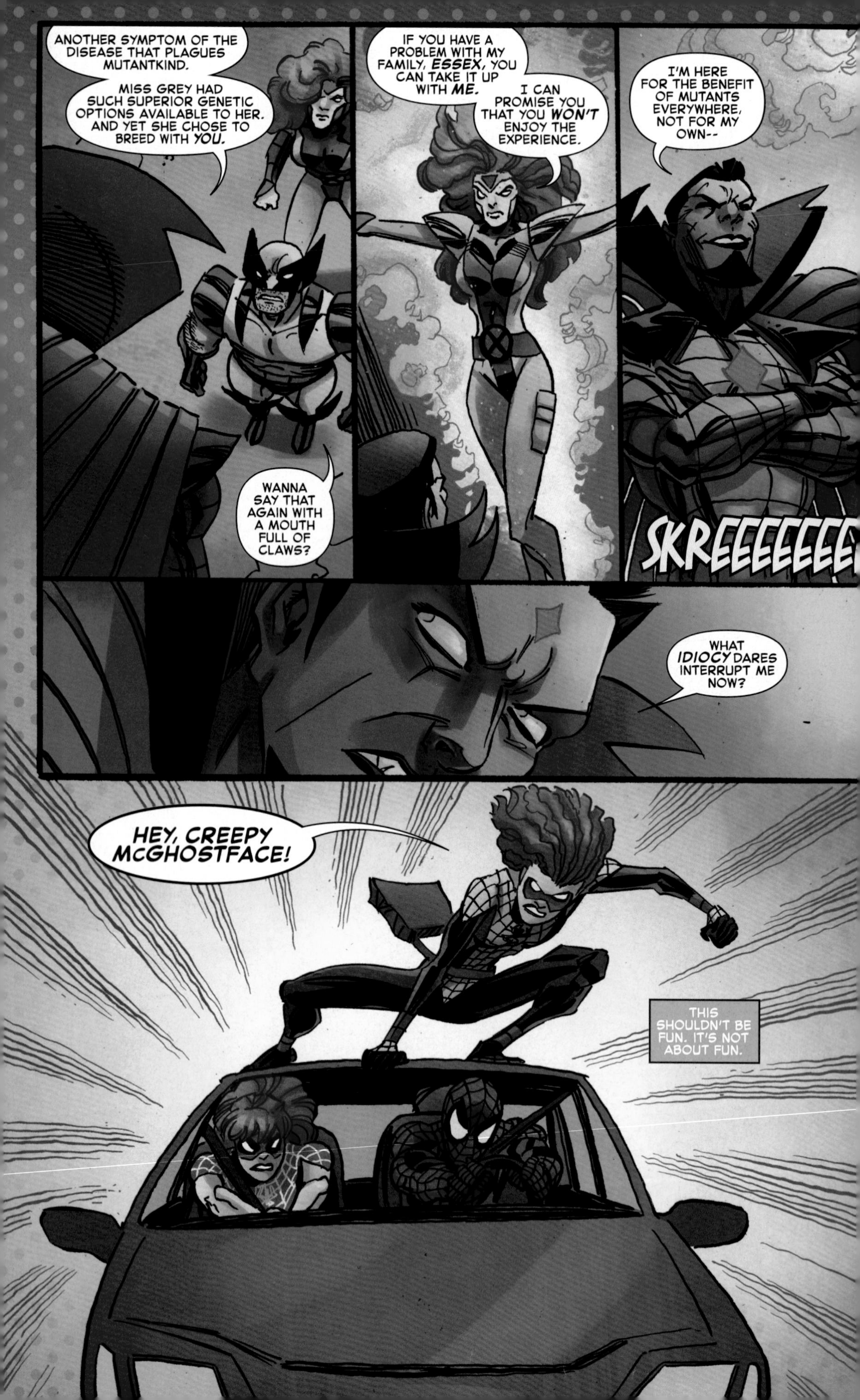
ANOTHER SYMPTOM OF THE DISEASE THAT PLAGUES MUTANTKIND.
MISS GREY HAD SUCH SUPERIOR GENETIC OPTIONS AVAILABLE TO HER. AND YET SHE CHOSE TO BREED WITH *YOU.*
WANNA SAY THAT AGAIN WITH A MOUTH FULL OF CLAWS?
IF YOU HAVE A PROBLEM WITH MY FAMILY, *ESSEX,* YOU CAN TAKE IT UP WITH *ME.*
I CAN PROMISE YOU THAT YOU *WON'T* ENJOY THE EXPERIENCE.
I'M HERE FOR THE BENEFIT OF MUTANTS EVERYWHERE, NOT FOR MY OWN--
SKREEEEEEEE
WHAT *IDIOCY* DARES INTERRUPT ME NOW?
HEY, CREEPY McGHOSTFACE!
THIS SHOULDN'T BE FUN. IT'S NOT ABOUT FUN.

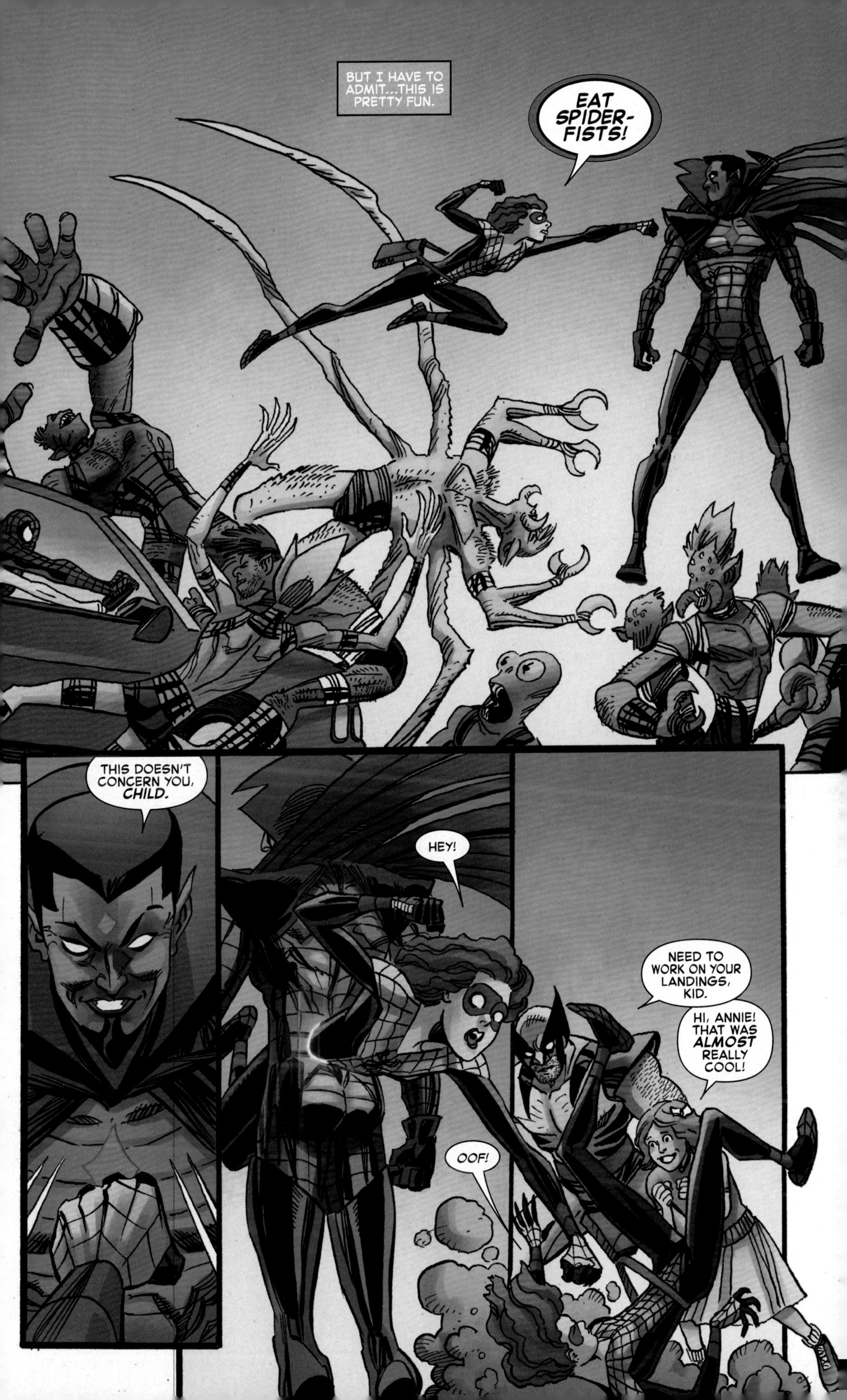
BUT I HAVE TO ADMIT...THIS IS PRETTY FUN.
EAT SPIDER-FISTS!
THIS DOESN'T CONCERN YOU, CHILD.
HEY!
NEED TO WORK ON YOUR LANDINGS, KID.
HI, ANNIE! THAT WAS ALMOST REALLY COOL!
OOF!

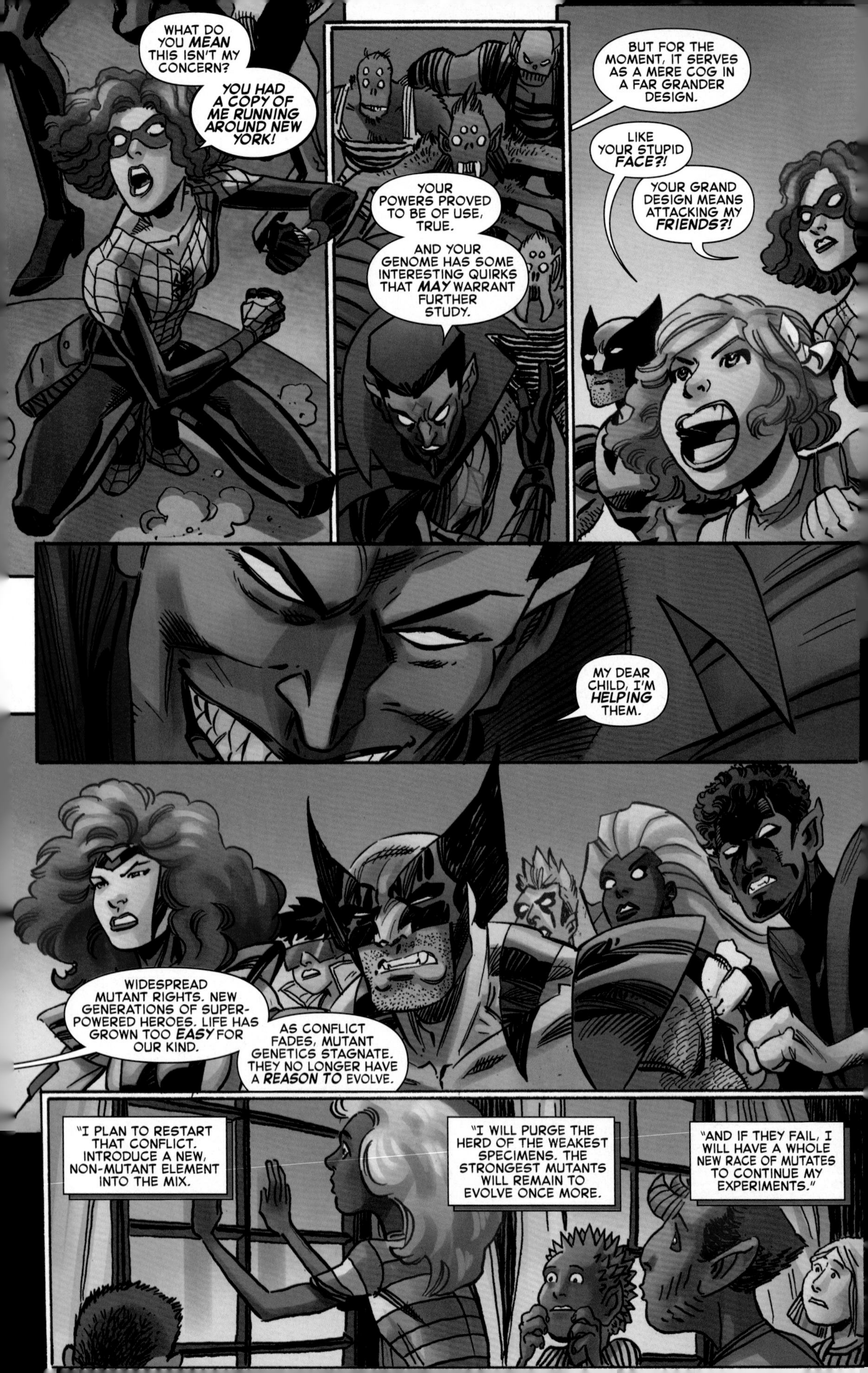
WHAT DO YOU MEAN THIS ISN'T MY CONCERN?
YOU HAD A COPY OF ME RUNNING AROUND NEW YORK!
YOUR POWERS PROVED TO BE OF USE, TRUE.
AND YOUR GENOME HAS SOME INTERESTING QUIRKS THAT MAY WARRANT FURTHER STUDY.
BUT FOR THE MOMENT, IT SERVES AS A MERE COG IN A FAR GRANDER DESIGN.
LIKE YOUR STUPID FACE?!
YOUR GRAND DESIGN MEANS ATTACKING MY FRIENDS?!
MY DEAR CHILD, I'M HELPING THEM.
WIDESPREAD MUTANT RIGHTS. NEW GENERATIONS OF SUPER-POWERED HEROES. LIFE HAS GROWN TOO EASY FOR OUR KIND.
AS CONFLICT FADES, MUTANT GENETICS STAGNATE. THEY NO LONGER HAVE A REASON TO EVOLVE.
"I PLAN TO RESTART THAT CONFLICT. INTRODUCE A NEW, NON-MUTANT ELEMENT INTO THE MIX.
"I WILL PURGE THE HERD OF THE WEAKEST SPECIMENS. THE STRONGEST MUTANTS WILL REMAIN TO EVOLVE ONCE MORE.
"AND IF THEY FAIL, I WILL HAVE A WHOLE NEW RACE OF MUTATES TO CONTINUE MY EXPERIMENTS."

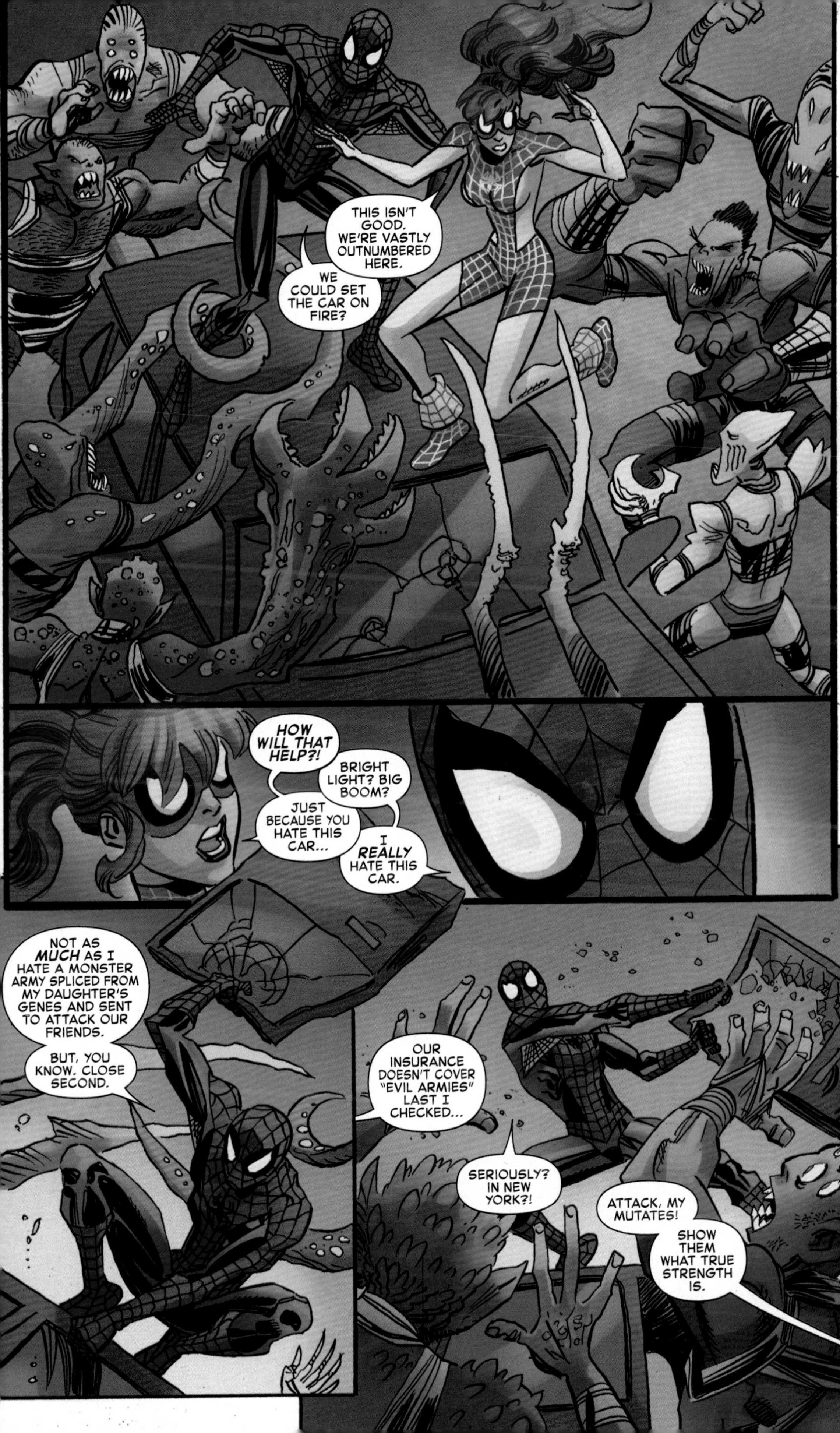
THIS ISN'T GOOD. WE'RE VASTLY OUTNUMBERED HERE.
WE COULD SET THE CAR ON FIRE?
HOW WILL THAT HELP?!
BRIGHT LIGHT? BIG BOOM?
JUST BECAUSE YOU HATE THIS CAR...
I REALLY HATE THIS CAR.
NOT AS MUCH AS I HATE A MONSTER ARMY SPLICED FROM MY DAUGHTER'S GENES AND SENT TO ATTACK OUR FRIENDS.
BUT, YOU KNOW. CLOSE SECOND.
OUR INSURANCE DOESN'T COVER "EVIL ARMIES" LAST I CHECKED...
SERIOUSLY? IN NEW YORK?!
ATTACK, MY MUTATES!
SHOW THEM WHAT TRUE STRENGTH IS.

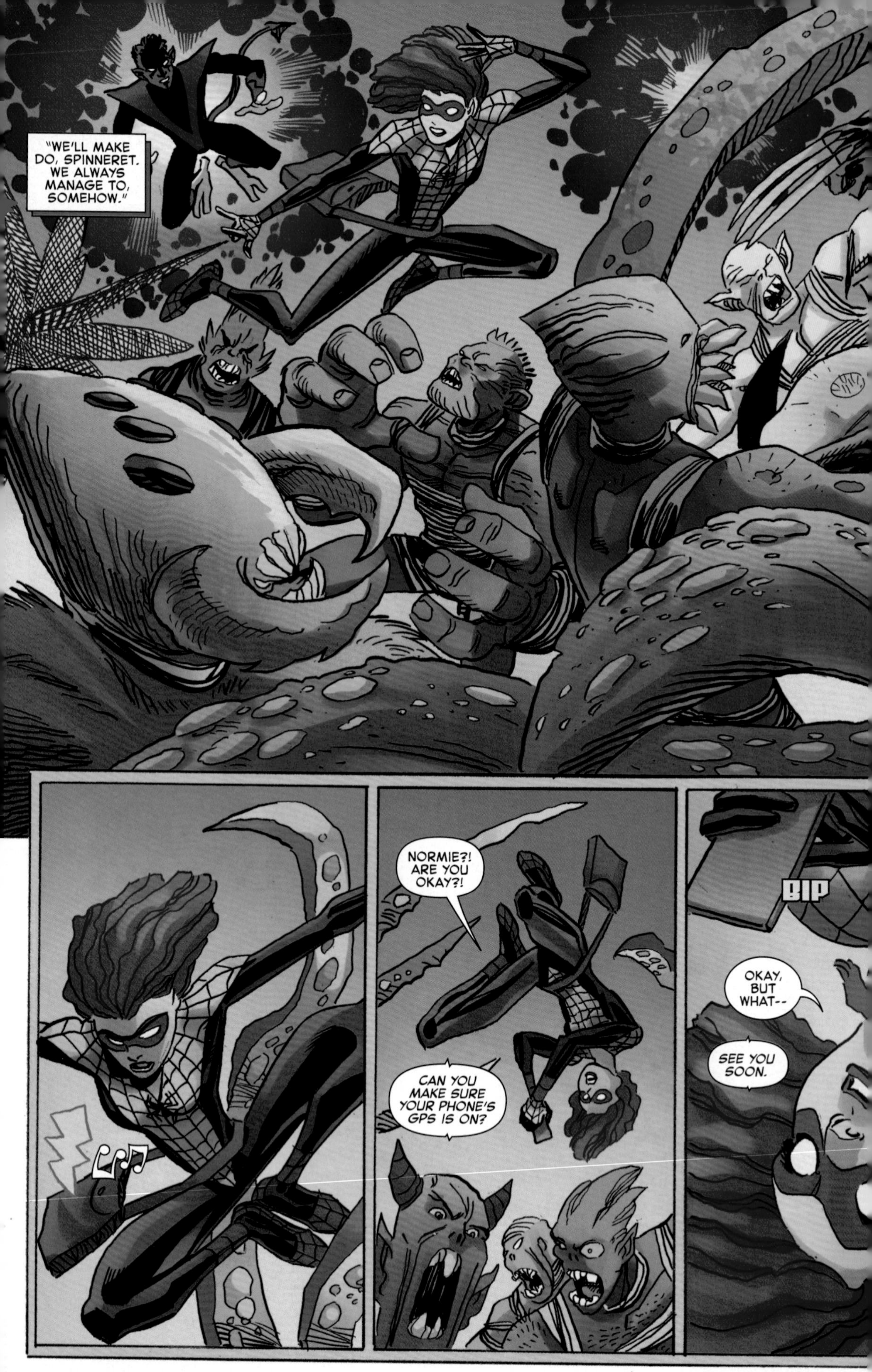
"WE'LL MAKE DO, SPINNERET. WE ALWAYS MANAGE TO, SOMEHOW."
NORMIE?! ARE YOU OKAY?!
CAN YOU MAKE SURE YOUR PHONE'S GPS IS ON?
BIP
OKAY, BUT WHAT--
SEE YOU SOON.

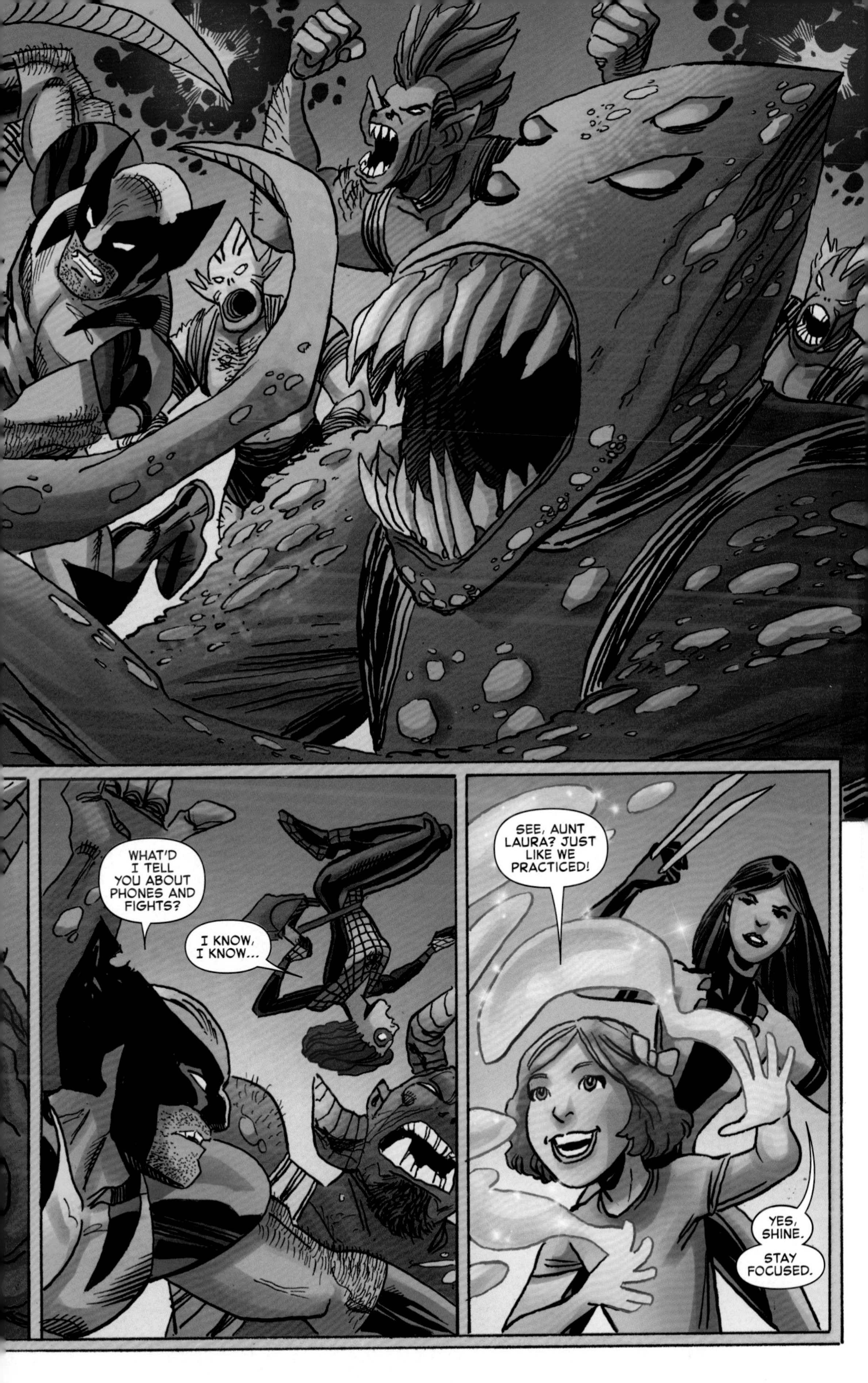
WHAT'D I TELL YOU ABOUT PHONES AND FIGHTS?
I KNOW, I KNOW...
SEE, AUNT LAURA? JUST LIKE WE PRACTICED!
YES, SHINE.
STAY FOCUSED.

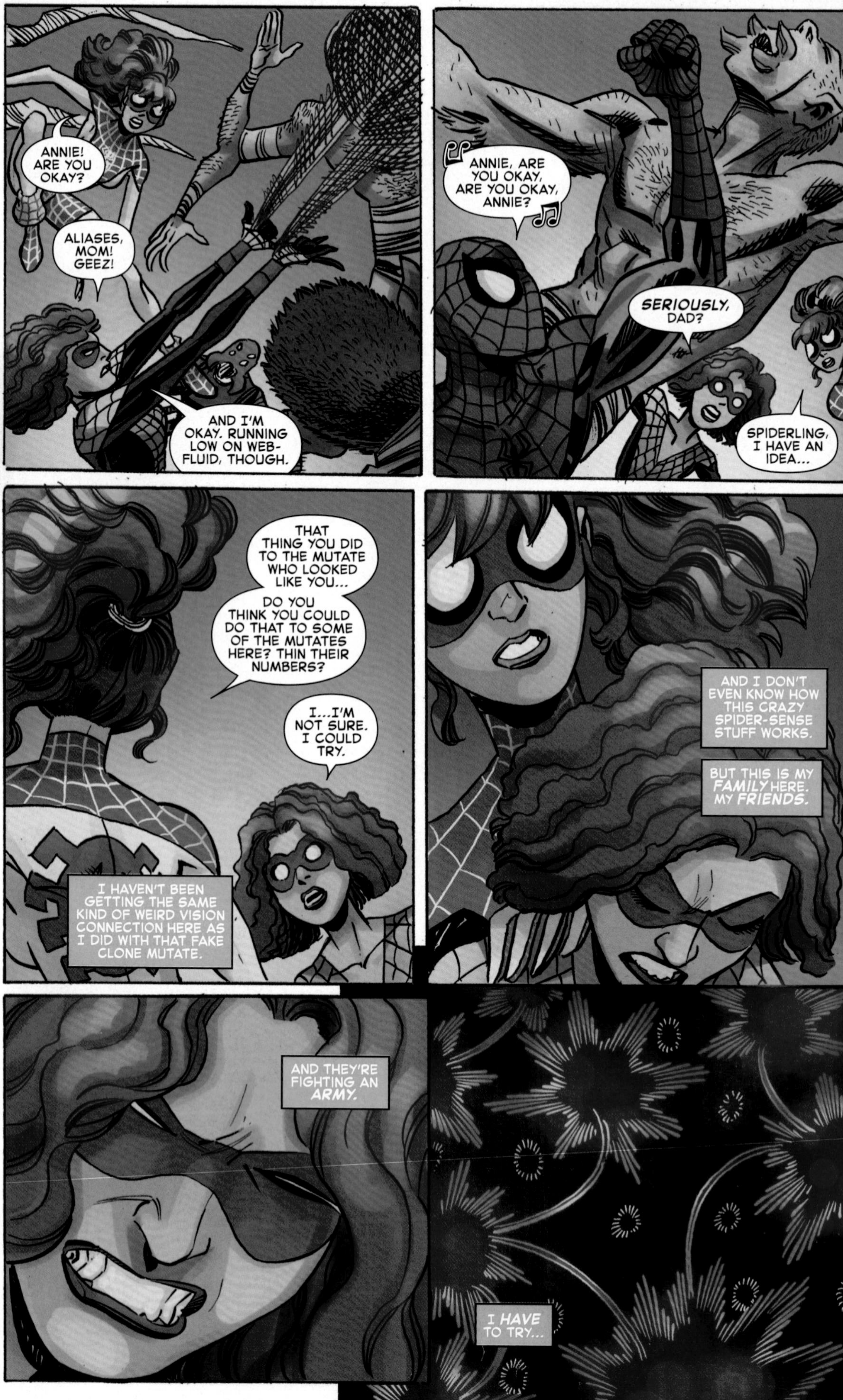

ANNIE! ARE YOU OKAY?
ALIASES, MOM! GEEZ!
AND I'M OKAY. RUNNING LOW ON WEB-FLUID, THOUGH.
ANNIE, ARE YOU OKAY, ARE YOU OKAY, ANNIE?
SERIOUSLY, DAD?
SPIDERLING, I HAVE AN IDEA...
THAT THING YOU DID TO THE MUTATE WHO LOOKED LIKE YOU...
DO YOU THINK YOU COULD DO THAT TO SOME OF THE MUTATES HERE? THIN THEIR NUMBERS?
I...I'M NOT SURE. I COULD TRY.
I HAVEN'T BEEN GETTING THE SAME KIND OF WEIRD VISION CONNECTION HERE AS I DID WITH THAT FAKE CLONE MUTATE.
AND I DON'T EVEN KNOW HOW THIS CRAZY SPIDER-SENSE STUFF WORKS.
BUT THIS IS MY FAMILY HERE. MY FRIENDS.
AND THEY'RE FIGHTING AN ARMY.
I HAVE TO TRY...

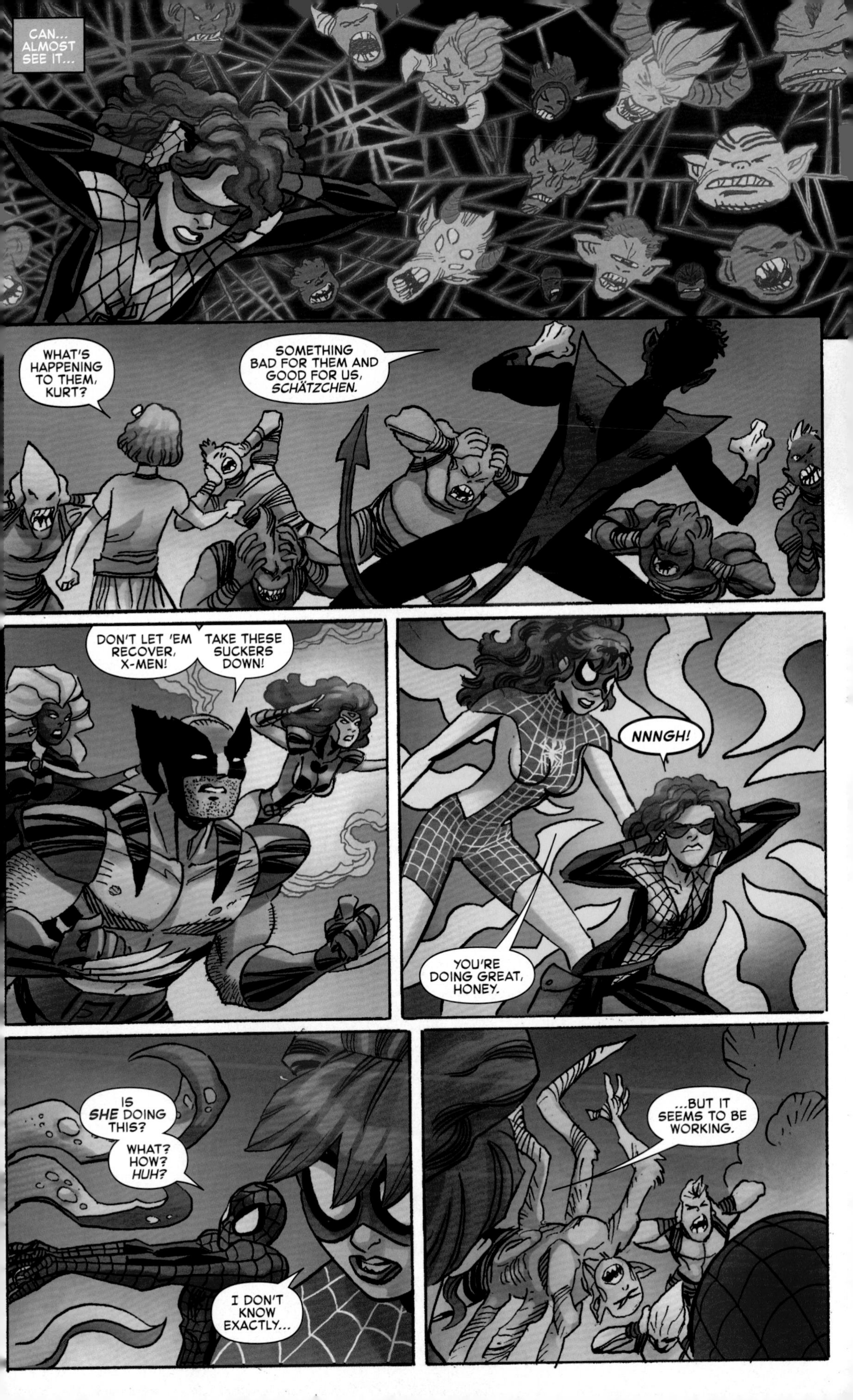
CAN... ALMOST SEE IT...
WHAT'S HAPPENING TO THEM, KURT?
SOMETHING BAD FOR THEM AND GOOD FOR US, *SCHÄTZCHEN.*
DON'T LET 'EM RECOVER, X-MEN!
TAKE THESE SUCKERS DOWN!
NNNGH!
YOU'RE DOING GREAT, HONEY.
IS *SHE* DOING THIS?
WHAT? HOW? *HUH?*
I DON'T KNOW EXACTLY...
...BUT IT SEEMS TO BE WORKING.

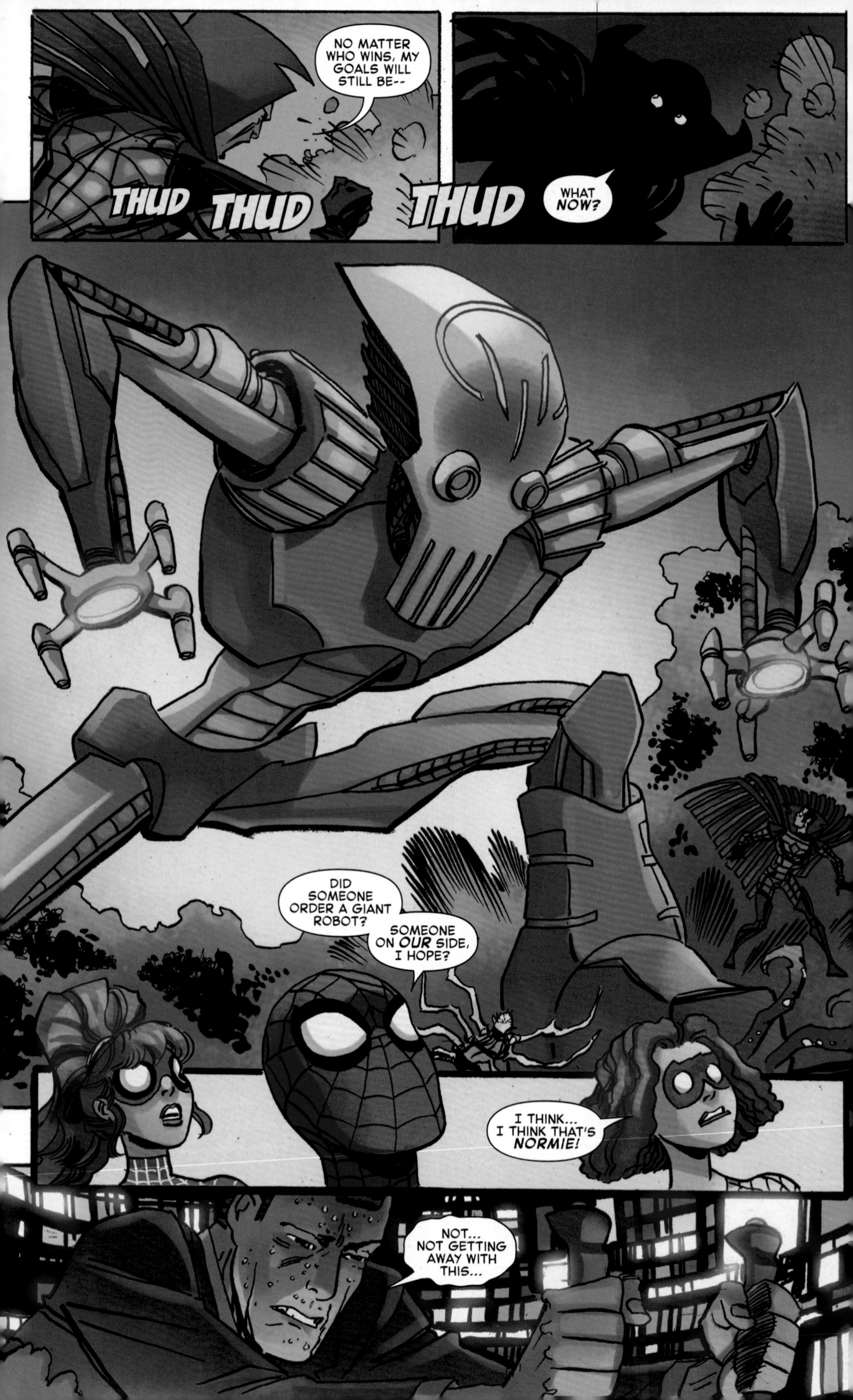
NO MATTER WHO WINS, MY GOALS WILL STILL BE--
THUD THUD THUD
WHAT NOW?
DID SOMEONE ORDER A GIANT ROBOT?
SOMEONE ON OUR SIDE, I HOPE?
I THINK... I THINK THAT'S NORMIE!
NOT... NOT GETTING AWAY WITH THIS...

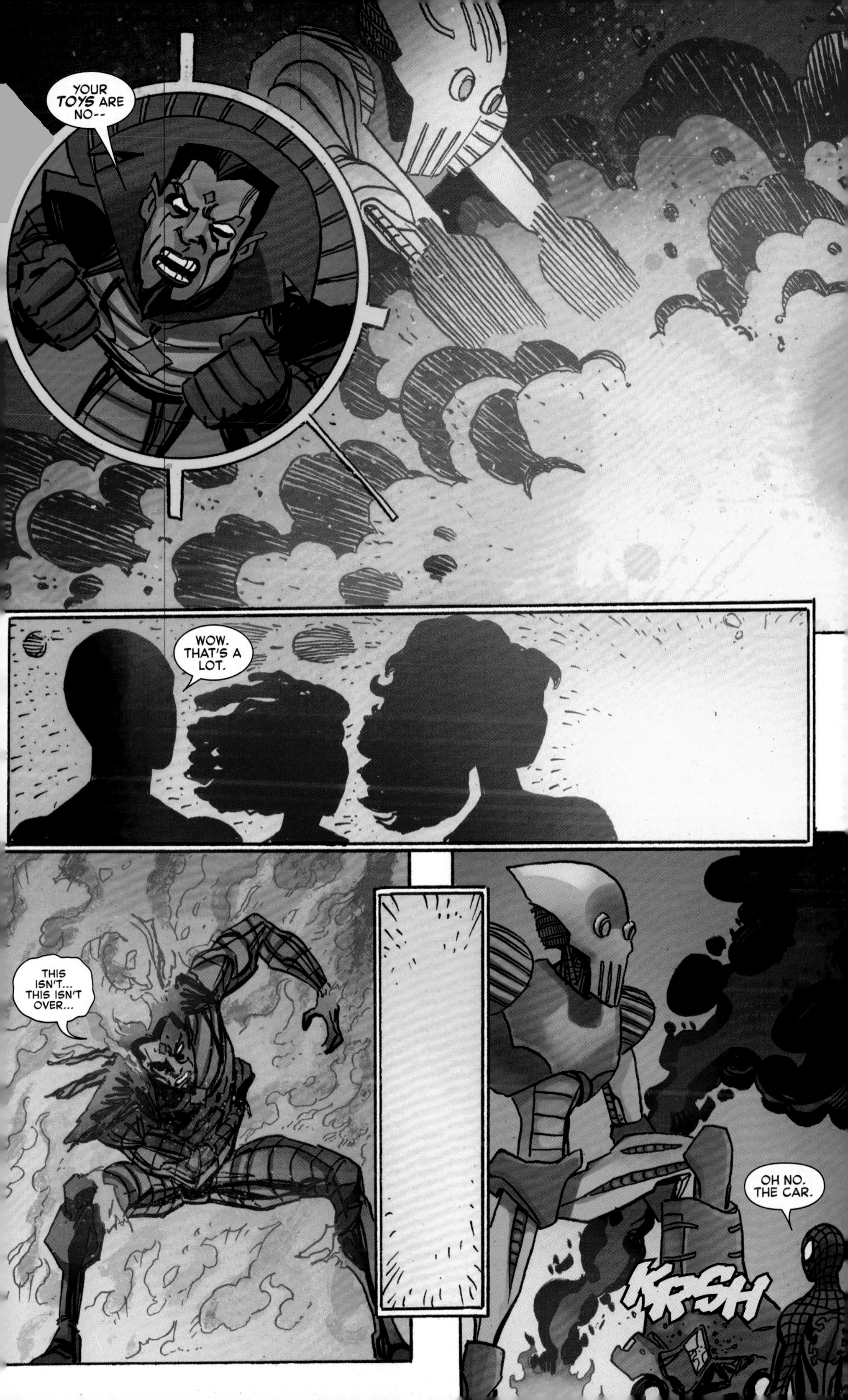
YOUR TOYS ARE NO--
WOW. THAT'S A LOT.
THIS ISN'T... THIS ISN'T OVER...
OH NO. THE CAR.
KRSH

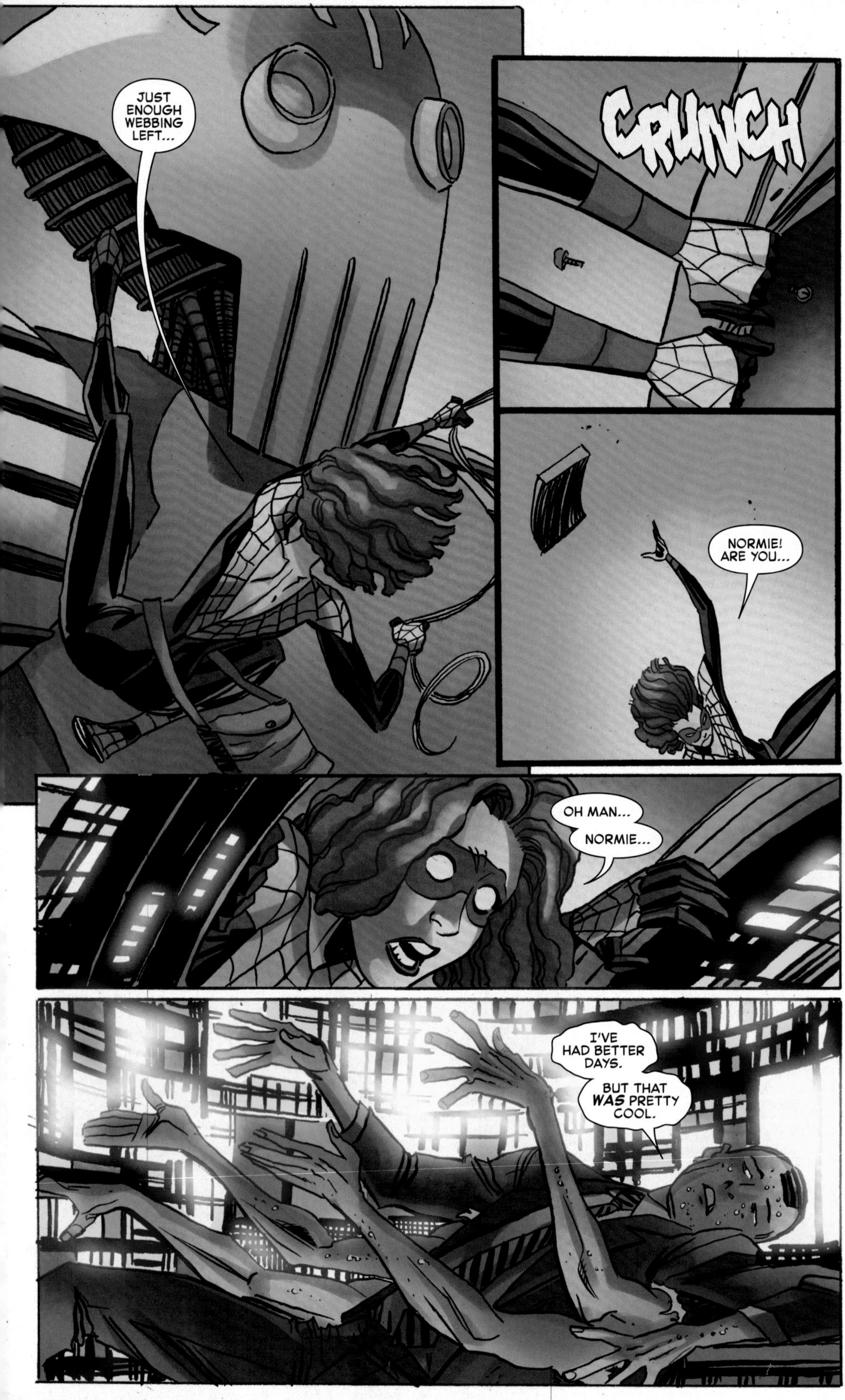

JUST ENOUGH WEBBING LEFT...
CRUNCH
NORMIE! ARE YOU...
OH MAN...
NORMIE...
I'VE HAD BETTER DAYS.
BUT THAT **WAS** PRETTY COOL.

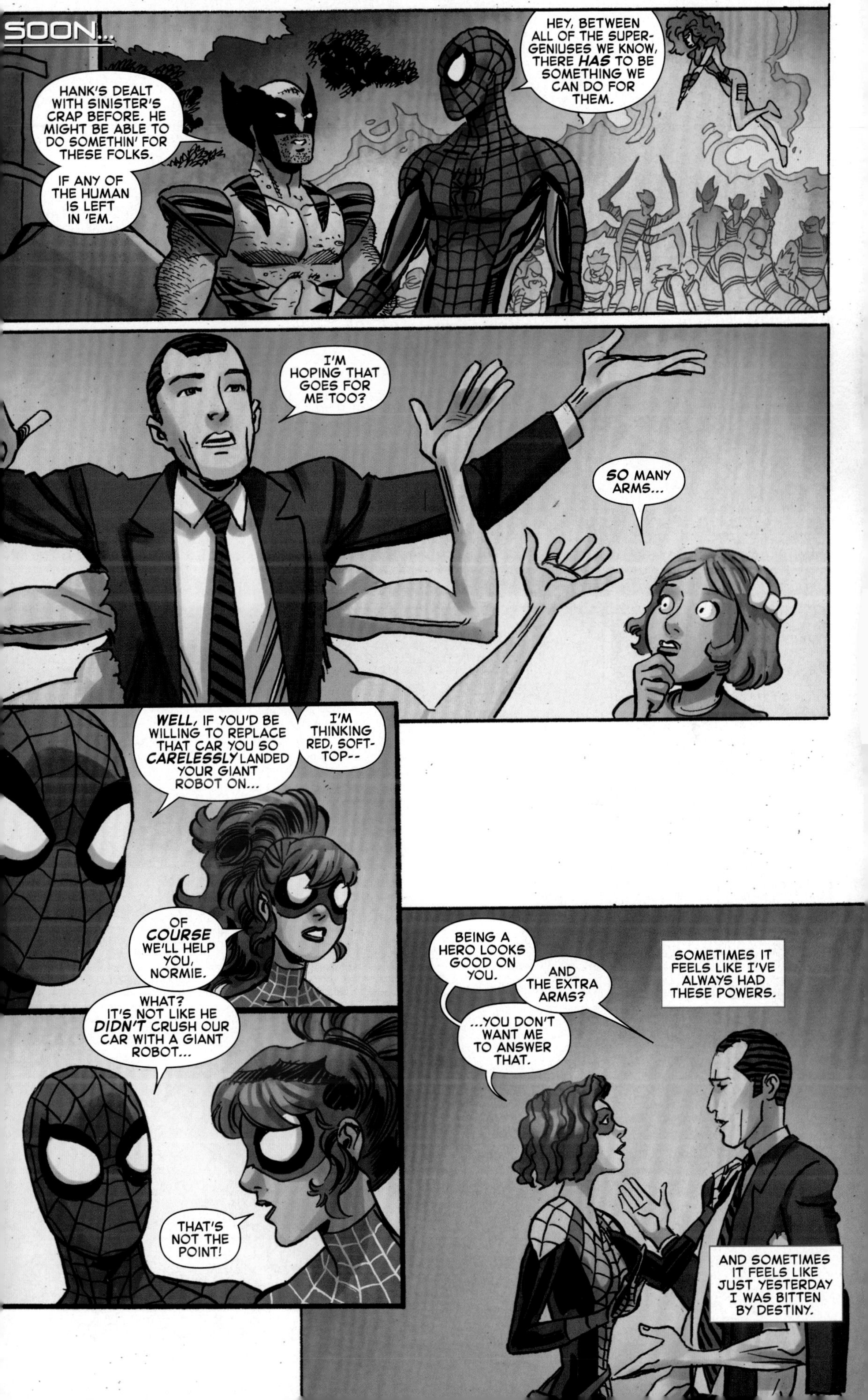
SOON...
HANK'S DEALT WITH SINISTER'S CRAP BEFORE. HE MIGHT BE ABLE TO DO SOMETHIN' FOR THESE FOLKS.
IF ANY OF THE HUMAN IS LEFT IN 'EM.
HEY, BETWEEN ALL OF THE SUPER-GENIUSES WE KNOW, THERE HAS TO BE SOMETHING WE CAN DO FOR THEM.
I'M HOPING THAT GOES FOR ME TOO?
SO MANY ARMS...
WELL, IF YOU'D BE WILLING TO REPLACE THAT CAR YOU SO CARELESSLY LANDED YOUR GIANT ROBOT ON...
I'M THINKING RED, SOFT-TOP--
OF COURSE WE'LL HELP YOU, NORMIE.
WHAT? IT'S NOT LIKE HE DIDN'T CRUSH OUR CAR WITH A GIANT ROBOT...
THAT'S NOT THE POINT!
BEING A HERO LOOKS GOOD ON YOU.
AND THE EXTRA ARMS?
...YOU DON'T WANT ME TO ANSWER THAT.
SOMETIMES IT FEELS LIKE I'VE ALWAYS HAD THESE POWERS.
AND SOMETIMES IT FEELS LIKE JUST YESTERDAY I WAS BITTEN BY DESTINY.

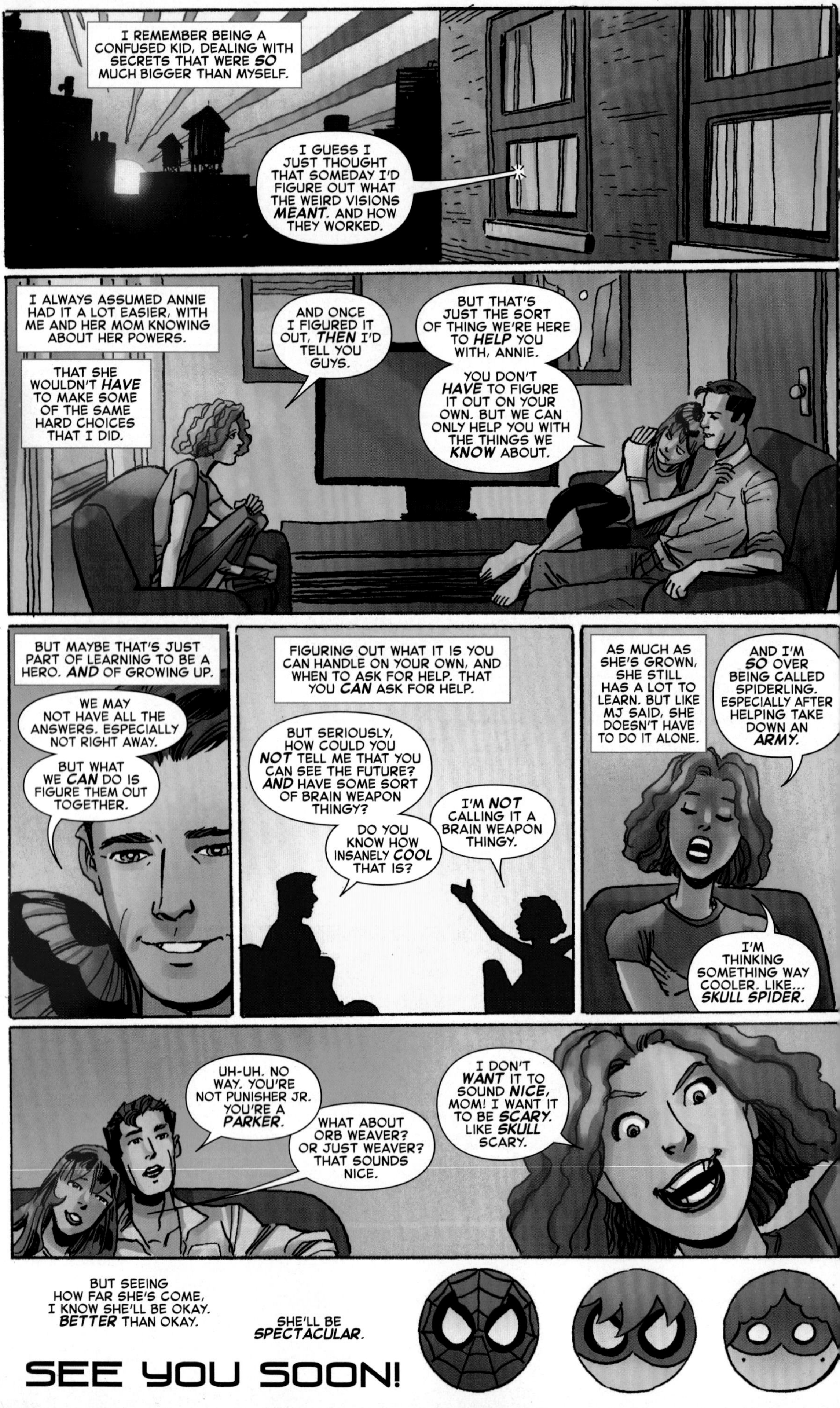
I REMEMBER BEING A CONFUSED KID, DEALING WITH SECRETS THAT WERE SO MUCH BIGGER THAN MYSELF.
I GUESS I JUST THOUGHT THAT SOMEDAY I'D FIGURE OUT WHAT THE WEIRD VISIONS MEANT. AND HOW THEY WORKED.
I ALWAYS ASSUMED ANNIE HAD IT A LOT EASIER, WITH ME AND HER MOM KNOWING ABOUT HER POWERS.
THAT SHE WOULDN'T HAVE TO MAKE SOME OF THE SAME HARD CHOICES THAT I DID.
AND ONCE I FIGURED IT OUT, THEN I'D TELL YOU GUYS.
BUT THAT'S JUST THE SORT OF THING WE'RE HERE TO HELP YOU WITH, ANNIE.
YOU DON'T HAVE TO FIGURE IT OUT ON YOUR OWN. BUT WE CAN ONLY HELP YOU WITH THE THINGS WE KNOW ABOUT.
BUT MAYBE THAT'S JUST PART OF LEARNING TO BE A HERO. AND OF GROWING UP.
WE MAY NOT HAVE ALL THE ANSWERS. ESPECIALLY NOT RIGHT AWAY.
BUT WHAT WE CAN DO IS FIGURE THEM OUT TOGETHER.
FIGURING OUT WHAT IT IS YOU CAN HANDLE ON YOUR OWN, AND WHEN TO ASK FOR HELP. THAT YOU CAN ASK FOR HELP.
BUT SERIOUSLY, HOW COULD YOU NOT TELL ME THAT YOU CAN SEE THE FUTURE? AND HAVE SOME SORT OF BRAIN WEAPON THINGY?
DO YOU KNOW HOW INSANELY COOL THAT IS?
I'M NOT CALLING IT A BRAIN WEAPON THINGY.
AS MUCH AS SHE'S GROWN, SHE STILL HAS A LOT TO LEARN. BUT LIKE MJ SAID, SHE DOESN'T HAVE TO DO IT ALONE.
AND I'M SO OVER BEING CALLED SPIDERLING. ESPECIALLY AFTER HELPING TAKE DOWN AN ARMY.
I'M THINKING SOMETHING WAY COOLER. LIKE... SKULL SPIDER.
UH-UH. NO WAY. YOU'RE NOT PUNISHER JR. YOU'RE A PARKER.
WHAT ABOUT ORB WEAVER? OR JUST WEAVER? THAT SOUNDS NICE.
I DON'T WANT IT TO SOUND NICE, MOM! I WANT IT TO BE SCARY. LIKE SKULL SCARY.
BUT SEEING HOW FAR SHE'S COME, I KNOW SHE'LL BE OKAY. BETTER THAN OKAY.
SHE'LL BE SPECTACULAR.
SEE YOU SOON!

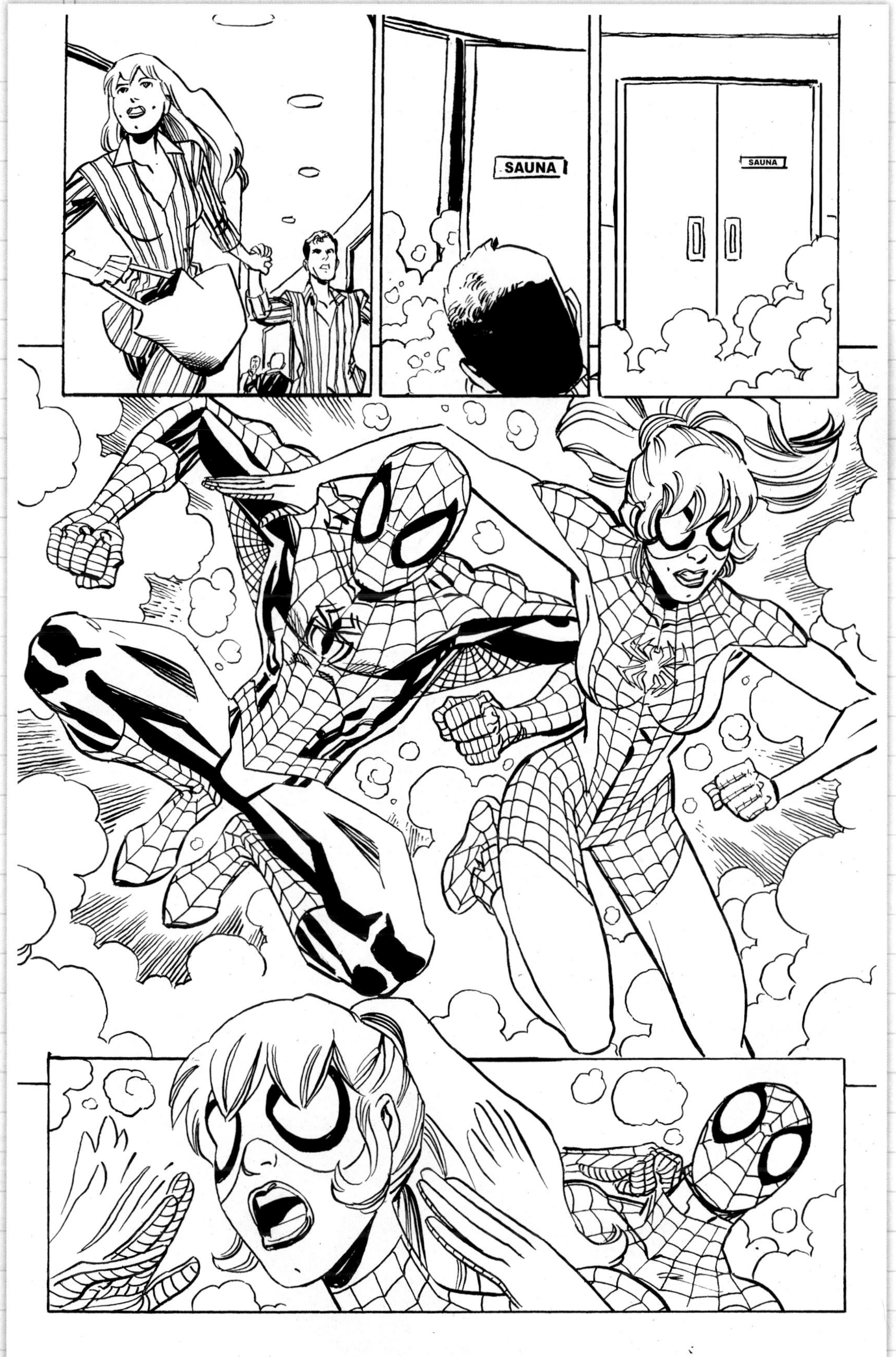
SAUNA
SAUNA

19. PAGE 10 ART BY SCOTT KOBLISH

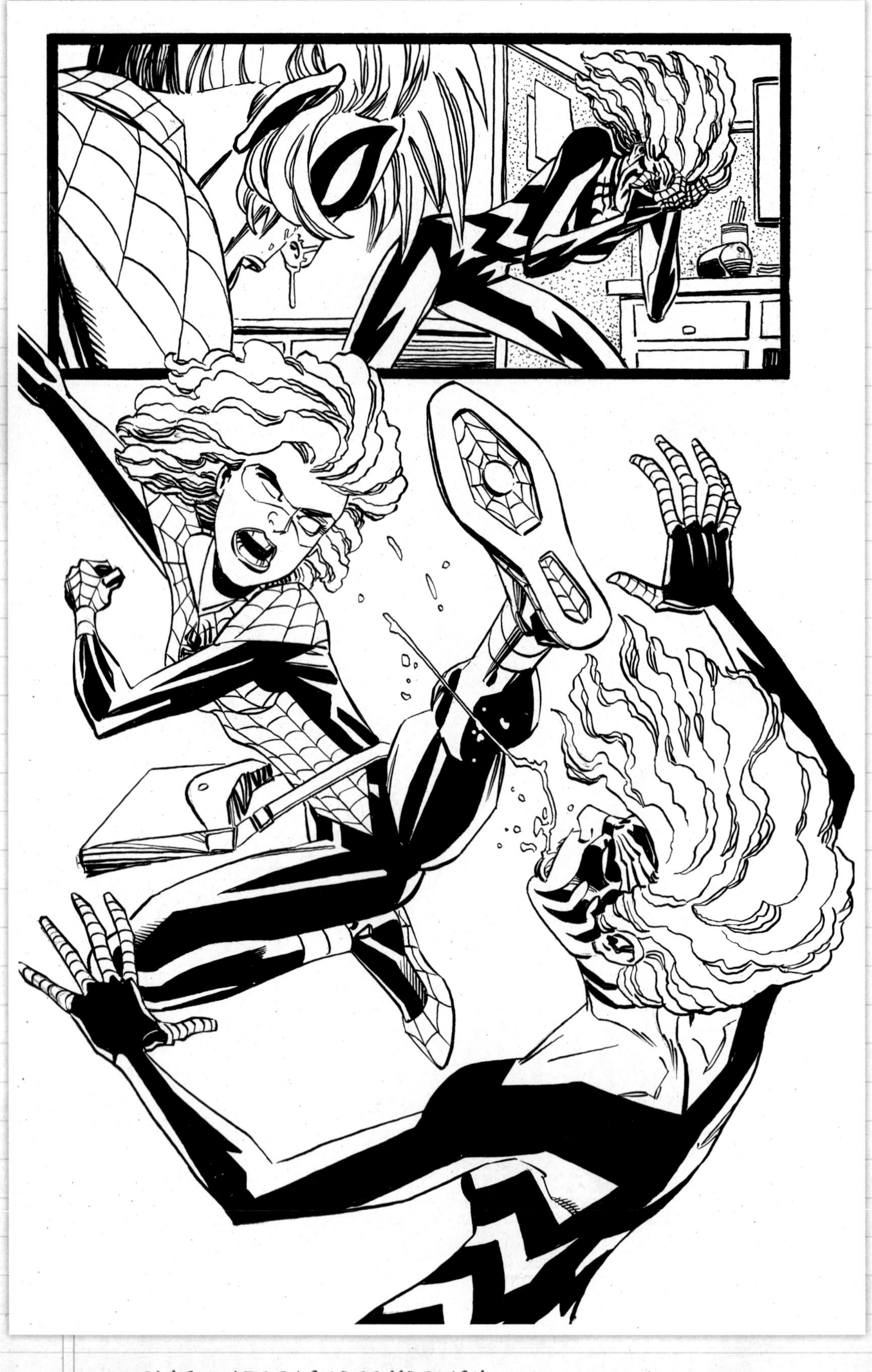

22, PAGE 12 ART BY SCOTT KOBLISH